Critical International Relations Theory after 25 years

Edited by Nicholas Rengger
and Ben Thirkell-White

T0345812

CAMBRIDGE
UNIVERSITY PRESS

CAMBRIDGE UNIVERSITY PRESS
Cambridge, New York, Melbourne, Madrid, Cape Town, Singapore,
São Paulo, Delhi, Dubai, Tokyo, Mexico City

Cambridge University Press
The Edinburgh Building, Cambridge CB2 8RU, UK

Published in the United States of America by Cambridge University Press, New York

www.cambridge.org
Information on this title: www.cambridge.org/ 9780521714259

First published 2007

A catalogue record for this publication is available from the British Library

ISBN 978-0-521-71425-9 Paperback

Critical International Relations Theory after 25 years

CONTENTS

Preface

NICHOLAS RENGGER AND BEN THIRKELL-WHITE

This is the first of four edited books, drawn from Special Issues, which will be produced while the *Review of International Studies* is based at the University of St Andrews. Editorship of the *Review* provides a unique opportunity to assemble the leading scholars from particular areas of the field, and all of us involved in the *Review* at St Andrews are conscious of, and grateful for, the opportunity that presents.

Early on in our term, the editorial team decided that while, of course, we would stand collectively behind all of the Special Issues, we would also allocate the specifics of organising and running them to two designated members of the team who would be responsible, as it were, for 'their' Special Issue and the ensuing book. The carrot that went along with that particular stick was that, as a result, the two specific members of the team who had done the work for that Special Issue would 'edit' the book version of the Special Issue. Thus, in this case, Nick Rengger and Ben Thirkell White took that task on.

A word about the topic chosen for this first issue. While, again, it was a collective decision, Rengger and Thirkell-White proposed it, each for slightly different reasons, but in the joint belief that this was a good moment to look at the evolution, current state and trajectories of 'Critical Theory' in International Relations at its broadest. Given that we would have less time than normal to prepare the Issue, it was very important not only that we had authors who were prepared to write to pretty strict deadlines, but we also wanted to range fairly widely across the various branches of critical international theory. A few people we asked to be involved and whose contributions we would really have liked to have, couldn't do it in the time frame we gave them, but we are very grateful for their interest and contributions along the way: Craig Calhoun, James Der Derian and Nancy Fraser.

Obviously, we are especially grateful to those who did contribute and who put up with our constant reminder of approaching (or exceeded) deadlines with grace and humour – and even, on occasion, with their contribution. We think the quality of the contributions speaks for itself. It is all the more remarkable given the very tight deadlines imposed by badgering editors. We would also like to thank Patrick McCartan, our editor at Cambridge University Press, for the time he took to explain to a neophyte editorial team the Byzantine process of putting one of these things together, to Emma Pearce and Gwenda Edwards, for their mastery of the technical side of that process and Mike Cook for a Herculean job of copy-editing. We would also like to thank our two anonymous referees who did an astonishing job in very short order and who deserve more than our thanks (but sorry, the royalties our ours!). Perhaps most of all, we would like to thank Mary Kettle, our indefatigable editorial assistant for the *Review* at St Andrews, who did a fantastic job (as she always does) of keeping the editors on their toes and reminding us of the nuts and bolts of this whole process.

On a more personal level, Kate Schick not only put up with Ben Thirkell-White working on the book whilst on honeymoon but also provided very useful pointers on early Frankfurt School critical theory that considerably improved the Introduction. Ben would also like to credit the cocktails at Taros in Essouira for some useful inspiration. Nick Rengger would like to thank Ben, for agreeing to co-edit this Special Issue (and now book) and for doing such a great job, and Chris Brown, James Der Derian, Mark Hoffman, Fritz Kratochwil and Andrew Linklater for discussions about critical theory, IR and much else over many years.

NJR, St Andrews
BTW, Paris
April 2007.

Richard Devetak is Senior Lecturer in International Relations at the University of Queensland. He completed his Ph.D at Keele University (UK) and has published on contemporary theoretical debates in IR, theories of the state, justice and globalisation, humanitarian intervention, terrorism and the war on terror, as well as foreign policy, refugees and national identity in the Australian context. He is co-author of *Theories of International Relations* (2005), and co-editor of *Security and the War on Terror* (forthcoming 2007) and *The Globalization of Political Violence* (forthcoming 2007).

John Hobson is Professor in the Department of Politics at the University of Sheffield. He gained his Ph.D from the LSE (1991) and joined the Department in 2004 as Reader in Politics and International Relations. Previously he taught at La Trobe University in Melbourne (1991–97) and the University of Sydney (1997–2004). His main research interests have been in the areas of historical sociology, International Relations theory, state theory and IPE, and increasingly in civilisational analysis.

Kimberly Hutchings is Reader in International Relations at the London School of Economics. Her publications include *Kant, Critique and Politics* (Routledge, 1996); *International Political Theory: Re-thinking Ethics in a Global Era* (Sage, 1999); *Hegel and Feminist Philosophy* (Polity, 2003) and, co-edited with Roland Dannreuther, *Cosmopolitan Citizenship* (Macmillan, 1999).

Fritz Kratochwil studied Classics, Philosophy and Political Science in Munich and received, as a Fulbright scholar, an MDd in International Politics from Georgetown University (1969) and a Ph.D from Princeton (1976). He taught at Maryland, Princeton, Columbia, Delaware and Pennsylvania before returning to Germany in 1995 and taking the Chair of International Politics at the European University Institute in Florence (2002). He has published widely on International Relations, social theory, international organisation and international law in US and European journals. His latest book, edited with Doris Fuchs, is entitled *Transformative Change and Global Order* (LIT Verlag, 2002).

Andrew Linklater is the Woodrow Wilson Professor of International Politics at the University of Wales, Aberystwyth. His most recent book, co-authored with Hidemi Suganami, is *The English School of International Relations: A Contemporary Reassessment* (Cambridge University Press, 2006).

1

Craig N. Murphy is M. Margaret Ball Professor of International Relations at Wellesley College and past-President of the International Studies Association. His most recent books are *The United Nations Development Programme: A Better Way?* and *Global Institutions, Marginalization, and Development.*

Ronen Palan is Professor of International Relations and Politics at the University of Sussex. He obtained his undergraduate and doctoral degrees from the Department of International Relations, London School of Economics. His first academic job was at the University of Newcastle-upon-Tyne, and he moved to the University of Sussex in 1996. He has also served as a Visiting Professor at the Hebrew University, Jerusalem; York University, Canada; and ULB, Brussels. He was a co-founder and an editor of Review of International Political Economy (RIPE), and is currently the co-director of the Centre for Global Political Economy and a member of the Steering committee of the International Political Economy Group (IPEG).

Nick Rengger is Professor of Political Theory and International Relations, University of St Andrews. He is currently Editor of The Review of International Studies.

Ben Thirkell-White is Lecturer in International Relations at the University of St Andrews and Associate Editor of the *Review of International Studies*. His research is concerned with the political economy of development finance at various levels from the political economy of Southeast Asia to critical approaches to global financial governance. He is author of *The IMF and the Politics of Financial Globalisation*, published by Palgrave (2005).

Introduction

Still critical after all these years? The past, present and future of Critical Theory in International Relations

NICHOLAS RENGGER AND BEN THIRKELL-WHITE*

Twenty-five years ago, theoretical reflection on International Relations (IR) was dominated by three broad discourses. In the United States the behavioural revolution of the 1950s and 1960s had helped to create a field that was heavily influenced by various assumptions allegedly derived from the natural sciences. Of course, variety existed within the behaviourist camp. Some preferred the heavily quantitative approach that had become especially influential in the 1960s, while others were exploring the burgeoning literature of rational and public choice, derived from the game theoretic approaches pioneered at the RAND corporation. Perhaps the most influential theoretical voice of the late 1970s, Kenneth Waltz, chose neither; instead he developed his *Theory of International Politics* around an austere conception of parsimony and systems derived from his reading in contemporary philosophy of science.[1]

These positivist methods were adopted not just in the United States but also in Europe, Asia and the UK. But in Britain a second, older approach, more influenced by history, law and by philosophy was still widely admired. The 'classical approach' to international theory had yet to formally emerge into the 'English School' but many of its texts had been written and it was certainly a force to be reckoned with.[2]

---

* The authors would like to thank all the contributors to this special issue, including our two referees. We would also like to thank Kate Schick for comments on drafts and broader discussion of the subject matter.

[1] Discussions of the development and character of so-called 'positivist' IR are something of a drug on the market. Many of them, of course, treat IR and political science as virtually interchangeable. For discussions of the rise of 'positivist' political science, see: Bernard Crick, *The American Science of Politics* (Berkeley and Los Angeles, CA: University of California Press, 1960). Klaus Knorr and James Rosenau (eds.), *Contending Approaches to International Politics* (Princeton, NJ: Princeton University Press, 1969) highlight the emergence of what might be termed 'classical' behaviouralist approaches. The growing diversity of the field can be seen in K. J. Holsti, *The Dividing Discipline* (London; Allen and Unwin, 1985) and the debates between positivism and its critics traced ably in the introduction to Steve Smith, Ken Booth and Marysia Zalewski (eds.), *International Theory; Positivism, and Beyond* (Cambridge: Cambridge University Press, 1996). Waltz's move from a traditional to a much more scientific mode of theory is found, of course, in *Theory of International Politics* (Reading, MA: Addison Wesley, 1979).

[2] The exhaustive (and exhausting) history of the 'English School' is given in Bruno Vigezzi, *The British Committee for the Theory of International Politics 1954–1985: The Rediscovery of History* (Milan: Bocconi, 2005), though good accounts of the structure and types of argument typical of it can also be found in Andrew Linklater and Hidemi Suganami, *The English School of International Relations: A Contemporary Reassessment* (Cambridge: Cambridge University Press, 2006).

Relatedly, there were voices within the realist tradition, elsewhere, drawing on older traditions of thinking about international relations. Most notably of these was Hans Morgenthau, whose first (and most powerful) English language book was a concerted reaction against the 'scientific' approaches dominant in his adopted homeland.[3]

The third approach,[4] often neglected in overviews of the discipline, was to draw on some form of Marxism. Much of this literature, though plainly relevant to international relations in the world, came from outside 'International Relations' as an academic subject. World Systems analysis, for example, was largely done in departments of sociology or history rather than in departments of political science or international relations.[5] Much the same is true of the peace research of Johan Galtung and his colleagues.[6]

Into this rather static world, in 1981, two articles were published that announced the arrival in International Relations of forms of theory long familiar outside it. These essays were Robert Cox's 'Social Forces, States and World Orders' published in the LSE journal *Millennium* and Richard Ashley's 'Political Realism and Human Interests' in *International Studies Quarterly*.[7] Both these essays deployed variants of Frankfurt School critical theory to analyse the problematic of modern international relations. They were joined the following year by perhaps the single most influential book-length treatment of International Relations from a similar trajectory, Andrew Linklater's *Men and Citizens in the Theory of International Relations*.[8] If these works could be seen as the breach in the dyke, the torrent soon became a flood as theoretical ideas from many other areas of contemporary social theory began to be deployed in the context of international relations: feminism, Neo-Gramscianism, post-structuralism, post-colonialism; the list grew exponentially.

Twenty-five years on, International Relations theory looks very different. A robust, analytical and still heavily 'scientific' US academy now has strong elements of critical theory of various sorts lodged within it. The so-called 'constructivist turn', which is so influential in contemporary IR theory, draws very heavily on aspects of the critical turn that preceded it.[9] In the UK and Europe, it is probably fair to say that various forms of 'critical theory', alongside the now relaunched (and very

---

[3] This was *Scientific Man versus Power Politics* (Chicago, IL: University of Chicago Press, 1946), though this was a view Morgenthau retained. See, for example, *Truth and Power: Essays of a Decade* (New York: Praeger, 1970).

[4] It is worth adding that there have been many ways of cutting up the evolution of IR theory: 'Great Debates' (such as Realism versus Idealism), Traditions (like Wight's Realism, rationalism and revolutionism); and Paradigms, such as the alleged 'inter-paradigm debate much discussed by some British IR scholars in the 1970s and 80s. We do not take a view on these readings, rather we are simply situating the emergence of critical theory against other reigning kinds of theory.

[5] For some internal treatments of Marxism and IR, see Andrew Cruickshank and Vendulka Kublakova, *Marxism and International Relations* (Oxford: Oxford University Press, 1985). Wallerstein's major statement of world systems theory remains *The Modern World System* ((New York: Academic Press, 1974).

[6] For Galtung's most explicit and detailed formulation of his approach, see his *Essays on Methodology*, 3 vols. (Copenhagen: Eijlers, 1977).

[7] Robert Cox, 'Social Forces, States and World Orders: Beyond International Relations Theory', *Millennium: Journal of International Studies*, 10:2 (1981), pp. 126–55. Richard K. Ashley, 'Political Realism and Human Interest', *International Studies Quarterly*, 25 (1981), pp. 204–36.

[8] Andrew Linklater, *Men and Citizens in the Theory of International Relations* (London: Macmillan, 1982).

[9] We will discuss the constructivist elements in the critical turn in more detail later on.

different) 'English School',[10] constitute the main theoretical alternatives within the discipline. Cox and Ashley's interventions have also helped to open space for a growing body of normative thinking on international issues and a burgeoning interest in the intellectual history, including history of international thought, even if these developments are often not self-consciously part of the tradition of critical IR theory.[11] This interest crosses the Atlantic as well as involving philosophers, lawyers and political theorists from outside the study of international relations.[12] In short, critical theory – in all its various guises – has had a huge impact on the study of international relations over the last twenty-five years.

Now is an appropriate time, then, for a closer look at precisely what that impact has been, where the various strands that have made up 'critical theory in international relations' now stand, what problems they face and what their future might be. That was the brief given to the contributors to this Special Issue of the *Review of International Studies*. The third section of this Introduction will introduce the essays that make it up. First, though, we lay the groundwork by providing an overview of the main strands of critical IR theory that have emerged since 1981. We go on to outline some of the most important reactions to the critical turn, both hostile and sympathetic. The essays can then be read in that intellectual context, as defences of critical theory against its more radical critics or as engagements with controversies that have taken place within the critical camp. We conclude with a short exposition of what we see as the state of critical theory within the IR discipline.

Trajectories in critical theory

This section draws out what we see as the four core strands of critical IR theory: Frankfurt School critical theory, neo-Gramscian theory, feminism and various strands of post-structuralism. Obviously, this is a somewhat restrictive conception but it was already more than enough to deal with in a single Special Issue. In the next section, we draw out the relationship between these strands of theory and other critical approaches that might have been included, notably critical constructivism, the 'new normative theory' and some kinds of critical IPE.

The influence of the Frankfurt School

In retrospect, it was predictable that, just as the scientific assumptions that generated much of the dominant work in International Relations from the 1960s onwards came

---

[10] See, for example, Barry Buzan, *From International to World Society : English School Theory and the Social Structure of Globalization* (Cambridge: Cambridge University Press, 2004).

[11] Good examples would include, David Boucher, *Political Theories of International Relations* (Oxford: Oxford University Press, 1999); Thomas Pangle and Peter Ahresndorf, *Justice Among Nations: The Struggle for Power and Peace* (Kansas, KS: University of Kansas Press, 1999); and Brian C. Schmidt, *The Political Discourse of Anarchy* (New York: SUNY Press, 1998).

[12] See, for example, the discussions in Chris Brown, *Sovereignty Rights and Justice: International Political Theory Today* (Cambridge: Polity Press, 2002).

into the subject from other fields (natural science, mathematics, and economics),[13] other theoretical innovations would make their way into the study of international relations. It was also predictable that they would initially be couched largely in opposition to those trends. It should not be surprising, then, that it is Frankfurt School critical theory[14] that was the first on to the field. Cox's *Millennium* essay, made use of the founding document of Frankfurt School critical theory to illustrate the differences between the approach he saw as dominant, and that which he saw as necessary. That document was Max Horkheimer's essay 'On Traditional and Critical Theory'.[15] Cox pointed out, as Horkheimer had, that 'traditional theory' – represented, for Cox, by US style 'positivist' International Relations – assumed that it somehow stood 'outside' the phenomena it was investigating. This forced it to assume a stance of evaluative neutrality ('value-free social science') and to adopt an effective complicity with the world as it was. It became, in Cox's words, 'Problem-solving theory', taking the world as an untheorised given and trying to work out how better to theorise, given that world.

Critical theory, on the other hand, recognises that the theorist is situated as much as a creature of the historical circumstances of the time as that which is being investigated. 'Theory', Cox said, is 'always for someone and for some purpose';[16] it speaks *from* a particular socio-historical situation and *to* one. As such it recognises the historical particularity of that situation and seeks to understand why and how it came to be as it is and what possibilities for change there might be implicit in it. Critical theorists refer to this method as immanent critique.

This method raises a second concern that is present in Cox's work but became much more explicit in Andrew Linklater's *Men and Citizens* the following year, and in Mark Hoffman's influential *Millenium* article from 1987. The search for the possibilities of change should be anchored in an emancipatory project that seeks, not just the possibility of change as such, but rather points to change in a certain – progressive – direction. This is what led Hoffman to suggest, in his article, that critical IR theory was, as he put it, 'the next stage' of IR theory, since it included a normative, emancipatory element.[17]

In a later essay, Linklater neatly summarises the main planks of what we might now call 'Frankfurt School' critical international theory as follows. First, that it takes issue with 'positivism' (as critical theorists of all stripes tend to refer to the allegedly scientific mainstream of IR theory). Second, it opposes the idea that the existing structures of the social world are immutable and 'examines the prospects for greater freedom immanent within existing social relations'. Third, it learns from and overcomes the weakness inherent in Marxism by emphasising forms of social learning

---

[13] For the integration of these fields into political science, see William Poundstone, *Prisoner's Dilemma* (New York: DoubleDay, 1992).

[14] The literature on the Frankfurt School is now vast. The most exhaustive general history is Rolf Wiggershaus, *The Frankfurt School* (Cambridge: Polity Press, 1994); the best account of its origins, Martin Jay, *The Dialectical Imagination* (Boston, MA: Little, Brown, 1973); and perhaps the clearest exposition of its central tenets, David Held, *Introduction to Critical Theory: From Horkheimer to Habermas* (Berkeley and Los Angeles, CA: University of California Press, 1980).

[15] Horkheimer's original essay was published in the *Zeitschrift fur Sozial Forschung* (the house journal of the Institute for Social Research which he directed and which was the institutional home of the School) in 1937, as 'Traditionelle und kritische theorie', *ZfS*, 6:2 (1937), pp. 245–94.

[16] Cox, 'Social Forces', p. 128.

[17] Mark Hoffman 'Critical Theory and the Inter-Paradigm Debate', *Millennium*, 16 (1987), pp. 231–49.

(drawing on Habermas' reconstruction of historical materialism) and opening up new possibilities for constructing an 'historical sociology with an emancipatory purpose'.

Linklater suggests, then, that critical theory:

judges social arrangements by their capacity to embrace open dialogue with all others and envisages new forms of political community which break with unjustified exclusion ... [it] envisages the use of an unconstrained discourse to determine the moral significance of national boundaries and to examine the possibility of post-sovereign forms of national life.[18]

This account, particularly in its stress on social learning through open dialogue, indicates just how powerfully critical theory in International Relations has been influenced by the work and thought of Jurgen Habermas. In fact, Habermas' influence in theoretical debates in International Relations extends far beyond self-confessed critical theorists. He has been an undoubted influence on Construc-tivist thought and has also influenced many figures who are much closer to the 'positivist' mainstream, for reasons that we shall return to shortly. But his first – and still most important influence – has been on the work of those, like Linklater, who did most to establish the trajectory of critical theory in International Relations.

Critical theory and social movements?

If Linklater has become the most influential Frankfurt school 'critical theorist' in International Relations, then Robert Cox's lasting influence has been in a slightly different direction. Cox came to the academy from a career in international organisations[19] and has had a lasting interest in questions of international institu-tional and economic organisation. He has been most influential in promoting 'neo-Gramscian' critical theory.

Italian communist Antonio Gramsci has had a pronounced influence on the European new left since the end of the Second World War.[20] But especially since the 1970s his ideas, developed in his so-called *Prison Notebooks*, had become increasingly influential. Ernesto Laclau and Chantal Mouffe's 1985 volume *Hegemony and Socialist Strategy*, in particular, quickly achieved cult status on the left.[21] The idea of hegemony was one they picked up and developed from Gramsci. Cox, and soon after a number of others, were following a similar trajectory in International Relations scholarship. Craig Murphy, Kees Van der Pijl, Barry Gills, Tim Sinclair and Steven Gill and a growing number of younger scholars, have all helped to develop what is now usually referred to as 'Neo-Gramscian' critical theory. They have elaborated

---

[18] Andrew Linklater, 'The Changing Contours of Critical International Relations Theory', in Richard Wyn-Jones (ed.), *Critical Theory and World Politics* (Boulder, CO: Lynne Rienner, 2001).

[19] For an account of Cox's career and its significance for his theoretical development see chapter 2 ('Influences and Commitments') in Robert Cox with Tim Sinclair, *Approaches to World Order* (Cambridge: Cambridge University Press, 1996).

[20] Good treatments of Gramsci can be found in A. Showstack-Sassoon, *Gramsci's Politics* (London; Croom Helm, 1980), Chantal Mouffe (ed.), *Gramsci and Marxist Theory* (London: Routledge and Kegan Paul, 1979), J. Larrain, *Marxism and Ideology* (London; Macmillan, 1983) and James Martin, *Gramsci's Political Analysis: An Introduction* (London; Palgrave Macmillan, 1998). See also James Martin (ed.), *Antonio Gramsci: Contemporary Philosophical Assessments*, 4 vols. (London: Routledge, 2001).

[21] Ernesto Laclau and Chantal Mouffe, *Hegemony and Socialist Strategy* (London: Verso, 1985).

and expanded on its insights, particularly in subfields such as International Political Economy (IPE) and Global Governance.[22]

Gill (in 'Gramsci', 1993 – see n. 22) outlined the hallmark of the 'Gramscian' research programme in International Relations as follows: First, ongoing attempts to reconsider epistemological and ontological aspects of world order, in the context of past, present and future. Second, continuous efforts in methodological, theoretical and conceptual innovation. Third, concrete historical studies of the emerging world order in terms of its economic, political and sociocultural dimensions with a view to its emerging contradictions and the limits and possibilities these may imply. Fourth, addressing and developing related ethical and practical approaches to global problems.

There are obvious parallels here to the Frankfurt inspired agenda outlined by Linklater above, but also some differences. Much less emphasis is placed on the kind of dialogic and discursive elements that interest Linklater, much more on the concrete empirical analysis of 'real world' processes and the linking of that to theoretical and emancipatory reflection and concrete political struggle. It is no accident that it is in IPE that Gramscian critical theory has established itself most firmly.

A not dissimilar trajectory is visible in another body of theory that emerged in International Relations at the same time: feminism. If neo-Gramscian theorists primarily tried to uncover the ways in which economic activities had shaped the international world that the mainstream tended to take as a given, feminist theorists pointed to the ways in which gender had done so. Given the diffusion of feminist scholarship through the academy over the last thirty to forty years in a wide range of fields,[23] this development was long overdue. Though not all feminist writers set out to be critical theorists, there are clear affinities between the feminist project of uncovering the gendered nature of contemporary social reality and the broader critical project in IR, with its emphasis on theorising the untheorised in an effort to promote emancipatory change. Thus books like Cynthia Enloe's *Bananas Beaches and Bases* became part of the critical turn, as much as Ann Tickner's *Gender in International Relations* and Jean Bethke Elshtain's *Women and War*.[24] Indeed, much

---

[22] Volumes that have contributed to this developing position would include: Stephen Gill, *American Hegemony and the Tri-Lateral Commission* (Cambridge: Cambridge University Press, 1990), Stephen Gill (ed.), *Gramsci: Historical Materialism and International Relations* (Cambridge: Cambridge University Press, 1993); Craig Murphy, *Global Institutions, Marginalization and Development* (London: Routledge, 2005), and Kees Van Der Pijl, *Transnational Classes and International Relations* (London: Routledge, 1998).

[23] The influence and growth of feminist scholarship across the humanities and social sciences since the mid–late 1960s awaits its major historian. Provisional assessments can be found in Margaret Walters, *Feminism: A Very Short Introduction* (Oxford: Oxford University Press, 2005), and Nancy Cott, *The Grounding of Modern Feminism* (New Haven, CT: Yale University Press, 1987).

[24] Major statements of feminist IR scholarship of this sort would normally be held to include Ann Tickner, *Gendering World Politics* (New York: Columbia University Press, 2001); Jean Bethke Elshtain, *Women and War* (Brighton: Harvester Press, 1987); Cynthia Enloe, *Bananas, Beaches and Bases: Making Feminist Sense of International Politics* (Berkeley, CA: University of California Press, 1989). For an excellent overview by an important voice, growing in influence, see Kimberly Hutchings, 'Feminist Philosophy and International Relations Theory: A Review'. *Women's Philosophy Review*, 27 (2001), pp. 31–60. For more post-structurally inclined feminist writers see below.

of the best and most acute writing in all the traditions that make up critical IR acknowledges the (sadly often unfulfilled) potential for fruitful two-way interaction between feminist writing and other critical traditions. In this issue, for example, Craig Murphy suggests that neo-Gramscian scholars could learn more from the relationship between scholarship and activism in the international feminist movement and Kimberly Hutchings points to the importance of feminist explorations of the relationship between difference and universality for broader thinking in IR.

Deconstruction

Although the opening shots in the critical campaign were fired by what we might call the 'emancipatory' wing of critical theory, they were swiftly joined by writers coming out of a different theoretical trajectory. From the mid to late 1960s onwards, one of the most important of all late twentieth century intellectual fashions began to influence (or infect, according to taste) a wide range of fields in the humanities and social sciences. Usually called post-structuralism (and often, though not very helpfully, postmodernism) this was actually a catch-all term for a loosely related set of theoretical positions derived from two principal sources, the diffuse but very real influence of Heidegger in France in the 1950s and the disillusion with traditional versions of Marxism that accompanied the rise of the student left and the events of 1968. In the 'deep background', as it were, and connected with the influence of Heidegger, was the growing stature of Nietzsche as a thinker. The two major thinkers to ride the crest of these waves were Michel Foucault and Jacques Derrida and their work became the most influential on scholars in International Relations.

Perhaps the first IR scholar to really develop a post-structural position was Richard Ashley. Moving beyond the argument he had outlined in *Political Realism and Human Interests*, Ashley began to develop a more radical critique of conventional discourses of IR. Initially, on the basis of a reading of Foucault's work, Ashley argued that 'post-structuralism' was a permanently 'critical' discourse, indeed the only *really* critical theory, since it did not, indeed could not, offer an alternative position or perspective to any other as there was no ground upon which such a perspective could be established. This he took to be the logic implicit in Foucault's view that all claims of knowledge implied a regime of power and *vice versa*, and that you could not therefore establish a position outside the competing power/knowledge claims.[25]

Elements of this reading persist in post-structurally influenced IR theory – as witnessed by David Campbell's claim that his work should be seen as a form of political criticism, though one which significantly he sees as an ethos – but it has also changed in important ways. Now, most post-structurally influenced scholars would agree with William Connolly's gentle critique of Ashley to the effect that:

---

[25] These arguments are perhaps most fully developed in his critique of Kenneth Waltz, 'The Poverty of Neo-Realism' [in R. Keohane (ed.), *Neo-Realism and Its Critics* (New York: Columbia University Press, 1986)] and in his essay 'Living on Borderlines: Man, Post-Structuralism and War', in James Der Derian and Michael J. Shapiro, *International/Intertextual Relations: Postmodern Readings of World Politics* (New York: Lexington Books, 1989).

(we) contend, in a way that overtly presents itself as a contestable supposition, that we live in a time when a variety of factors press thought into a rather confined and closed field of discourse . . . the political task at a time of closure and danger is to try and open up that which is enclosed, to try to think thoughts that stretch and extend the normal patterns of insistence'.[26]

Although this is the general position that post-structurally influenced critical IR theory has taken, there remain a wide variety of approaches to applying post-structural insights. Rob Walker, following perhaps Derrida more than Foucault, has sought to focus on the way in which a range of dichotomies can be read as having structured the conditions of modern IR: inside/outside (to use the title of his best known book) but also identity/difference, time/space, self/other, inclusion/exclusion, unity/diversity and universality/particularity.[27] James Der Derian shares something of this sensibility, particularly the focus on the time/space dichotomy, but has chiefly focused on the implications of this for what he calls the chronopolitics of security in today's world where chronology is elevated over geography and pace over space.[28] There are also feminist readings of not dissimilar problematics, such as those of Christine Sylvester and Spike Peterson on IR and IPE in general and, in the UK, Jenny Edkins' meditation on Trauma and Memory in IR, Cindy Weber's work on gender, representation and film in Contemporary IR and Kimberly Hutchings' articulation of a broadly post-structural feminist sensibility.[29]

Reactions to critical theory

Rejection

The critical turn was a self-conscious attack on the mainstream of International Relations. It should not surprise us, then, that most leading so-called 'positivist' scholars, largely, though by no means exclusively, in the US, have tried to reject the entire critical project. They have two grounds for this rejection. The first is based on a largely methodological assumption – rarely argued for in any detail – that IR should be subsumed into something called 'political science' and the methods that govern political science are essentially akin to the natural sciences. The assumptions

---

[26] See Connolly, 'Identity and Difference in Global Politics', in Der Derian and Shapiro, *International/Intertextual Relations*. See also Connolly's arguments in *Identity/Difference: Democratic Negotiations of Political Paradox* (Ithaca, NY: Cornell University Press, 1991).

[27] The only major statement of Walker's view remains *Inside/Outside: International Relations as Political Theory* (Cambridge: Cambridge University Press, 1993).

[28] Der Derian has explored these positions in three major books plus a host of articles, op-eds and other writings plus at least one filmed documentary. For the evolution of his views, see *On Diplomacy* (Oxford: Oxford University Press, 1987); *Anti-Diplomacy: Speed, Spies, Terror and War* (Oxford: Blackwell, 1992); and *Virtuous War: Mapping the Military Industrial Media Entertainment Network* (Diane, 2001).

[29] See, for example, Christine Sylvester, *Feminist International Relations* (Cambridge: Cambridge University Press, 2001), Jenny Edkins, *Trauma and the Memory of Politics* (Cambridge: Cambridge University Press, 2003), Cindy Weber, *Imagining America at War: Morality, Politics and Film* (London: Routledge, 2005). Hutchings' work on feminist IR has been mainly in essays so far (such as the one cited above and the one in the present issue). But see also her studies *Hegel: A Feminist Revision* (Cambridge: Polity, 2002) and *International Political Theory* (London: Sage, 1999).

on which critical theory (of any sort) have always been based, then, are simply mistaken.

The second assumption, often spelt out in greater detail, is that critical theory can offer neither a proper explanation of IR nor appropriate normative reflection since it is essentially 'relativist' and cannot offer anything by way of guidance for action or policy. This was broadly Keohane's strategy in his 1988 Presidential address to the ISA (later published), 'International Institutions: Two Approaches'.[30] Keohane sought to suggest that IR scholarship was divided between a rationalist 'mainstream; and a range of (very diverse) so called 'reflectivist' approaches. Until (reflectivist) critical theory developed its own 'research design' it would remain forever on the fringes of the field.

Some postmodern accounts, such as Ashley's, would accept the charge of relativism. The vast majority of critical writers, though, would not. As we saw above, even many contemporary post-structuralists see themselves as engaged with the world of practice. When it comes to feminist IR, Frankfurt School and neo-Gramscian writing, the criticism is clearly too scattershot to hit the mark. Even those that it does catch – chiefly post-structurally inclined IR theory – are not really relativists in the rather 'straw man' sense usually implied. Taking a hermeneutic stance 'beyond objectivism and relativism' may be contestable but it is not, by definition, relativistic.

A minor variant of this critique has also been to suggest that critical theory is essentially what one prominent contemporary realist – Randall Schweller – has called 'fantasy theory',[31] that it consists chiefly of ever more ingenious attempts to build castles in the air but meantime, he suggests, the rest of us have to live in the real world of states and their conflicts. There is much that might be said about this astonishingly bad reading of what most critical theorists have been saying but one obvious point is simply to aver that few, if any, critical theorists of any stripe would take the royal road to what, in a different context, John Rawls called 'ideal theory'. The critical theorists' concern has always been, first and foremost, with the situation of the here and now and how it came about: only then might we find possibilities of change immanent within it. Their analysis might be wrong, of course, but it is no more a fantasy than is Schweller's.

The original, methodological critique fairs no better, we suggest. It is simply a restatement of the claims to science that have been attacked by a succession of theorists of various stripes, at least since Hans Morgenthau's withering critique in *Scientific Man versus Power Politics* in 1946. The 'Critical' version of it comes, as we have suggested, in a variety of forms, all of which are certainly arguable, but simply restating the equally contestable claims of science in an ever louder voice hardly seems likely to persuade.

What we might term the 'rejectionist' critique therefore, seems to us to fail, both on its own terms, and because it does not really engage seriously with the arguments put forward by critical theorists.

---

[30] Included in his *International Institutions and State Power* (Boulder, CO: Westview, 1989).
[31] The title of his contribution to the forum on Andrew Linklater's, *The Transformation of Political Community*, in these pages. See *Review of International Studies*, 25:1 (1999), pp. 147–50.

Springboarding

A more significant response to the critical turn has been to use the intellectual space that was opened up by writers such as Cox and Ashley to push a wide range of intellectual projects. The rise of critical International Relations theory started to re-embed the discipline of International Relations more firmly within the broader social sciences.[32] This has triggered a rapid expansion of the theoretical scope of the discipline. It may be a slight overstatement to claim that all these new intellectual developments are a direct consequence of the arrival of critical theory, but the critical turn was certainly an important factor in legitimating a wide range of borrowings from social and political philosophy. The result has been a huge increase in the diversity of perspectives within the discipline.

Keohane's 1988 lecture was bracketed by two books each of which could be seen to make common cause with aspects of the critical turn but which were also rather different in both form and content. The first, Nicholas Onuf's *World of Our Making*[33] appeared the year before Keohane's lecture, and was the first to suggest that IR should draw on the wide range of work that had been generically termed 'constructivist' in other areas of the academy and which drew on, for example, the later philosophy of Ludwig Wittgenstein. To see the world as a construction, Onuf suggests, liberates us from the flat and sterile materialism of conventional IR theory and allows us to investigate the manner in which the construction was achieved and thus also the possibilities for change and reconstruction within it. This was obviously close to the kind of things the emancipatory wing of critical theory had been saying, though in Onuf's hands the emancipatory element was far less pronounced.

The second book, appearing the year after Keohane's lecture, overlapped considerably with Onuf's but was also much less Wittgensteinean. This was Friedrich Kratochwil's *Rules, Norms, Decisions*.[34] Kratochwil's book was a study of the manner of practical reasoning through rules and norms as it affected both domestic politics and international relations, and argued that in this context the character of international relations was established through such norms and such practical reasoning. He too, therefore, was arguing for a 'constructivist' account of international relations.

Again, much of the theoretical apparatus deployed so ably by Onuf and Kratochwil came from outside IR, indeed outside the social sciences. The 'constructivist turn' had been influential in philosophy and social theory for some fifteen years before it reached International Relations but, unlike the critical theories just discussed, it could be read in a more or a less 'critical' way. In the hands of Onuf and Kratochwil, it shared a good deal with aspects of critical international theory, but in other hands, for example those of Peter Katzenstein and especially Alexander Wendt, it came much closer to a modification of more conventional IR theory than an outright challenge to it. Saying the world is 'constructed' can be taken in more or less radical ways. For Wendt, for example, it led to the view that 'ideas mattered' in

---

[32] See, particularly, Palan's contribution in this issue.

[33] Nicholas Onuf, *World of Our Making: Rules and Rule in Social Theory and International Relations* (University of North Carolina Press, 1987).

[34] *Rules, Norms, Decisions: On the Conditions of Practical and Legal Reasoning in International Relations and Domestic Affairs* (Cambridge: Cambridge University Press, 1989).

IR – that for example 'anarchy is what states make of it'[35] – but this was still understood within a framework that owed a good deal to more 'conventional social scientific' assumptions than was the case with Onuf and Kratochwil. His closeness to those assumptions was perhaps indicated in the title he chose for his major book, *Social Theory of International Politics*; quite explicitly aligning his argument with that of Waltz (although also obviously criticising it as well).[36]

'Constructivism' quickly became the acceptable face of 'reflectivism', at least in the United States, a development which to some extent sundered the link of constructivist scholarship with the wider critical turn. However, the extent to which that is true depends on which constructivist one looks at.

The critical turn also opened space for a far wider range of 'critical' approaches than we have been able to focus on in this special issue. In particular, there are now a bewilderingly wide range of critical approaches in contemporary IPE.[37] Generally, these approaches are more empirically driven than the work we have focused on and have had less impact outside questions of political economy, but there are often clear overlaps with themes we have addressed.

Perhaps the writing that has broadest significance in the wider literature comes from other versions of Marxism – for example those developed by Fred Halliday, Kees Van der Pijl and, perhaps more powerfully still, by Justin Rosenberg.[38]

The other major source of inspiration has been the impact of globalisation, which has added powerful empirical impetus to consideration of key critical themes – identity, difference, meaning, discourse, the double implication of 'domestic' and 'international', the role of conceptions of space and time, the importance of the 'destruction of distance', the ambivalent but always present role of technology and so on. This empirical impetus has triggered work that is closer to a more mainstream, albeit still largely constructivist, set of debates (for example in the work of Jan Art Scholte or Richard Higgott) as well as some work in sociology and wider areas of social theory that was much closer to other areas of critical theory (for example the work of Zygmunt Bauman or Saskia Sassen).[39]

Finally, one should also include the 'new normative theory' – some of which was actually very old – which also supported these developments even if the actual positions adopted were not always close to those taken by critical theorists. Perhaps especially notable here is the evolving work of David Held, Antony McGrew and their various collaborators around the ideas of globalisation, global governance and

---

[35] Alexander Wendt, 'Anarchy is What States Make of it: The Social Construction of Power Politics', *International Organization*, 46:3, pp. 391–425.

[36] For Katzenstein's view of 'constructivism', see his edited book *The Culture of National Security: Norms and Identity in World Politics* (New York: Columbia University Press, 1996). For Wendt, of course, most importantly, *Social Theory of International Politics* (Cambridge: Cambridge University Press, 2003).

[37] For an overview, see Ronen Palan (ed.), *Global Political Economy: Contemporary Theories* (London: Routledge, 2000).

[38] See, for example, Fred Halliday, *Rethinking International Relations* (London: Macmillan, 1994); Van Der Pijl, *Transnational Classes*; and Rosenberg, *The Empire of Civil Society: A Critique of the Realist Theory of International Relations* (London: Verso, 1994).

[39] See, for example, Jan Art Scholte, *Globalization* (London: Palgrave, 2000, 2nd edn. 2005); Richard Higgot and Morton Ougard (ed.), *Towards a Global Polity* (London: Routledge, 2002); Zygmunt Bauman, *Globalization: The Human Consequences* (Cambridge: Polity Press, 1998), Saskia Sassen, *Globalization and its Discontents* (New York: The Free Press, 1998).

cosmopolitan democracy which links with many of the ideas motivating critical theory in IR.[40]

Assessment

Overall, the critical turn has opened space for an enormous expansion of methodological variety within the IR discipline. However, the consequences of that are by no means set in stone. As we saw in the previous section, Frankfurt School and neo-Gramscian theorists both expected a more complex understanding of the historical evolution of the international system to uncover the potential for emancipatory change. Post-structuralists, on the other hand, were inclined to draw the message that almost nothing can be predicted and were concerned that any attempt to do so would be implicated in coercive structures of power/knowledge. The constructivist position seems to be sufficiently open to allow one to adopt some of the new methodological insights of the broader social sciences without necessarily adopting a recognisably critical position.

This variety of new approaches emphasises just how significant the critical turn has been in bringing the discipline of International Relations into closer contact with the broader social sciences. In the process, though, it has raised a whole new set of questions about the relationship between a variety of ontological and epistemological positions on the one hand, and different normative and political commitments on the other.

Immanent critique

Within the critical camp, debate has focused on exactly the questions that were raised at the close of the previous section. At its most basic, one might think of the conflict as between the post-structuralists on the one hand and 'the rest' on the other. The issue goes right back to Theodor Adorno and Max Horkheimer's *The Dialectic of Enlightenment*.[41] Adorno and Horkheimer set out to challenge the danger of scientific totalitarianism that they saw in both liberalism and classical Marxism. They were concerned about the dominance of instrumental reason, which threatened to overwhelm the concern with human freedom and emancipation ushered in by the Enlightenment. Their hostility to prescription and social engineering, though, tended to deprive them of the philosophy of history that, for Marx, had grounded a steadfast confidence in progress. Adorno, famously, despaired to the point where all he could do was cling to the hope that his writing would be a 'message in a bottle' for future generations.[42]

---

[40] See especially, amongst a large and growing literature, Held, *Democracy and Global Order* (Cambridge: Polity Press, 1995); Held, McGrew, Goldblatt and Perraton, *Global Transformations: Politics, Economics, Culture* (Cambridge: Polity Press, 1999); and Held and McGrew, *Globalization and Anti-Globalization* (Cambridge: Polity Press, 2002).

[41] Theodor Adorno and Max Horkheimer, *The Dialectic of Enlightenment* (London: Verso, 1997).

[42] The quote appears to be anecdotal. For discussions of Adorno's ethical thought, see Martin Jay, *Adorno* (Cambridge, MA: Harvard University Press, 1984), and Kate Schick, 'Outside International Ethics: Adorno, Suffering and Hope' (University of St Andrews, September 2006, mimeo).

The Habermasian response was a highly complex and sophisticated rehabilitation of reason as a non-instrumental, radically democratic, 'dialogic' collective enterprise.[43] The neo-Gramscian response is less well articulated. Gramsci himself seems to have maintained a broad faith in the potential for a transition to socialism on essentially Marxian historical materialist grounds. IR neo-Gramscians clearly accept Marxist accounts of the development of capitalism. They are historically materialist in that the social relations of production are seen as a key driver of history. However, they are also generally inclined to keep potential 'progress' more open, seeing it as contingent on the forms of social movement and struggle that emerge in practice, rather than dictated by the inevitable triumph of the 'universal class'. That has the advantage of the potential to sidestep the narrow Marxian focus on class exploitation, but it does undermine the solid ground that Marx claimed to have for believing that progress would take place.[44]

Contemporary critical theorists working in both these traditions are clearly uneasy about the post-structuralist challenge. The more rigid one's philosophy of history (and therefore the firmer the basis of confidence in emancipation), the greater the danger of subsiding into undemocratic and closed forms of instrumentalism becomes. On the other hand, the more one accepts contingency, uncertainty and the multiplicity of political projects, the less guidance emerges for concrete political action.

Much of the debate within the critical camp, then, revolves around this central question. Some theorists see others as having overly closed emancipatory projects. Feminist writers, in particular, have often rightly felt marginalised from neo-Gramscian writing.[45] As we will see in this issue, others have argued that there is a critical silence surrounding the developing world and, perhaps particularly, post-colonial questions about culture. Habermasians and neo-Gramscians, on the other hand, both criticise the post-structuralists for a radical openness that cuts out the ground on which to stand in making a critique or looking for progress.

The problems raised, of course, also have an impact on debates with those outside the critical camp. In an exchange with William Wallace, for example, Ken Booth rejected the charge that critical theorists were 'monks' – flippant, self-indulgent, with nothing to offer those who were engaged in, for example, talking to diplomats in newly emerging democracies about the difficulties and concerns that would inevitably confront them. In response, he claimed that critical theorists were speaking to a practical audience, but a different practical audience; civil society, social movements, activists, those in the international community) which certainly might include some working within state governments) who were working for a better world and perhaps

---

[43] For an excellent overview, see Held, *Introduction to Critical Theory*.

[44] The criticism is our own, but compare, for example, Robert Cox, *Production Power and World Order: Social Forces in the Making of History* (New York: Columbia University Press, 1987) with Cox's 'Reflections and Transitions', in Robert Cox, *The Political Economy of a Plural World* (London: Routledge, 2002), and Craig Murphy, *Global Institutions*.

[45] Cox has recently explicitly suggested that counter-hegemonic struggles might embrace racial, cultural or gender emancipation (see, for example, Cox, 'Reflections and Transitions'). In practice, though, even critical IPE rarely engages with feminist concerns – see Georgina Waylen, 'You Still Don't Understand: Why Troubled Engagements Continue between Feminists and (Critical) IPE', *Review of International Studies*, 32:1 (January 2006), pp. 145–64.

also for a different world. That was to be preferred to the role of 'technocrats, simply trying to make the existing machine work better'.[46]

Underlying this tension, between more and less open political projects and conceptions of social causation, there is a very fundamental philosophical question that is not often addressed about the extent to which there is any relationship at all between knowledge of the world and action in it. It is a question that has been relatively well rehearsed in a wide range of philosophical literature. There are a variety of approaches, ranging from some interpretations of Wittgenstein, to readings of Heidegger, which suggest that the relation is nowhere near as clear or direct as it would have to be for the kind of carryover on which critical theory has wanted to rely. Once one engages with the kind of idealist, linguistic and phenomenological debates that triggered the critical turn, this kind of fundamental philosophical question can no longer be sidestepped.

Contents and themes of this Special Issue

Having reviewed the main strands of critical theory and the kinds of debate that they have triggered within the IR discipline, we now turn to the main body of the issue. The contributions all engage with this context in one way or another. In particular, most of them can be seen as providing answers to the questions we raised in the previous section. We have chosen to arrange them so that they begin with articles that focus primarily on methodological questions about the philosophy of history and conclude with more practically-oriented contributions on the role of critical theory in promoting political change. This section provides a brief summary of each contribution, relating it to the themes and criticisms raised above. We then conclude with a brief evaluation of the past contribution and future potential of critical IR theory.

The issue begins with Friedrich Kratochwil's assessment of critical IR theory from the point of view of a 'sympathetic [constructivist] outsider'. Perhaps predictably, Kratochwil is inclined to see the principal contribution of critical theory in terms of an opening up of methodological space in the discipline. He argues that critical theory is 'critical' primarily in its reluctance to treat social 'facts' as natural kinds. Theory in the social sciences should be evaluated on the basis of ideas such as completeness, relevance and appropriateness, rather than simply the positivist criteria of logical rigour, demonstrable proof and universal validity.

However, he is less sympathetic to Ashley's particular project in his 1981 article. He argues that Ashley's issues with the 'silences' of neorealism did too little to uncover the silences of *classical* realism. Instead, Kratochwil raises three challenges that he feels critical IR theory should address.

Firstly, in good constructivist fashion, he calls for a rediscovery of politics in terms of 'which types of constitutive understandings authorise particular practices'. Hobbesian theory, for example, was politically significant because it helped both to authorise the sovereign state *and* the liberal distinction between public and private spheres. The place theorists can play in building the social world in this way places

---

[46] For this exchange, see William Wallace 'Truth and Power, Monks and Technocrats: Theory and Practice in International Relations', *Review of International Studies*, 22:3 (1996), pp. 301–21, and Ken Booth, 'Discussion: A Reply to Wallace', *Review of International Studies*, 23:3 (1997), pp. 371–7.

a responsibility on all academics as 'experts', one which is sometimes neglected at the expense of career building. Yet the issues of the constitution of the international system are increasingly crucial under globalisation and even critical theories have more to do in theorising these changes.[47] Secondly, Kratochwil takes issue with variants of critical theory that continue to hold philosophies of history that expect the triumph of Enlightenment: the transformation of human beings into 'rational actors' engaged in the 'pursuit of happiness'. He argues that the resurgence of complex and significant identity politics continues to place straightforward assumptions about future universality in serious question. Finally, and most fundamentally, he raises questions about the adequacy of contemporary theories of action. If we reject the 'rational actor' model, how do we account for the relationship between rationality, desire, appropriateness and duty in accounting for human action?

Kratochwil avoids taking any position on specific political projects. Instead, he concentrates on methodological terrain, arguing that critical theory has raised new questions for International Relations. It has, appropriately, complicated the task of assessing different theories and views of the world. However, it may not have done enough to question old orthodoxies, particularly in terms of the assumptions of progressive Western Enlightenment.

Kratochwil's article raises challenges that are most directly relevant to our first three articles by self-consciously critical theorists. Although they might not describe what they are doing in his terms, all three raise questions about how we should conceive the constitution of global politics and all three, to different degrees, question any conception of progression towards enlightened modernity. In their different ways, they all do this through an interrogation of the philosophy of history.

Coming from a background in IPE, Ronen Palan is particularly conscious of the difficulties of discussing the contemporary globalised economy within the framework of state-centric IR theory. He argues that these difficulties cannot be resolved by 'bolt-on' additions ('institutions', 'interdependence' 'domestic politics', and so on). Rather IR theorists should be (and critical theorists often are) resituating international relations within the broader social scientific enterprise of understanding the human condition. This includes a sociological reflection on some of the questions Kratochwil raises about the nature of human agency. Drawing on Deleuze and Guatarri, Palan suggests that the 'rationality' of orthodox IR is something that has been produced through historical social processes. If orthodoxy asks how (rational) people achieve what is good for them; heterodoxy asks why people desire what is bad for them, how particular structures of motivation are produced. The result is a vision of international relations theory as analysis of a far more complex set of social processes, with a particular focus on those with an international dimension, which are often missed by other social science disciplines. (There are echoes, here, of Linklater's 'sociology of global morals with emancipatory intent'). We need an approach that is 'globally encompassing, historically oriented and focused on political institutions'.

Palan goes on to sketch what such a critical IR/IPE would look like. It is a vision that might be particularly associated with a British approach to critical IPE that sees

---

[47] For instance, he points to the weaknesses of neo-Gramscian theory in understanding the global constitution of class in a context in which there are as many conflicts of interest as there are points of contact between the workers of the world.

itself as following in the footsteps of Susan Strange. He argues that even the neo-Marxism of someone like Cox retains a somewhat mechanistic, structural picture of global political economy. Instead, we should work towards a more contingent, evolutionary conception, drawing on a conception of the state that can be found in rather different readings of Marx and Hegel, reaching its fullest expression in French regulation theory.

We should see the state as a historical juncture; as the mediator between a variety of social forces. Similarly, we should see capitalism as evolving as much through specific historical institutions and inter-state struggles (or emulation) as through some grand process of the unfolding of an abstract 'mode of production'.[48] The evolution of capitalism is full of experiments, some of which have proved abortive but others of which have diffused through a process of learning and adaptation in ways that have stabilised capitalist states against their expected collapse. We need a critical global political economy that understands the general tendencies of capitalism but also looks at the specifics of individual jurisdictions.

On the whole, Palan celebrates a newfound heterodoxy in the International Relations discipline. He provides an optimistic picture of a discipline that already partly exists. His principle criticism is of an overly deterministic and mechanistic conception of history that pays too little attention to the changing, historical, social construction of human agency and to the complex interactions that shape it. Instead, he calls for a more evolutionary conception of history that has some broad tendencies but also much more space for unexpected contingencies. It is a much more plural vision of international relations than the mainstream provides. We may find, therefore, that interesting things go on in the margins, as well as at the centres of power (one might think of Palan's own work on 'offshore').[49]

In the end, though, Palan does not question the idea that what will emerge is *one* history of the development of contemporary capitalism, albeit a more complex, nuanced and disorderly one than we often find in orthodox IR. Palan's attention to complexity, diversity and social construction in the understanding of history have echoes in our next two contributions, but these contributors also set out to question the idea that there may be 'one' understanding of history at all.

Kimberly Hutchings makes an argument about conceptions of time that run through different strands of critical theory. Like Kratochwil, she is anxious about an uncritical assumption of progress towards Western modernity. Echoing Adorno and Horkheimer's critique of modernity, she argues that Marxian accounts of critical theory (including the Frankfurt School and neo-Gramscian writing) tend to be tainted by a conception of unitary progress, embedded in particular philosophies of history (Gramsci's progress to socialism) or a faith in supposedly transcendental human capacities for freedom and reason (in more Habermasian writing such as Linklater's or Ashley's 1981 article).

The postmodern alternative, she argues, provides a powerful corrective to the danger of 'messianic' theories, that can only be redeemed by the future. Postmodernists are right to be concerned that even aspirations towards justice will frequently fail to do justice to the indeterminacy of the future. However, postmodern

---

[48] This is very much the Marx Hutchings discusses as Derrida's 'hauntological' Marx, later in this issue.

[49] Ronen Palan 'Tax havens and the commercialisation of state sovereignty', *International Organization*, 56:1 (2002), pp. 153–78.

writing can still be deterministic in its own way. Postmodern writing in the style of Virilio or Der Derian, continues to privilege the shift from modern to postmodern time in a way that privileges an accelerated temporality, which is primarily an experience of the West. A Western experience of time comes to stand for international political time in general. Although postmodern writing that draws more from Derrida avoids this problem, it too is forced to rely on an unjustified and only allegedly transcendental preference, in this case for the 'inexhaustibility of the possibilities of deconstructive critique'.

Hutchings argues for an approach that 'embraces analytical reason in pursuit of social justice but does not allow it to erase the question of heterotemporality from the history of the modern subject'. She suggests that this kind of theory may be assisted through a multiple conception of time, which acknowledges a range of intersecting histories that evolve concurrently, each with their own logic and meaning, but also each vulnerable to unexpected and unpredictable interactions with other processes and other histories.

In more concrete terms, this kind of theorising would need to learn some of the lessons that feminist theory has learnt in dealing with the contradictions between universal values and particular historical circumstances. As with Palan's writing, the vision is one of a mixture of predictability and contingency. Hutchings argues that this 'permits a lateral kind of theorising in which multiple, parallel and interacting presents may be understood in relation to one another, in this sense it is systemic as well as pluralist'. The hope is to avoid, on the one hand, subsuming different histories under one privileged master narrative and, on the other, retreating into an ethical commitment to a mysterious 'difference'.

Hutchings' writing is based on some very abstract considerations of the temporal logic of particular forms of explanation. Hobson provides some concrete historical reasons for drawing similar conclusions. He argues that even much critical IR theory remains tied within a Eurocentric outlook that tends to read history backwards from contemporary Western hegemony. The result is a misunderstanding of both the way the current international system was constructed historically (an overly endogenous and predetermined understanding of the rise of the West), and of the potential sites of agency for future change (a systematic undervaluing of Eastern agency). The East is seen as a residual that either inevitably succumbs to the rise of Western modernity or as a place in which Western practices and values are adopted and corrupted.

Hobson briefly sketches some of the lost East–West interactions that have shaped important parts of the modern world, through processes of interaction, of 'interstitial surprise'. He highlights the way in which the thirst for Chinese technology sucked the Europeans into international expansion in the first place (in attempts to acquire gold to exchange for Chinese goods) and went on to drive military revolutions in Europe. He cites the way financial techniques 'developed' by Italian bankers were borrowed from the Islamic world and beyond. He also traces the interactions between Western and Eastern black liberation movements from the abolition of slavery to the French revolution, to Haiti and back to anticolonial movements and the civil rights movement in the US. We can see echoes here of Hutchings' discussion of separate but intersecting histories.

Hobson argues for what he provocatively calls a 'post-racist' IR, which would read history in a less-Eurocentric way. In the process, it would recover Eastern agency in the past and open space for East–West dialogue in the present. In a move that is very reminiscent of Linklater's 'praxeological' approach, Hobson argues for a dialogical uncovering of neo-racist histories so that neo-racism can be held up against the professed ideals of the West in the same way that racist colonialism once was. In other words, where Hutchings draws largely post-structuralist conclusions (though non-relativist ones), Hobson calls for a more Habermasian use of public debate and reason to challenge existing conclusions.

So far, our discussions have been predominantly theoretical and methodological. They have primarily addressed questions about the philosophy of history and how those questions shape our understanding of possible political futures. All three have drawn attention to the need to continue to open up discussion further and to allow for more contingency than is present in much existing critical theory. On the other hand, all three have conceptualised that relationship differently. Palan comes closest to retaining a Marxist philosophy of history in which our knowledge of the world is not fundamentally problematic. However, we should constantly guard against the risk of over-simplifying causal processes and over-determining our expected findings. Hobson, too, sees problems with our actual understanding, more than with our potential ability to understand. His solution is very much a Habermasian one of improved dialogue but there is a particular emphasis on dialogue about history and with Eastern 'others'. Hutchings is more radical still, implying at least that even our ways of knowing about history need to be problematised and unsettled.

All three contributions, though, concentrate primarily on ways of understanding the world and move only a short distance in the direction of thinking about how to change it. Hobson and Hutchings both suggest that rethinking history and historiography is, itself, a potentially emancipatory exercise but say little about the potential political agency that might be involved in any subsequent struggles. In our next contribution, by Craig Murphy, that balance is reversed. Murphy has something to say about rethinking international relations but he is primarily concerned with the relationship between academic endeavour and political action.

He argues that Cox, and particularly Ashley's interventions, chimed with a mood that was already present amongst many American graduate students involved in peace research. Increasingly complex game theory which revealed the potential for learning in repeated games, had paved the way for an acceptance of the second of Habermas's three kinds of science, introduced in Ashley's article: the historical-hermeneutic sciences with their focus on *verstehen*, or empathic understanding of other human beings, their histories and world views. Murphy argues that critical IR has managed to hold open a place for this kind of endeavour within the US academy but has struggled to avoid being marginalised.

He suggests that there is still much more that could be done to listen to 'voices from below'. For Murphy, though, that is more likely to mean connections with anthropological and comparative work, rather than the postcolonial cultural theorists referred to by Hutchings and Hobson. He argues for greater attempts to think oneself into the world views of the marginal or, better still, to lend them a voice directly. Here, some feminist scholars have led the way in uncovering women's experiences at the 'margins' of the international system.

Murphy also argues that feminist scholars have been better at creating work that forms a bridge between academics and activists: work in which theorists take seriously the potential to change the world through what they write. He argues that critical IR scholars have much to learn from the feminist movement's success in creating UN resolution 1325 on 'Women, Peace and Security' or from Mahbub ul Haq's role in producing the UN Human Development Reports. While the human development approach may be reformist, rather than revolutionary, Murphy argues that there is much to be learned from it. To change the world, academic work needs to create an inspiring vision but one that is incorporated into and comes to inform real struggles. It must be accessible and contain concepts that can be reinterpreted to be meaningful in a wide range of vernaculars, informing struggles worldwide. The overall message is one of (partial) success in the academy that has yet to be matched in terms of practical global impact and influence. Murphy is inclined to concede Wallace's allegation that critical theorists tend to be 'monks'. What is required is greater scholarly engagement with the world's marginalised and with social movements in order to challenge political structures more directly than simply through engagement with problematic forms of knowledge in the academy.

In his recent writing, Robert Cox has acknowledged that he has perhaps been better placed to theorise the world as it is than to perform the role of a Gramscian 'organic intellectual', articulating a new common sense that can intellectually unite a potential counter-hegemonic block. Murphy praises his honesty (one of the attractions of Murphy's work, here and elsewhere, is his realistic pragmatism; implicitly academics should strategically consider how they can best change the world).[50] However, he also challenges academics to seek out opportunities to become *better* placed and to create opportunities for those that are to create academic work. That will help academic practice in lessening the distance between theorist and political actor, enhancing hermeneutic understanding of the objects of research, and ensure closer links between critical theory and political action.

Andrew Linklater's piece appears, at first sight, to provide a sharp contrast to Murphy's. Linklater's work continues his attempts to create critical theory on a grand scale, looking for the forms of immanent sensibility that can be built on to create a more inclusive and cosmopolitan global order. However, his piece also offers a corrective to his earlier work, grounded in a concern with uncovering new resources that can be drawn on to increase the motivational purchase of cosmopolitan ethics.

He argues that Kantian inspired critical theory, such as the work of Habermas, can privilege reason as a source of morality, at the expense of other potential sources. He argues that there is scope for an investigation of an 'embodied cosmopolitanism' building on the relationship between suffering and solidarity found in early Frankfurt School writing. Linklater draws on the writings of Weil, Schopenhauer, Horkheimer and Adorno to emphasise the importance of the recognition of suffering, revulsion at inhumane acts, and the idea of 'injurability', rather than the fear of sanction or meditation on categorical imperatives, in driving our ethical convictions. These themes are also echoed in approaches to human rights that centre on vulnerability to harm. He suggests that these primal ethical sensibilities may represent the immanent potential of a cosmopolitan ethics, to be realised fully through a long process of social learning, in the same way that Habermas famously argued that the first speech act contained the potential for communicative action.

---

[50] See also *Global Institutions* where Murphy points to the role of middle-class intellectuals, in contact with more radical social movements, in creating more solidarist global governance from the top down.

Linklater calls for a rediscovery of these themes and an investigation of their role in collective social learning over time. The impulse to assist suffering strangers, that is present universally but activated to varying degrees in different societies, points to a need for further exploration of the ways in which this immanent ethical impulse can be built on to create a cosmopolitan ethic that is based on more fundamental human impulses than the claims of reason.

Murphy and Linklater, in their different ways, raise doubts about the motivational purchase of contemporary critical IR theory. Nonetheless, they are calling for a continuing reinvigoration of the critical enterprise, rather than a rejection of it.

Richard Devetak provides us with a robust defence of the fundamentals of critical theory, against charges of utopian imperialism. His article, then, can be seen as a response to some of the rejectionist critiques that we reviewed earlier in this Introduction. Devetak tries to show that critical cosmopolitanism steers a middle-course between statism and anti-statism. He begins with a review of statist claims that any support for humanitarian intervention reopens space for metaphysically sanctioned, violent, moral crusading, that transgresses the limits to violence inaugurated by the modern states system.

Devetak traces this kind of critique back to the statism of Pufendorf who was concerned to prevent the kind of religious warfare that plagued early modern Europe. He deploys an eminently critical theoretic critique of statist claims to an autonomous, value-free sphere of the political. He argues that this conception of world order in fact privileges the normative value of security over claims for freedom. As Kant pointed out in his own criticism of Pufendorf, law that is bereft of moral standards pertaining to freedom is morally and politically dangerous.

However, one does not have to be fully Kantian to offer this kind of critique. For one thing, Habermasian critical cosmopolitanism shifts the imaginary dialogue of rational individuals to a communicative form of actual public dialogue. Perhaps more importantly, Kant saw law as ultimately subordinate to morality, while Habermas sees the two as complementary. Human rights, then, are not some form of ghostly authority that descends from the heavens. Rather, they are the product of socially produced temporal authority in the form of constitutionalism and democracy. Likewise, the authority of law must be morally questionable but through public debate and constitutional processes, rather than unilateral violent challenges.

When we return to the challenge of humanitarian intervention, then, critical theorists proceed cautiously. There is a recognition of the role the sovereignty principle plays in the constitution of world order but also a reluctance to see that sovereignty principle as transcendent and absolute. Humanitarian intervention should only be authorised through constitutionalised public channels such as the UN system and decisions should be made on a case by case basis, weighing the evidence and the important role that the non-intervention principle has in limiting violence.

Conclusions

We should not expect everyone to endorse the critical project in International Relations – one of the authors of this Introduction broadly does, one is broadly, though sympathetically, sceptical. However, we would argue that it is increasingly difficult to deny its importance to the discipline. For some, who would like to see the discipline settle into a single paradigm of 'normal science', that may be unsettling or even a sign of weakness. For the rest of us, though, it is a sign of strength. If Cox and Ashley are right, critical theory in its broadest and most fundamental sense, is necessary and, indeed unavoidable. All theory is situated and a single theory means that we only get a view from one place in the world, with its particular goals and purposes. A diversity of theories helps us to understand, argue over, and, for the more optimistic, even accommodate a far wider range of political positions. Critical theory has moved the discipline a long way in the right direction even if there continue to be problematic silences – most notably about the role of the non-Western world in shaping contemporary international relations.

Within this widely shared enthusiasm for a more complex and nuanced understanding of the production of the social world, though, there is room for a good deal of variety and disagreement. In particular, as we suggested in the section on 'immanent critique', there continue to be divergent views about the relationship between understanding the world and changing it. For post-structuralists, any contribution academia can make to change is largely through adopting the attitude of critique – through setting up constant challenges to orthodox narratives and the power they embody. For neo-Gramscians, on the other hand, for whom there is generally greater faith in the potential for social movements to pursue active emancipatory projects, there needs to be a closer relationship between new understandings and active political action. Frankfurt School theory seeks more to lay out a road-map for forms of increasingly inclusive collective reasoning that, presumably, take place out in the world. Academics may play some role in these processes but, for Habermas at least, there is some danger in crossing the line between theorist and activist.[51]

We see those differences of opinion and orientation in the different ways in which our contributors propose engaging with the 'East', the 'postcolonial' or the 'developing world'. Hutchings and Hobson see that engagement in terms of postcolonial theory, while Murphy points to involvement with concrete political struggles in the developing world (postcolonial theorists might question the distinction but many others would not).[52]

These differences certainly illustrate that critical theory has not produced *a* definitive answer to the ways in which emancipation is to be promoted. At the same time, though, they point to the potential for an ongoing and creative process of mutual engagement between different strands of critical theory. It is this debate and interaction that forces theorists to clarify their answers to difficult questions and challenges, such as the prospects for emancipation in the developing world or the precise relationship between academia, activism, and political change (if any such

---

[51] See his exchange with Nancy Fraser in the final section of Craig Calhoun (ed.), *Habermas and the Public Sphere* (Cambridge, MA: MIT Press, 1997).

[52] One of us, at least, would suggest that there is a far wider literature on the developing world that IR has yet to fully engage with than simply postcolonial literature (for some emerging correctives to this, see for example Anthony Payne, *The Global Politics of Unequal Development* (Basingstoke: Palgrave, 2005), and William Brown, 'Africa and International Relations: A Commentary on IR Theory, Anarchy and Statehood', *Review of International Studies*, 32 (2006), pp. 119–43). One does not have to be 'orthodox' to question the postcolonial or 'post-development' approach – see for example Jan Neverdeen Pieterse, 'My Paradigm or Yours? Alternative Development, Post Development, Reflexive Development', *Development and Change*, 29:2 (1998), pp. 343–73.

relationship can exist). Hopefully, the essays in this special issue will encourage exploration in all these issues.

Regardless of the outcomes of that exploration, critical theory has provided vital new resources for our understanding of international relations. Many issues of contemporary importance, particularly the continuing salience of identity politics, non-state violence and global economic processes, simply could not be addressed with the theoretical resources available within the discipline in the 1970s. The critical turn has forced scholars to develop a more nuanced understanding of the historical development of the world we inhabit and of the ways in which it is sustained by highly complex social processes. For some, that understanding provides important resources for confronting forms of exclusionary power. For others it simply makes the discipline of International Relations a far more intellectually stimulating and satisfying one to be working in. There is no reason to think that critical theory will cease to contribute to both these tasks in the years to come.

Looking back from somewhere: reflections on what remains 'critical' in critical theory

FRIEDRICH KRATOCHWIL

Abstract. This article revisits some of the theoretical debates within the field of IR since Ashley and Cox challenged the mainstream. But in so doing it attempts also to show that the proposed alternatives have their own blind spots that are subjected in the second part to discursive criticism. Neither Ashley's celebration of the wisdom of old realists nor their 'silence' on economics, nor the notion of 'internationalisation of the state' and of the world order are adequate for understanding politics in the era of globalisation. Instead, a critical theory has to examine the political projects that were engendered by the Hobbesian conception of order and rationality. Highlighting the disconnect between our present political vocabularies and the actual political practices, I argue that a critical theory has not only to 'criticise' existing approaches but has to rethink and re-conceptualise *praxis*, which is ill served by the analytical tools which are imported to this field from 'theory'.

Introduction

The task assigned to me here is to provide the view of a sympathetic 'outsider' assessing the project of critical theory. This charge, entailing some notion of objectivity that one cannot expect from the protagonists engaged in a pitched battle or long drawn out fight, seems fair enough. However, given that it is critical theory which is being discussed, it is somewhat ironic that some notion of scientific detachment and objectivity is invoked, although critical theory has always pointed out that the 'view from nowhere' is impossible. It is impossible not only in the sense that all theories are 'for' someone and naturalising the social world mystifies power through an hegemonic discourse. But it is also impossible because we never see the 'world out there' as it is, but comprehend it through our concepts. Thus even if we do not raise the *cui bono* question which the first issue addresses, we only observe observations, not things as they are. This realisation, of course, has implications for the assessment of our theories, as their truth can no longer simply be read off from the matches they provide between the concepts and 'the world'.

Given this predicament I think the term 'sympathetic' attains its full meaning. Precisely because I cannot claim an unassailably objective point of view, I have to engage with the arguments, have to give them a hearing, critically examine them, and weigh the evidence, instead of dogmatically asserting that 'science' or epistemology provide the applicable *a priori* standards. One need not rehearse the sometimes tedious epistemological debates over the last three decades when logical positivism was bolted together with empiricism, grafted upon Kuhnian notions of paradigms,

25

was modified by Lakatosian 'generative problem shifts' and pepped up by some notions of 'instrumentalism' *à la* Milton Friedman, in order to realise that such constructions are neither able to provide an accurate account of scientific 'progress' nor define usable demarcation criteria for distinguishing 'science' from other activities.[1]

Even if this nearly mindless borrowing of bits and pieces of rather different epistemologies had been done with greater sophistication and circumspection, the bitter truth is that in view of the problems encountered in logic (Gödel) and the Wittgensteinian turn to 'normal' language rather than relying on an ideal language, the foundationalist project of epistemology has failed. It has failed because it cannot account for the fact that science is an actual practice among a group of people who are not only deeply implicated in setting the research agenda, but in the construction of the very problems they investigate. Kant here once used the metaphor that scientists are no longer the pupils of nature but have become judges that compel nature to answer in a court of reason.[2] But the foundationalist project has also failed because harnessing the logical principle of the excluded middle (either something is or is not, a third possibility does not exist) turns out to be a poor philosopher's stone when applied to experiments that are inconclusive or 'indecidable'.[3] Thus instead of clear demonstration and incontrovertible evidence, debates and argumentation, burdens of proof, procedures introducing 'relevant' points or judgements of 'reputable' fellow scientists, and so on, become necessary. All this is a far cry from the near automatic process of conjectures and refutations that is supposed to provide us with 'truth' or at least transport us nearer and nearer to it.[4]

Aside from the issue of 'sympathy' there is also the temptation deriving from the charge of stocktaking some twenty-five years after. By definition such an undertaking has to become 'historical' in that the selection of issues, their embeddedness in a plot, the omissions and silences that are thereby created will carry much of the persuasiveness of the argument. We all know that there is of course no problem in selecting a turning point and then describing the sharp contrasts of the world 'before' and thereafter, as for example David Kennedy[5] has so nicely shown in the case of the League of Nations. Similarly, it is no secret that in selecting two points we always can draw a straight line through them and thus represent them either in terms of a causal or an evolutionary relationship. Although this provides illumination by low wattage as, of course, the narrative structure rather than the events themselves do most of the explaining, it is surprising how popular these stories still are. Similar plots – either of cycles as approvingly mentioned by Ashley, or of 'spirals' as sometimes suggested by the sequence of 'great debates' allegedly propelling IR theorising to a more encompassing view[6] – should be equally critically examined, even if their shortcomings are not as patently obvious. Again, the 'debates' turn out to be largely

---

[1] See, for example, the discussion by the philosopher of science Diesing concerning the Lakatosian attempt to save the Popperian notion of a demarcation criterion, in Paul Diesing, *How Social Science Works* (Pittsburgh, PA: University of Pittsburgh Press, 1991), ch. 2.

[2] See Immanuel Kant, *Critique of Pure Reason*, 2nd edn. (Preussische Akademieausgabe, vol. B, p. xiii).

[3] Here, a physicist and philosopher of science, John Ziman, *Reliable Knowledge* (Cambridge: Canto, 1991).

[4] See Karl Popper, *Conjectures and Refutations* (New York: Harper 1965).

[5] David Kennedy, 'The Move to Institutions', *Cardozo Law Review*, 8 (April 1987), pp. 841–988.

[6] See Yosef Lapid, 'The Third Debate', *International Studies Quarterly*, 33, pp. 235–54.

ex post facto constructions provided by the historical narrative rather than by the events themselves. Thus, as Peter Wilson reminds us, the first debate hardly took place and the exchanges were quite different from the sparring between well-identified opponents, as the disciplinary history suggests. Finally, given that we are not even sure how many debates we had[7] – and here the controversy that Cox and Ashley created does not even 'make it' in the official disciplinary catalogue – this should give us pause and caution us against disciplinary tales. The remedy again is not a 'totalising' history of the discipline, simply because any history has to have a 'point' and that inevitably requires selection and recollection of those things important and those which are left in the background or are passed over. The remedy consists rather in the realisation of the inevitable limitations of any 'story' and their critical examination through other (possible) stories.

With these caveats in mind, it is clear that the following discussion will not be a story of who influenced whom. It will not be a story of triumph – after all both Ashley and Cox were trail-blazers who made it possible for others to raise new issues and pursue a research agenda significantly different from 'mainstream' IR – or of despair, since the success might have come at a heavy price, at least in the American community. (Europe for obvious historical reasons admittedly presents a different lie of the land.) For one, the reigning orthodoxy is far from having been emasculated. The fact that 'primers' of political science, such as King, Keohane and Verba's new 'bible',[8] has been the most successful book ever published by Princeton University Press, speaks for itself. Thus the vast majority of students are still being 'trained' (not to say indoctrinated) in 'the scientific method' no matter what area or problem they want to investigate. Apparently, as in the case of the Midas muffler, 'one size fits all'. Why? Because we (the authors) say so! Similarly, the power structure within the profession and reflected in the 'top departments' has remained predictably stable. Journals have proliferated and certainly enabled younger scholars to have some 'voice', but proliferation has also had a downside. The ability to provide for a wide public forum has decreased, and thus different segments of the profession preach to the choir instead of to the congregation. Finally, it is the 'constructivists' who have mainly profited from both the demise of orthodox Marxism and the new openings created by the scholarly attack on the old bastions of structuralism and statism and by the changing agenda of world politics. But constructivists seem quite busy fighting among one another for the 'middle ground',[9] trying to build bridges to old projects that were better forgotten, instead of fighting the barbarians at the gates.

So all is not well in the academic citadel, but this is hardly news. In the following I shall, therefore, not concentrate on showing who influenced whom in an attempt to 'measure' (or better assess) the impact of Cox's and Ashley's work – an assessment that hardly could be done in the time and the pages accorded to me – but rather take their central point of a critical theory seriously and ask what a critical turn of theorising about (inter)national politics entails today. In short, I am more interested

---

[7] See, for example, Ole Waever's argument in his 'The Rise and Fall of the Inter-Paradigm Debate', in Steve Smith, Ken Booth and Marysia Zalewski (eds.), *Positivism and Beyond* (Cambridge: Cambridge University Press, 1996), ch. 7.

[8] Gary King, Robert Keohane and Sidney Verba, *Designing Social Inquiry: Scientific Inference in Qualitative Research* (Princeton, NJ: Princeton University Press, 1994).

[9] See here both the attempts of Emmanuel Adler, 'Seizing the Middle Ground', *European Journal of International Relations*, 3 (September 1977), pp. 319–63; and also Alexander Wendt, *Social Theory of International Politics* (Cambridge: Cambridge University Press, 1999).

in the meaning of the term for our present predicament as 'theorists' of IR whose familiar parameters from the 'state' to 'power' and 'rationality' seem to dissolve before our very eyes. Thus, rather than attempting to focus on a story that traces the influence of certain 'ideas' one finds in these two seminal articles, I want to 're-read' and reflect on these manifestos and examine what our present task is now, at a time when the old verities have gone, and even history – the mainstay of prudential realism celebrated by Ashley – has ceased to 'throw much light on the future', as de Toqueville has already suggested.[10]

For that purpose I shall briefly review in the next section both contributions – being aided by one of my former commentaries written when Ashley's article originally appeared[11] – before I identify some critical areas for further theoretical development and also suggest some significant changes in the conceptualisations and research agenda of a future critical theory.

What is 'critical' in critical theory: some thoughts on re-reading Ashley and Cox

Since we cannot be 'critical' in general – as little as we can be doubtful of everything, Descartes speculation notwithstanding – we always are critical of something and that means that getting the context right in which the specific criticisms are voiced is a crucial first step. But since every theory criticises some other theory and its results, as criticism is the main way in which we attempt to attain warranted knowledge,[12] the distinct objective of the critical theory project seems to be indistinguishable from 'normal science'. That is after all what most exponents of positivist and mainstream approaches suggest when they point to the importance of 'tests' and to the controversies concerning the datasets or the techniques and procedures that fuel the debates in the journals of political science. Thus while this observation disposes quickly of the frequently made argument that critical theory is somewhat autistic since it only 'criticises' but does not provide a more 'positive' prospect of how to go about or research, it does so by subverting at the same time the *raison d'être* of the critical project.

I think it is here that both Ashley and Cox have pointed to a crucial conceptual distinction that also provides the justification for theorising in a critical mode. Cox's felicitous distinction between a 'problem solving' and a 'critical' theory, going back to Horkheimer and the Frankfurt school, and Ashley's perhaps less felicitous but extensive argument about neo-realism's 'orrery of errors' speak exactly to this issue. Both identify the treatment of the 'facts' of the social world as if they were 'natural kinds' as a step in the wrong direction, quite aside from the question whether even in the natural sciences the notion of natural kinds is still tenable. If our concepts are not simply describing the world but are actually 'constitutive' of what we see, as Kant has already pointed out, then the 'received model' of science has little to offer, and certainly does not provide the *via regia* to a theory of action that is indispensable for understanding the world of practice.

---

[10] Alexis de Toqueville, *Democracy in America* (New York: Knopf, 1991).
[11] Friedrich Kratochwil, 'Errors Have Their Advantage', *International Organization*, 38 (Spring 1984), pp. 305–20.
[12] See here the pragmatist critique by William James, *Pragmatism* (New York: Dover, 1995).

Furthermore, except when we bracket issues of responsibility and are simply concerned with selecting the appropriate means to a chosen goal that is treated as given, the reduction of praxis to one of *techne* denies the role of practice in establishing and changing of social orders. But such a reduction might also result from habit, from the inability to image alternatives – a point made by Gramsci and reintroduced by Cox – or it might derive from the fascination with the means, as when in 'strategic studies' the discussion is frequently reduced to issues of tactics, or to the technical fine-tuning of force, or even the identification of the law as generalisations in social life. Clausewitz had already warned of such a reduction of strategic problems in his controversies with the 'theoretically'-oriented von Buelow. He was quick to point out the disastrous consequences such an approach might entail,[13] but his well-supported arguments have, of course, not prevented subsequent authors from modelling wars in terms of the exchange ratios produced by weapons systems, and predicting 'victory' on the basis of marginal utility calculations derived from body counts. If we needed any further proof of the dangers of such undertakings we just have to look at the present situation in Iraq which demonstrates what happens if one mistakes capabilities for power, and force as the first and foremost *ratio* of politics.[14] The point is not only that such a conceptualisation of power simply ignores the fungibility problem, it also misconceives of power as a 'possession', leaving out the social context. But whether, for example, a threat works depends not only on the stick I wield, or the commitment I try to communicate, but also on the response of the threatened and his ability of communicating how 'un-impressed' he is, his 'faking it', that is, his apparent compliance with the demands while working around them, as both Saddam and Milosevic have so amply demonstrated.

Putting these issues squarely on the table it is clear that critical theory is heir to many controversies, such as the distinction between technical knowledge and practice, the humanist critique against Descartes' obsession with certainty, as exemplified by Vico, the Marxist notion of 'false consciousness' and fetishisation, the explaining/understanding controversy and the latest debate concerning 'structuralism's scandalous anti-humanism' as Giddens once called it,[15] which Ashley takes as his foil for making the same point. But precisely because critical theory raises such existential issues and does so in a systematic fashion rather than by paradigmatic example (as for example the drama), or by telling a story (as is the case in myths), it is clear that its claim to 'truth' cannot be one of a proper conceptual matching some pre-existing reality. Besides, if the problem of praxis were one of simply arriving at the truth we should be going around muttering tautologies, '*a* is *a* is *a*, is *a* . . .', as the latter statement is definitely 'true'. Obviously we are after something more when we deliberate about actions, or ask for advice. Consequently, we are not mistaken when we believe that there is something terribly amiss in a perspective on action that orients itself mainly on logical rigour, demonstrative proof, and universal validity,

---

[13] See, for example Peter Paret, 'Clausewitz', in Peter Paret (ed.), *Makers of Modern Strategy* (Princeton, NJ: Princeton University Press, 1986), ch. 7.

[14] See, for example, Waltz's remark in his *Theory of International Politics* (Reading, MA: Addison Wesley, 1979): 'In politics force is said to be the *ultima ratio*. In international politics force serves not only as the ultimate reason, but indeed as the first and constant one.' Ibid. p. 113.

[15] Anthony Giddens, *Central Problems in Social Theory* (Berkeley, CA: University of California Press, 1979), p. 38.

instead of being attentive to issues of completeness, relevance, and appropriateness, even if considerable difficulties arise from the multiplicity of criteria which we have to employ.

There are several corollaries that follow from these initial remarks. One is that critical theory has always to move on two levels. Precisely because it cannot take the 'givens' of the social world for granted, be it a state, a technique or a political project, it has to examine the issues raised in the context of a problem-solving exercise, while at the same time it has to question the naturalist accounts that endow these 'givens' with their facticity. Consequently, it cannot rely on some ultimate tests that could settle the issues by some deictic procedure – as the validity of 'tests' on the lower level are usually called into question by the considerations on the meta-level, and tests on the latter would have to assume some ultimate incontrovertible foundations. In short, critical theory cannot invoke a 'view from nowhere' and use the traditional instruments available to its adherents: clear, stipulative definitions, acceptance of ready-made datasets, methods of 'inference', and so on. Instead, it has to do its work by engaging with the vocabulary of theorists, or with a generally accepted 'truth', and has to subject it to cross-examination. Here, not the 'correspondence' of its terms to 'the world', but its relations to other terms in a semantic field, as well as their archaeology, are at issue. What the terms hide or reveal, what questions they allow and how the bounds of sense are thereby drawn, now become the decisive questions.

Thus Andrew Moravcik', articulating the objection of many 'mainstreamers', that the main difference between, for example, constructivists and the adherents of mainstream approaches (counting at least some of the constructivists and exponents of critical theorising) is that the latter believe in testing while the others go about their business in a somewhat woolly-headed fashion,[16] is getting the story precisely wrong. The issue is not test versus non-test but what 'can count' as a test or provide sufficient evidence to establish a proposition (or rather justify a particular judgement) at least presumptively. Part of the difficulty has of course to do with the problems that in practical matters the choice situations (or cases) can be subsumed under certain generalisations, but that the latter are usually far from providing conclusive grounds for subsuming a case (or cases) under this or another generalisation. Under these circumstances substantive rather than formal criteria have to be adduced to justify an interpretation and come to some conclusions as to what this 'whole thing is about'. Again, if the situations are well specified, and independent of each other, large numbers will help us in our 'inferences'. But if we have only a few and know that they are not independent of each other, no positive 'test' will be decisive. It can be at best a part of an argumentative strategy that has to stand on other than formal grounds.[17]

A second corollary following from the considerations above is that the critical intent can easily get lost or crowded out when the examination proceeds by the exegesis of the texts. Thus arguing the finer points of 'structure' and charging the neorealists with 'stasis' can be countered by the observation that, after all, some neorealists do explicitly focus on change and that 'therefore' the charge against

---

[16] Andrew Moravcik, 'Theory Synthesis in International Relations: Real not Metaphysical', in *Forum: Are Dialogue and Synthesis Possible in International Relations? International Studies Review*, 5 (2003), pp. 123–56, at 131.

[17] For a further discussion of problems of practical reasoning, see Albert Jonsen and Stephen Toulmin, *The Abuse of Casuistry* (Berkeley, CA: University of California Press, 1988).

neorealism is invalid. Here the heuristic devices we usually employ in our research as part of our good practice actually can misguide us. As I suggested twenty-five years ago, when writing a comment on Ashley's article for the International Organization symposium,[18] using ideal types, such as 'neo-realism', might entail certain costs. Since ideal types are not based on simple inductive generalisations it might not be instantiated by any one writer, or not all of them might share all the characteristics identified by the ideal type.

Thus given the 'polemic' character of the original indictment and the charged atmosphere in the court of academia, it is likely that by showing, for example, that 'change' is a topic which (some) neorealist addressed, not only is a particular writer absolved from the indictment of 'stasis', but 'neorealism' itself might get off the hook. The larger and actually more important questions then remain unexamined, whether the processes of change that can be analysed in terms of shifting capabilities or even in terms of the 'uneven law of growth' that Gilpin uses in order to distinguish between positional and hegemonic wars,[19] do justice to phenomena like transformative change. An instance of the latter type we encountered when the bipolar structure of the postwar order melted into thin air with the demise of the Soviet Union. Similarly, the even more general problem that remains unexamined is that of 'history', that is, not the notion of history as the teacher (*magistra vitae*)[20] through examples, or of the construction of long waves that can be made out (with some imagination and the massaging of data), but of the 'historicity' of political action to which Nietzsche alerted us. It was precisely that point that inspired Bull's plea in the second debate for what he called a 'classical approach'.[21] Here the crucial issue is how, from the present, a particular past is 'recollected', which in turn shapes our preferences by evoking an identity and constitutes the set of alternatives for realising our future projects.[22]

Under these circumstances debates easily get confusing, as even single writers often use contradictory assumptions and thereby make – wittingly or unwittingly – their 'theory' refutation-proof. Much of the controversy then clouds the relevant issues, as suggested above, or bogs them down in a scholastic exercise of compiling citations and exhaust themselves in proving that so-and-so is or is not 'really' a realist, constructivist and so on. Such is the case, for example, if a Marxist writer suddenly discovers a theory of the state, or transforms Marx's well known dialectics into a 'structure',[23] or suddenly includes in the notion of 'production' not only work in the traditional sense, but also ideas, thereby voiding the notion of 'materialism' of any meaning. When we are dealing with such moving targets, the request that the 'real' Marx please stand up is not an irrational *crie de coeur*. Nevertheless, some of these debates are of course inevitable, as an approach pioneered by one thinker

---

[18] Kratochwil, 'Errors Have Their Advantage'.

[19] Robert Gilpin, *War and Change in World Politics* (Cambridge: Cambridge University Press, 1981).

[20] See the discussion of the topos of History as Teacher of Life by Reinhart Koselleck, 'Historia magistra vitae', in Reinhard Koselleck, *Futures Past: On the Semantics of Historical Time* (Cambridge, MA: MIT Press, 1985), pp. 21–39.

[21] See Hedley Bull, 'International Relations Theory: The Case for a Classical Approach', *World Politics*, 18 (April 1966), pp. 361–77.

[22] For a further discussion see my 'History, Action and Identity', *European Journal of International Relations*, 12 (March 2006), pp. 5–9.

[23] This after all engendered Thompson's criticism of Althusser and provided Ashley with his opening argument. See E. P. Thompson, *The Poverty of Theory and Other Essays* (New York: Monthly Review Press, 1978).

might be developed further by another. Here consistency with any particular canonical text might be the virtue of small minds, given the purposes of analysis and the fact that even in canonised writings there are different emphases and contradictions usually abound, as, for example, the debate about the early and the late Marx showed.

The inevitable picking and choosing from the canonical texts might disturb the purist whose concern is with keeping the orthodox lore free from any contamination. It might also be of concern to the intellectual historian, but for those of us who are concerned with understanding practice the proof of the pudding will always be in the eating, not in the ingredients or where they came from. Here Cox's use of Marx and Gramsci provides a good example. Irrespective of whether his interpretation of Marx is in tune with the best available interpretation of Marx's oeuvre as a whole – given also that Gramsci's interpretation seems quite unorthodox – Cox's framework for analysing change on the social, the state and international level is a creative adaptation that has to be recognised on its own merits irrespective of whether or not it accords with the original Marxian template.

When we compare this creative adaptation with much of the debate on realism, the differences could not be more striking. Most of these discussions were rather useless since their generation was nearly entirely driven by scholastic interests rather than by the analysis of actual practical political problems to which the critical reflections on a theory should be addressed. To that extent perhaps the whole detour to return to classical realism as suggested by Ashley, which set off the subsequent debate, was an exercise in over-kill. The case against a structuralist theory *à la* Waltz could have been made by pointing out that this 'theory' is based on what is called in logic a simple category mistake, even if it was one of the first order. After all, from the fact that something is possible we cannot infer without further information what is probable. It does not allow one to specify even 'the range', as Waltz suggests, within which the predicted outcome falls. Thus even if we have bought Waltz's 'systemic' argument on the effects of anarchy – a rather tall order at that, given that many governments are the reason for domestic violence spilling over into civil war – no particular conclusions follow, unless and until I provide further information that allows me to make risk assessments. Thus one really has to wonder how the conjuring up of the 'ghosts' of realism could have improved on these objections.

How convoluted and confused things got is evidenced by the fact that sometimes the simple self-definition of people as 'realists' (only to be later repeated by 'constructivists' of various stripes) was enough to count them among the fraternity, with little concern for whether they were subscribing to any of realism's tenets or were simply shamelessly engaged in theorists' favourite game of '*ad hocery*'. The fact that in the end even emotional dispositions, such as 'optimism' or 'pessimism'[24] were invoked to lend some force to some theoretical claims, does not betoken critical awareness but is only one step ahead of utilising the zodiac as an *explanans*. The assertion that realists are pessimists somehow always brings to my mind the image of the 'soooo sad' clown which (for instance) Venetian souvenir shops try to pawn off

---

[24] See, for example Charles Glaser, 'Realists as Optimists', *International Security*, 19 (Winter 1994/95), pp. 50–90. As for the prevailing view that realists view the world as a cruel place and thus are pessimistic about sustainable cooperation see, for example, John Mearsheimer, 'The False Promise of International Institutions', *International Security*, 19 (Winter 1994/95), pp. 5–49.

on the gawking tourists, while it took admittedly an even larger leap of imagination to discover the optimism that is supposed to shine through the Hobbesian conception of man in the state of nature.

This leads me to a third corollary. Since critical theory cannot resort to some incontrovertible foundations, it inevitably has to engage in some 'translations' in making its points and has to make use of the hermeneutic circle in establishing its case. The first problem is that something might get lost in translation, or it might not be directly translatable, as the vocabulary of one 'theory' emphasises different problems and backgrounds to others. Thus the social contract theory that, within roughly two generations, supplanted in the seventeenth century the notion of the 'body politic', cannot be understood as a more 'accurate' representation and thus an improvement in theorising, as a polity is neither a contract nor a body. Rather, both 'theories' (or better, basic metaphors, serving as the basis for further theorising) emphasise different problems and provide different answers to the problems of order, obligation, opposition to authority, and political change.

Understanding these changes, then, entails not relying on normalised datasets or searching for transhistorically valid generalisations, but tracing the changes in the constitutive and regulative rules underlying the institutions and practices. This then requires a reliance on reasoning from 'case to case',[25] and on analogies, rather than on deductions and inductive generalisations. And it requires the evidence to be 'weighed' rather than assumed to speak for itself. To that extent a 'fact' attains its meaning from its place in the whole semantic field, but the whole, in turn, is constituted by the facts. Here the 'criticism of sources' used by historians, or the law of evidence in law, provide probably better templates for the necessary critical evaluation procedures than the experimental design used in natural sciences, or the multivariate analysis familiar from the large-*n* research in social science.

Since the fraternity of international relations specialists is usually not familiar with these methodologies, there exists the tendency to use some 'proxies', either an 'ideal type' or a 'tradition' which however usually have serious problems. After all, the invention of a 'tradition' which establishes a true 'canon' sits quite uneasily with the 'critical' element in critical theorising. Even worse is the problem when such an analysis tries to explain political change not only through 'translations' and interpretation but attempts to make a virtue out of the difficulties that arise in translation. Hence Ashley's attempt to create a cohort of real 'realists', whose wisdom allegedly far transcended the intellectually flat-footed attempts of present neo-realists, that only resulted in a 'grotesque mediocrity',[26] but whose neglect of (for instance) economic questions in international relations is celebrated as a 'silence' that implies some deep insight. Although Ashley later admits that this 'silence' of classical realism cannot provide a template for our present political practice and that actually the present era is characterised by the 'economisation of politics and loss of political autonomy',[27] the celebration on the one hand and the denial of its relevance for our present predicament on the other hand, deserve some further comment. As Ashley writes somewhat opaquely:

---

[25] For a general discussion of casuistic reasoning, see Albert Jensen and Stephen Toulmin, *The Abuse of Casuistry* (Berkeley, CA and Cambridge: Cambridge University Press), ch. 8.

[26] Ashley, 'Poverty of Neorealism', p. 264.

[27] Ibid., p. 278.

Where competent statesmen are prepared to recognise problems, classical realism will give voice to problems. But where competent statesmen have an interest in silence, classical realism will be silent too. Among these problems are those that would call into question the tradition within whose context statesmen demonstrate their competence, secure recognition, and orchestrate the empowering of states. For the classical realist, as for the competent statesman, such questions are not literally forgotten. Rather they inhabit the domain of 'that which must not be said'. They are unspoken and unrecognised by competent parties as a condition of their competence.[28]

This is, however, a rather odd argument since it violates the critical intent of critical theory in important respects. For one, it is one thing to argue for the primacy of practice, rather than to begin with some assumptions, develop a model and then cast around for its application, as has become fashionable. It is another thing to celebrate silences or blind spots without further ado, by making them appear as part of the *arcana imperii*, too secret to be communicated to the unwashed masses.

Here, of course, we have a problem with the Hobbesian roots of realism on the one hand and the 'emancipatory project of critical theory' on the other. Hobbes' sovereign, after all, held power not only because he was in possession of the means of coercion, but also because he was the 'fixer of signs', decreeing what the authoritative meaning of our vocabulary was. This construction presupposes not only the mystification of power that is thereby achieved, it also prevents, under the guise of a pacifying function, dissent, disagreement and 'politics' within the commonwealth. Indeed, disagreements and discussion are 'silenced' as only one point of view is allowed, and politics as the negotiation among the free citizens is now substituted by the silencing logic of administration and a self-justifying decisionism of the sovereign. Nothing could be farther from the 'emancipatory' project of critical theory. Habermas's legitimisation crisis is explicitly mentioned by Ashley but the gist of the argument seems forgotten, that is, that the modern state loses legitimacy because of its persistent attempt to create administrative and technical structures in which 'experts', armed with the knowledge 'of how things are and how they cannot be otherwise', are exempted from control and the need of justification.

Even if we do not share the belief that all knowledge has to be emancipatory and will 'set men and women free' – here Greek tragedy and Oedipus in particular articulates a much less comforting truth that is also part of our predicament – the realist's silencing seems hardly an appropriate strategy for handling complex problems. As even administrative law recognises, the stakeholders must get a hearing and problems of development can hardly be reduced to the expertise derived from neoclassical equilibrium analysis, as the World Bank (and to a much lesser extent) the IMF found out. To that extent one also has to be a bit sceptical that the new 'dialectical competence model' that Ashley proposed, is able to take care of these objections. If this model is only another silencing strategy in newer garb, as Ashley is keenly aware of fundamental changes that cannot be treated by the old vocabulary, one has to wonder how it could fulfil its promise to explain and guide practice.

Thus, rather than celebrating realism – even if such a historical reflection might disclose important elements that have been lost and need to be recovered – a more critical historical reflection is needed. Here at least alternative explanations ought to have been entertained, aside from getting the historical record straight and submitting to hero worship. Thus realism's silence on economics might indeed have had

---

[28] Ibid., p. 274.

more to do with the demise of mercantilism and the liberal sequestering of 'property' to the 'private realm', mystifying power by making it appear non-political and establishing thereby the silent empire of civil society, as Justin Rosenberg has called it.[29] Such an explanation would fit Britain better than the continental states, where the notions of good governance by the 'sovereign' included until late into the nineteenth century explicit provisions for welfare and economic growth as proper functions of the state. It was ingrained not only in the self-understanding of rulers as good heads of the (state) who cared for their subjects in a way analogous to the *pater familias* of traditional estate society. This understanding was also supported by a widely shared notion of 'Polizey-Wissenschaft' as the proper form of knowledge for exercising power.[30]

Besides, in addition to a highly problematic reading of the historical record, Ashley seems also to have gotten the story of 'classical' realism in some respects wrong. After all, as Morgenthau – one of his key witnesses – suggests, the 'classical' realist looking over the shoulder of the statesman understands the latter's actions better than the decision-maker himself. The principle of national interest in terms of power, and the construction of a *homo politicus*, provides him with the necessary conceptual instruments for an 'objective' understanding of politics that at the same time frees us from investigating the motives of the actors. Thus many of the shortcomings criticised in neorealism, such as objectivism and the attempts to make the field more scientific via the construction of an ideal type of actor, have their identifiable roots in vintage realism.

To that extent the construction of a 'tradition' might be less advantageous than it at first appears. True, one has to begin somewhere, and entering the debate by using the realist vocabulary assures the familiarity of the audience with the terms used, an important asset for communication given that neologisms enhance the chance of misunderstandings. In addition, using a storyline and emplotting the facts and events in it, such as the narrative of progress – familiar from mainstream accounts – or of cycles or even decay which we encountered earlier – will already have shown us in a subtle way how things came to pass. It provides us with some assurances of what the field is and who the *dramatis personae* are. Certainly, therefore, such stories have to be told, as we create through them the protagonists in the real or imagined 'debates', as Cameron Thies[31] has shown, even when this type of recollection is most of the time less than accurate.[32] Nevertheless, it seems that redrawing the boundaries of sense this way – conjuring up the old ghosts and having them bear witness of how shallow their progeny has become – is not necessarily helpful for the critical theory project. Precisely because such an approach relies on the communication strategy of turning the 'originals' against their sorry later fakes, one might grant too much to the originals. One might forget to examine the naturalising moves they made and that deserve as much critical examination as the contemporary 'orrery of errors'. In

---

[29] Justin Rosenberg, *The Empire of Civil Society: A Critique of the Realist Theory of International Relations* (London: Verso, 1994).

[30] See, for example, the literature of the Holy Roman Empire the fundamental discussion of Hans Maier, *Die aeltere deutsche Staats- und Verwaltungslehre* (Neuwied, Germany: Luchterhand, 1966).

[31] See Cameron Thies, 'Progress, History and Identity in IR Theory', *European Journal of International Relations*, 8 (Summer 2002), pp. 147–85.

[32] See, for example Peter Wilson, The Myth of the First Great Debate, in Tim Dunne, Michael Cox and Ken Booth (eds.), *The Eighty Years Crisis: International Relations 1919–1999* (Cambridge: Cambridge University Press, 1998), pp. 1–16.

addition, one might also might become captive to an agenda and a research programme that falls dramatically short of the project of critical theory. To that extent it might be useful to outline a few areas which seem to me 'critical' not in the sense of simply subjecting the work of others to criticism – as important as it might be – but to provide an independently articulated positive heuristics for the field.

What needs to be done

In the following I want to focus on three areas that, without any suggestion of ranking in importance or completeness, seem to me topics of central importance to any work that aspires to be part of the critical project. The first is, of course, the focus on 'politics' – not only as a question of who gets what when and how – but also which type of constitutive understandings authorise particular practices and thus create or disable specific types of authority. Hobbes' move of creating a space for politics that is actually depoliticised by mystifying power in possessions, and by banning any form of public contestation, has briefly been mentioned. But the silencing went in a way even deeper to the 'subject' since even the 'individual' must now look for his satisfaction to the 'pursuit of happiness' rather than to achieving public recognition within a community. Similarly, as the feminist critique emphasised correctly, repopulating the shadowy Hobbesian 'public space' with new members by suddenly admitting women to it, will not do. Here the silencing proves more insidious. Women had not only been sequestered to the 'privacy' of household but their very subjectivity as political agents had been denied by the alleged 'weaknesses' of their sex or their 'irrationality', both of which rendered them powerless and subjected them to domination and even invisible 'domestic' violence.

The more general point is, therefore, that a critical theory has to address the problem of how modes of knowledge and political practices interact positively and negatively. This entails not only the tracing of parallels between women's struggles, social movements, indigenous resistance and anti-colonial efforts to regain some space for action by first and foremost reappropriating one's own history and identity. It will have to include the question which Steve Smith adumbrated in his ISA presidential address,[33] to what extent we as scholars aid and abet certain practices that reproduce and help traditional policies, but are inattentive to, or even hide, important issues that ought to receive a 'public' hearing. That this responsibility might be of a lesser kind than that of 'experts', who more often than not create havoc by providing wrong strategic and economic advice,[34] is arguable. But despite the 'many hands' problem involved here and the apparent remoteness of the activity from the actual harm done, it seems to me that it cannot be entirely evaded. Here more modesty and the observance of the Hippocratic principle 'above all do no harm', instead of the aggressiveness and arrogance that comes with privileged knowledge – who can reasonably oppose the expert? – would be required.

---

[33] See Steve Smith, 'Singing our World into Existence: IR Theory and September 11', *International Studies Quarterly*, 48 (September 2004), pp. 499–515.

[34] See, for example Joseph Stiglitz, *Globalization and its Discontent* (New York: Norton, 2002); *Joseph Stiglitz and the World Bank*: Selected Speeches by Joseph Stiglitz, with a commentary by Ha Joon Chang (London: Anthem 2001).

Similarly, given the 'professionalisation' of the field, 'seeing what one sees' and giving voice to it, seems to have become a commodity in diminishing supply. Getting along, worrying about one's career, building networks and vying for the position of a gate-keeper in the profession, seems considerably more important than pursuing necessary but unpopular topics and letting the chips fall where they do, as David Kennedy once acerbically remarked when contrasting the civil servants and experts of international law and organisation involved in creating the League of Nations with the new professionals who are part of the transnational elite of law firms, NGOs, bureaucracies and so on. While formerly the professionals were inspired by the image of forging swords into ploughshares, the contemporary young professional just tries to 'forge' (both in the sense of making and of 'faking') his CV into something useful for his later 'real' job.

Part of this phenomenon has of course to do with the transformation of politics and of the public weal. While states were previously relatively good containers of their populations and of most of their transactions, the communications revolution, the globalisation of production and of financial markets, as well as migrations, have altered this picture considerably. Thus, while formerly the 'inter' in international relations was quite well defined and the agents in charge for its regulation were clearly the states, the experience of the loss of steering capacity, decried in the first wave of the globalisation debate,[35] bears witness to the anxieties those changes generated, despite the fact that the 'internationalisation of the state' had grown by leaps and bounds. But while the naïve interpretation, that the market was now ascending[36] while the 'state' was on its way out, was clearly faulty, it did suggest that even the relatively sophisticated conceptual tools of Cox's approach are no longer sufficient for capturing the dynamics of the system. Thus while, for example, the theoretical proposition of the transnational formation of a managerial class might throw some light on the mobility and particular interests with which this class increasingly vocally defends its position – indicating that we have here no longer simply a class by itself, but a 'class for itself' with a specific awareness of its goals and position in the global market – it would be difficult to find such an awareness among the labouring masses. Here, the former food riots addressed to the national government have been followed by more spectacular protests at WTO meetings and at World Social Fora. But for the labour markets, which still remain mostly national and which, if anything, have become, through tougher immigration policies, more exclusive, nothing dramatic seems to be in the offing.

The reason for this is not only that solidarity indeed faces many hurdles when the interest between low-wage and high-wage countries have to be bridged, but that 'labour' plain and simple is steadfastly losing out to the more and more sophisticated skills that are required by an 'information society' and a 'knowledge economy', where they are the driving forces of the value-adding process and of productivity. Given also that more and more wealth will be derived from intellectual property rights – which, in contrast to the production of goods, are not subject to decreasing returns due to marginal utility – it is indeed rather strange how this topic has aroused – outside the circle of some specialists and some law journals – little interest

---

[35] See, for example Susan Strange, *The Retreat of the State* (Cambridge: Cambridge University Press, 1976).

[36] For a more extensive discussion of these points see Doris Fuchs and Friedrich Kratochwil (eds.), *Transformative Change and Global Order* (Muenster, Germany: LIT Verlag, 2003).

among the general public. If these property rights appropriate all the potential of future gains, there will be little to redistribute unless the 'silence' created by this 'privatisation' of the most promising avenues for future economic growth is broken.

But let us come back to the problems posed for critical analysis by the phenomenon of globalisation. As we observe, the internationalisation of the state has certainly not led to the demise of the state, even if it curtailed some policy options. While thus the original misinterpretations might have been the result of anxieties (as exemplified in the lament of loss of steering capacity) that later studies, such as that of Scharpf,[37] corrected, the psychologising of the analytical failure hides an important problem which critical theory ought to address: the problem of how logic can misguide actual research. As already suggested, the bivalence principle of logic, excluding any third possibility, here shows its drawbacks. To conclude that when one element becomes stronger it implies that the other is getting weaker is convincing only if we mistake a logical principle for an existential proposition. True, sometimes the two seem to coincide when, for example, someone's increase in security is likely to result in others' greater insecurity. But if we know anything about power it is that power is not a simple zero-sum concept and that much of it is generated not by traditional 'capabilities' but by institutions. Consequently the density of institutions might create 'islands' of order, as the former regime debate suggested against realism's anarchy *problématique*. Furthermore these islands of order might be sustained by state and non-state actors who cooperate in finding new organisational solutions to the problem of cooperation, and increase the effectiveness of their programmes in the pursuit of their mandated goals.[38] In doing so, these new organisational forms often move away from the traditional rule-based approach to administration and introduce private sector management techniques. As successful as such attempts might be in solving a particular problem by muddling through the otherwise impenetrable jungle of veto players and insoluble legal hurdles, such arrangements have also created some 'disorder' at the same time. We simply cannot assume without committing a grave fallacy of composition, that all these particular orders will fit 'hand in glove' into a comprehensive global order. What might make for non-discrimination in free trade might not make for good environmental protection or for the observance of human rights. Taking care of the potential externalities that such free-standing regimes are likely to engender would require other, well-institutionalised arrangements to deal with the inevitable irritations arising out of their interaction. In addition, the 'silent' and powerless have no means of linking themselves to some network or becoming part of a 'transnational coalition', even if their life is vitally affected by the operation of these networks. This was, after all, the function of the traditional 'public'. But where does one go now that the public has splintered into many single-issue regimes and networks and when it is no longer clear who or what the public or the 'we' is, in whose name issues can be raised? These points need not be rehearsed here any further, as the recent past provides sufficient examples.

---

[37] Fritz Scharpf and Vivian Schmidt, *Welfare and Work in the Open Economy* (Oxford: Oxford University Press, 2000).

[38] Here the Global Knowledge Partnership created in 1997 by the World Bank can serve as an example.

International lawyers have therefore raised the issue of the fragmentation of the international legal order,[39] have pointed to the dangers of 'forum shopping' by those who have the wherewithal to engage in costly litigation all over the world, and have asked for the 'constitutionalisation' of the international legal process. Here of course, the UN Charter presumably is the best candidate, but even some international lawyers promote the WTO and want to deduce from a free trade ideology 'consumer rights' which in turn should have the status of human rights.[40] As we can see, 'our dance-card probably ain't full yet' and one cannot but wonder what clever lawyers with other specialisations have yet in store. Nevertheless, the expectations placed in constitutionalisation are likely to be disappointed. For one, interpreting the Charter without further ado in constitutional terms creates its own difficulties, as Alvarez has pointed out.[41] Not the least of which is the fact that each organ of the UN develops its own law and practice, leading a few years ago to the debate whether, for example, decisions of the Security Council, particularly when based on the stretched meaning of Article 39, could be *ultra vires*. But even if the constitutionalisation progressed further and included a review of the decisions of the SC by the ICJ – an issue the Court has well-advisedly always side-stepped – constitutional adjudication is far from neutral and creates its own politics. It valorises expertise by creating its own political process as opposed to 'normal politics' that depends ideally on open discussion, deliberation and the agreement among free and autonomous actors.

As not only the adherents of the critical legal studies movement have pointed out, the idea that controversial choices can be mediated through the application of neutral principles is hardly tenable logically, and its political effectiveness depends upon whether or not the political process is well institutionalised and can withstand the dissent and the challenges to the finality of a constitutional decision. Here, obviously, two further prerequisites are necessary. One is that the constitutional decision can be made acceptable by appeal to both a self-understanding of 'who we are' and to the political project that unites us. Thus the Hobbesian notion of the individual as a maximiser of satisfaction was not only designed to create a stable political order but was crucially dependent upon refashioning the social institutions and individual life plans of a society that still was very much oriented to seeing the meaning of life in 'honour', instead of in the private pursuit of happiness. That the fear of violent death can only become the shared dilemma of aversion after the individual is virtually exclusively concerned with his present rather than his afterlife, be the latter inspired by the fear of eternal damnation or by the glory that accrues to the hero who has chosen death over a commodious life in obscurity, is one of the most important points to realise in regard to the Hobbesian project. Thus far from presenting a theory which is rooted in 'natural' tendencies he presents a political project that 'naturalises' certain desires and devalues other concerns, be they of religious origin or socially rooted in the tradition of glory within a 'status' society.

---

[39] See, for example Martti Koskenniemi, 'Fragmentation of International Law', *Leiden Journal of International Law*, 15 (September 2002), pp. 553–79.

[40] See Ernst Ulrich Petersman, 'Time for a UN Global Compact for Integrating Human Rights into the Law of Worldwide Organization', *European Journal of International Law*, 13 (April 2002), pp. 621–50. See also the reply by Robert Howse, 'Human Rights and the WTO: Whose Rights, Whose Humanity', ibid., pp. 651–9.

[41] Jose Alvarez, 'Constitutional Interpretation in International Organizations, in Jean Marc Caoincaud and Veijo Heiskanen (eds.), *The Legitimacy of International Organizations* (Tokyo and New York: United Nations University Press, 2001), ch. 3.

This leads me to a second set of concerns that ought to be addressed by a critical theory. If it is true, as we have seen, that appeals to neutral constitutional principles or even subjective rights will not do when political projects become contested again, even if they are even further mystified as is the case of the Rawlsian choice behind the veil of ignorance, then present international politics is characterised by a crisis much deeper than usually realised. It is not only a crisis of distribution that is its most visible and scandalous manifestation. It is also not only a crisis of the state around which debates about democratisation and the adoption of best practices revolve. As a matter of fact these debates take on an eerie quality the more we have to confront the apparently growing gap between the new technologies of peacekeeping and the political reality, between the universalistic prescriptions and claims to competence and the 'local' conditions. Here the UN's 'empire' at East Timor faces similar criticisms as the administration of Kosovo, the half-hearted attempts in Sudan or the totally out of control situation in the Middle East.

It seems to me that these are symptoms of the decay or even conscious rejection of the Western political project that was supposed to be universally applicable. The emergence of fundamentalism contests not only the status and the concomitant authority of the traditional actors, but also the rules of the game which realists assert to be transhistorically valid, and of the political project of 'rational' actors engaging in the 'pursuit' of happiness who see the world (like many of the 'scientists' who study this project) as a shop. Perhaps nothing is more telling than the apparently never-ending supply of suicide bombers, beginning with the Iranian youths that were sent into battle with aluminium keys for unlocking the gate of heaven, to the present perpetrators of terrorist attacks in Baghdad, Lebanon and elsewhere who keep the spiral of violence turning without any end in sight. While formerly there was still something in the tongue-in-cheek adage of an 'expert' in Middle Eastern politics 'to give war a chance' for settling scores, and then construct a new order on the basis of the realities of the battlefield, the experiences of the past few years have shown the imaginary character of such an analysis. As in the case of the child soldiers in some parts of Africa who, armed with amulets and Kalashnikovs destroy even the last vestiges of social order, as they have never known a non-violent life and never expect to be the satisfied consumers of the liberal economic project or even participating citizens in a well-ordered society, these examples confront us with ways of life and political projects that are hard for us to fathom. It is ironic that the old saw of peaceniks and war-resisters that 'force and violence never settle anything' has now more truth to it than it had in the past. That view was frequently contested, since war, despite the brutalities it involved, had a clearly defined institutional role, as Clausewitz suggested. However, it seems like cold comfort to boast that this adage now has a new claim to validity, a claim we probably all wished never to have encountered.

It is these phenomena that not only dash the hopes for the eventual universal realisation of the enlightenment vision of emancipation and of rule by reason, but also call attention to the powerful hold of issues of identity and of collective memories that have been neglected, or were even placed under a taboo, as they contradicted the expectation of development in which 'mankind' (of course modelled after the Western subject and not the particularities of the local) provided the stuff for politics. While certainly this 'local' predicament and the situatedness of the subject were neither natural, nor their identity primordial, as constructivists have correctly pointed out, I think frequently the conclusions drawn made the opposite mistake. Because identities were not fixed but malleable, and thus a matter of choice, anything seemed possible. Not only were 'multiple identities' discovered, the 'choice' of them seemed quite similar to that of deciding between apples and oranges or between becoming a member of a bowling team or a country club.

Of course, nothing of that sort follows, and a lot of bad scholarship ensued, more concerned with building up straw men to be knocked down in due course than with throwing light on these phenomena. Even if something is not fixed or natural not everything is possible – unless we cannot any longer distinguish between a logical and an empirical truth.[42] Thus both the fact that most nationalist projects have failed, and that that only a few combinations of ethnic identifications and modern political movements were viable, should give us pause and prevent us from 'constructing' new identities as if it were simply a matter of designing new car engines from freely combinable parts. In addition, an identity is not like a 'role' of which we all have many, since it serves precisely to mediate the conflicts of various roles and establish some coherence for the actor.

Indeed, issues of identity are crucial for both drawing the lines of social solidarity and of deciding which particular political projects to pursue, accepting the necessary sacrifices. The observation of Benedict Anderson, that in virtually every country one will find a grave of the unknown soldier but look in vain for one of the fallen Marxist,[43] should remind us that politics is always particular, and that the universalist dreams of a revolutionary change that catapults man from the realm of necessity into that of freedom are phantasmagorical eschatological speculations. Similarly, putting one's faith in 'progress' by 'finally' creating new international institutions like international criminal courts, by having the national bureaucracies interact in a more efficient manner, or by creating benchmarks and new forms of surveillance and capillary control, seems equally problematic. Both strategies are likely to draw our attention away from addressing the political issues we face and for which we bear responsibility.

The first fails us by making the transformation a sudden, nearly ineffable transformation, that just comes about, a heroic assumption that was entirely unconvincing even for one of the most ardent Marxists, Lenin. He at least realised that revolutions have to be made, but he had little grasp of how to translate the visions of an alternative order into concrete institutional terms. The result was a particularly oppressive mixture of repression, surveillance and bureaucracy – sometimes interrupted by episodes of state terrorism – that took its terrible toll and proved reform-resistant until it disintegrated. The second, more gradual strategy, does not, on the whole fare much better because it encases our political imagination in familiar organisational forms and often hinders us in diagnosing actual problems. Thus it might very well be 'good practice' in the first and second world to have the police in fitted uniforms, having accurate records, and relying on a 'neutral' dedicated staff to serve the public. But given the problems of a society in which literacy is minimal, in which no identity cards exist, in which knowledge of where

---

[42] For a critical discussion of the shortcomings of both primordial and constructivist accounts of national identity see Anthony Smith, *Nationalism and Modernism* (London: Routledge, 1998); Rogers Smith, *Stories of Peoplehood: The Politics and Morals of Political Membership* (Cambridge: Cambridge University Press, 2003).

[43] Benedict Anderson, *Imagined Communities*, revised edn. (London: Verso, 1991), p. 10.

someone lives does not go beyond a couple of villages, and in which minimal social order is maintained by local headmen (or gangsters), has the shipment of uniforms, computers and some instruction about 'proper' policing methods, anything to do with addressing the local problems of public order in a reasonable fashion, as was the case in Haiti? The uniforms might instil pride in the staff, the computers will prove useless for the actual work of record keeping, given the lack of infrastructure. They will therefore be used for other purposes and/or disappear, and the hours of instruction will be counted and reported 'upstairs', in the expectation that hours of contact and instruction translate into a sustainable change in practice, which is a heroic assumption as we all know. But the villager who has been wronged will know that redress, if at all possible, will depend on his family and their relationship to local power-holders, especially if he has lived through some former 'reforms' and knows that these efforts are marginal, as they cannot be sustained and the missions have to leave after having announced 'success'.

The surreal quality of many of these reforms is perhaps best illustrated by the creation of the International Criminal Court for Rwanda. Pushed on the people of Rwanda by the 'international community', we encounter the whole panoply of agents of change: judges in limousines, holding court in a far-off place dispensing a few cases after years of activity while the Rwandan society has to deal with more than 300,000 potential perpetrators.[44] Given the persistent problem of getting even children in school and kindergarten to cooperate and not reopen the old ethnic divisions by fighting and name-calling, is the money spent on prosecuting a tiny minority by an international tribunal (rather than by domestic courts), well spent, and ought not programmes to prevent further eruptions be given priority? How seriously can we take the argument that punishment also 'prevents' further violence in the face of the evidence that ethnic violence is not something like the murder perpetrated by an opportunistically-acting individual? Has justice really been done, and can it serve the purposes of local reconciliation, if the most prominent perpetrators are enjoying the special privileges of 'international criminals' while the ones of lesser complicity are judged by the national justice system. They face not only stiffer penalties but also cannot claim a violation of their human rights due to the long period before they come to trial, since the system is obviously over-taxed?

These are troubling and quite unpopular questions and it is therefore not surprising that there exists a tendency to charge the bringer of bad news with reactionary inclinations, even perhaps with complicity in the politics which brought about these disasters. But as popular as these argumentative gambits might be, they are certainly not productive. Rather, they prevent us from asking the right questions and addressing actual practical problems, since they proceed on the basis of organisational answers whose remedial capacities have no relationship to the local circumstances. As in the case of sanctions that were advocated both as an alternative to force and as a more humane form of coercion, recent experience has proved both assumptions wrong. This despite the various episodes of the sanctions debate which moved from the question of whether they worked, using totally unrealistic assumptions about their goal (such as displacing a dictator or getting right back to the *status quo ante* were made), to how they worked – where issues of the fine-tuning and

---

[44] For a critical assessment of the Rwanda experience, see Jose Alvarez, 'Crimes of State/Crimes of Hate: Lessons from Rwanda', *The Yale Journal of International Law*, 24 (1999), pp. 365–4483.

correct targeting of sanctions came to the fore. But even with important modifica-
tions as to the correct addressee of the sanctions, the investigation was usually limited
to the means, that is, getting the pressures and the incentives right. What remained
largely unexplored was the process by which compliance is sought and in which
ends and means interact in complex ways. Not only does the dichotomy between
compliance and non-compliance prove unhelpful as, for example, the sanctioned
party might subscribe to a certain provision by passing a law or statute safeguarding
for instance the property rights of a minority after some 'ethnic cleansing', but then
fail to execute its provisions in good faith, or drag its feet in implementing the
particular obligations that follow from it. Besides, compliance with goals so extensive
as to democratise the political process are hardly operational in a strict sense and
require a complex normative adjustment of the sanctioned party.

Thus while it is relatively easy to 'certify' whether or not a regime has complied
with certain provisions of the nuclear non-proliferation regime by giving an account
of declared fissionable material, it is hard to verify the actual commitment to the goal
underlying the treaty. Alternative sites which are not inspected might be used for
carrying out prohibited activities or for participating in clandestine networks of trade
in prohibited or dual-use technology, which might make available to the regime the
elements which the weapons regime and the inspection are designed to prevent. But
when we insist on compliance we often mean more the compliance with the 'spirit'
than with the 'letter' of the law, a problem that is not easily accommodated in the
procrustean bed of a means/ends rationality. Thus getting the 'incentives' right might
be one way of telling the story. But if we do not understand that here the calculations
do not simply involve the comparisons of costs among the different means of
reaching a given goal, but involves the continued interaction of means and ends as
pragmatists have pointed out,[45] we are likely to miss the forest for the trees.

This leads me to my third area of concern which a critical theory has to tackle. It
is a more adequate account of action. The complaints about the overly narrow
conception of rational action, and of the inadequacies of the traditional desire plus
belief model have often been mentioned. But a more adequate account still seems to
elude us, despite the addition of further assumptions that are supposed to take care
of the otherwise absurd consequences. Thus the inclusion of expected utilities and
of second-order preferences as suggested by Sen[46] are supposed to take care of the
most obvious shortcomings. But it is not clear how the expectation of a future gain
or the construction of a second-order preference can be 'motivating' in an action
scheme in which only desires count and reason remains 'the slave of passion' as
Hume suggested. Since desires are supposed to be immediate and not in need of
further reflection, a desire I do not have at present is hard to conceive of, especially
if the imagined 'future delights' are so powerfully counteracted by the urge to satisfy
my present needs. Either reason must then be able to motivate – as it allows for a
comparison of desires – in which case the desires are no longer 'original' and
immediate and thus in need of explanation (*de gustibus est disputandum!*) – or the
model becomes incoherent.

---

[45] See, for example Charles Sanders Peirce, 'We cannot begin with complete doubt. We must begin
with all the prejudices which we actually have', in his 'Some Consequences of Four Incapacities',
reprinted in Louis Menand (ed.), *Pragmatism: A Reader* (New York: Vintage Books, 1997), pp. 4–6.
[46] Amartya Sen, 'Rational Fools', in H. Harris (ed.), *Scientific Models of Man* (London: Oxford
University Press, 1978), pp. 317–44.

Similarly, the introduction of secondary preferences might accommodate larger life plans and subject primary goals to some critical evaluation, but it is still unclear how such preferences can be motivating, or how the extension of this model is able to account for long-term commitments and projects that unfold as we go along. Here we need something like a shared understanding of what the project is about, that is, some notion of a common intentionality,[47] requiring that we continuously adjust our preferences not only in the light of our own life plans but also taking others into account. This give and take is not seen as a happy coincidence of two strategies in equilibrium, but we should understand it as a common project that imposes some obligation to bring along others who are part of it. Nobody who has children or plans to get married will do so on the basis of cost calculations, not because we are 'altruistic' rather than self-interested (although again what counts as the self is not a straightforward matter as Hume wondered when he cited the example of a mother caring for her children) but because even within the limits of the rational action model it is impossible to do so, since future 'prices' are simply unknowable. Thus keeping commitments and sticking to some rules provides a better guide in all but the most simple situations than constant calculation and Bayesian updating.

Finally, the traditional rational-action model falls on its face for even the most simple social situations. Consider in this context two simple examples: one concerning the request, 'please pass me the salt', the other the payment of my bar bill. What desires can we invoke in either case? In the first one we could say that we want to be polite and this 'desire' explains our action. Furthermore, the action of passing the salt requires little sacrifice. But this is not the point. The point is rather that it is not my desire that I am following here in any recognisable way. If wanting to be good is introduced as an actual personal 'desire' – rather than a circumlocution to save the model – then where are all the puzzles of cooperation resulting from the disjunction of individual and collective rationality and from the assumption of the primacy of my wishes as opposed to the expectations of a generalised other? It seems to me that accommodating these considerations necessitates not simply adding auxiliary assumptions but requires the change from a *homo economicus* model of action to one of a *homo sociologicus*. The latter need not be a normative dope either, as suggested by some 'conflict theorists'[48] opposing the Parsonian paradigm of actors simply implementing the prescribed rules. For one, a *homo sociologicus* is aware that most situations are not simply available to us under one exclusive description, but are susceptible to various competing normative and factual characterisations. Deciding thus needs interpretation and introduces strategic elements as well as issues of appropriateness into the picture. The present tendency of playing off a logic of consequences against one of appropriates seems thus a rather futile exercise that has more to do with the scholastic desires to knock down straw men than with providing an explanation.[49]

---

[47] See, for example John Searle, *The Construction of Social Reality* (London: Penguin, 1995), particularly ch. 1.

[48] See, for example Ralf Dahrendorf, *Homo Sociologicus* (Opladen, Germany: 1977); Ralf Dahrendorf, *Class and Class Conflict in Industrial Society* (London: Routledge, 1959).

[49] See, for example Thomas Risse, 'Let's Argue: Communicative Action in World Politics', *International Organization*, 54 (Winter 2000), pp. 1–39; Frank Schimmelfennig, 'Liberal Norms, Rhetorical Action and the Enlargement of the EU', *International Organization*, 55 (Winter 2001), pp. 47–80.

The above articulated suspicion is enhanced by the second example, that of paying my bar bill. It is hot and I am thirsty. Consequently, I go to the next bar and order a beer. When I am nearly done the bartender ask me whether I want another one and I agree since I still feel thirsty. After the second beer I am satisfied and the barman presents me with the bill. But as much as I try to analyse my desires that did so well in explaining the purchase of the beer, I cannot for the world detect any 'desire' in me to pay my bill. However, if I tell this to the bartender and even express my regrets explaining that, due to the requirements of the science to which I am subject as a social scientist, I cannot pay him, as only desires can motivate, I should not be too surprised if this man considers me a prankster at best, or an actual nuisance at worst, who has to be brought to reason by a quick hook to the chin. Again, unless we admit in good *ad hocery* fashion the introduction of a desire to 'pay one's bill', we have to agree that some of the most important social interactions are governed by desire-independent reasons. Consequently, any theory of action that takes these reasons not seriously but insists on the psychologism of personal desires, does not deserve its name. So it is here that the greatest 'orrery of errors' still awaits us and requires the interventions of 'critical theory'.

Transnational theories of order and change: heterodoxy in International Relations scholarship

RONEN PALAN*

Abstract. In this article I argue that the very meaning of 'inter-national relations' is emerging as a focus of debate in International Relations, particularly among the critical traditions in the discipline. No longer seen as a mere study of peace and war, IR is viewed as a component of general pan-disciplinary theories or order and change. The international sphere is perceived, accordingly, no longer as a system in its own right, but rather as a gigantic transmission belt, and a huge communication device transmitting and diffusing ideas, practices, rules, norms and institutions throughout the world. The article examines the implications of such an approach on IR theory. In addition, the article revisits the works of Hegel, Marx and the French School of Regulation to demonstrate how they developed an empirical theory of international diffusion.

This special issue of the *Review of International Studies* aims to evaluate the impact and likely future direction of the so-called critical tradition in International Relations scholarship. But what precisely is this critical tradition? Is there one tradition, or a variety of traditions? Is it not the case that all theories and approaches are supposed to be critical? And who exactly has the right to proclaim themselves 'critical', and in doing so, by default pronounce their intellectual opponents uncritical?

For Robert Cox the critical tradition represents a certain sensibility, a historical awareness of the limitations and content of theory itself – an awareness that is presumably lacking in IR 'orthodoxy'. In a celebrated reference to the Frankfurt School (a School that is often described as 'critical theory') he says: '[t]heory is always for someone and for some purpose. All theories have a perspective'.[1] In a similar vein, 'post-structuralists' like Richard Ashley, employ techniques drawn from philosophy and literary criticisms such as deconstruction to comb through IR texts in order to 'reveal', as they put it, the historical specificity and power assumptions embedded in conventional IR theory.[2] The not-too-charitable implications are, of

---

* I would like to thank Anastasia Nesvetailova, Nick Rengger, Ben Thirkell-White and the anonymous reviewers for their helpful comments.

[1] Robert W. Cox, 'Social Forces, States, and World Orders: Beyond International Relations Theory', *Millennium: Journal of International Relations*, 10:2 (1981), reprinted in Robert W. Cox with Timothy J. Sinclair, *Approaches to World Order* (Cambridge: Cambridge University Press, 1996), p. 87. On theories as instrumental knowledge, see Jurgen Habermas, *Knowledge and Human Interest* (London: Heinemann, 1978).

[2] Whether the IR variant of post-structuralism may be considered post-structuralist in the first place is a matter of dispute. See Colin Hoadley, 'An Archaeology of Post-Structural Intent in

course, that 'mainstream' or 'orthodox' scholars are either willing servants of power (for what reason? power? money? prestige? In other words, for all the motives that realists tend to associate with some universal human nature! Sic!); or alternatively, are unaware, naïve conformists who fail to question the 'party line'.

Human failings, lack of curiosity or intellectual mediocrity are not to be discounted, but they are not the exclusive domain of orthodoxy. It is not entirely clear why, for instance, 'orthodox' IR scholars, educated as historians, such as Martin Wight, E. H. Carr, or, for that matter, Robert Keohane, 'an outstanding scholar of remarkably broad erudition' as Benjamin Cohen describes him,[3] should lack basic historical sensibility that seems to come so easily and naturally to those who choose to describe themselves as critical scholars. It is equally not clear why mainstream scholars, and only mainstream scholars, are so blind to their human failings. This is not to say that there are no important differences in approaches. Benjamin Cohen believes that there is a distinct 'British' School[4] which can be described as critical: 'Least of all did British academics require', he writes, 'any encouragement to question authority. So-called "critical" theory, challenging orthodoxies of all kinds, has long found a comfortable home in the country's universities.' A respectful and sympathetic observer of the British School, he nonetheless warns, 'The British school may be fairly criticized for its less rigorous approach to theory building and testing, which makes generalization difficult and cumulation of knowledge virtually impossible'.[5] I suspect that many IR scholars would readily sign up to this statement.

These conversations and debates are important and must continue. Nonetheless, I argue, they fundamentally miss the main cause for the bifurcation of the IR discipline between orthodoxies and the critical traditions. As Richard Marsden notes, a 'theory is a cluster of conclusions in search of premises'.[6] People tend not to chose to be mainstream or critical by patiently sifting through the evidence, examining the quality of research methodologies, historical evidence, and so on – these sorts of criticisms, justified or not, are retrospective. To understand the cause of the bifurcation of the IR discipline we need to enquire into the diverging clusters of conclusions that are currently in search of a premise. This seems to be the core of the debate.

Nor can we truly judge a school, an approach or a theory purely on the basis of material already published. Theories are changing, schools of thoughts are evolving, and traditions often develop in unpredictable ways. Writing in a different context, but in words that are wholly applicable to IR, Colander, Holt and Rosser argue: 'Standard classifications tend to miss the diversity that exists within the profession,

---

International Relations' (Thesis, University of Sussex, 2003); Earl Gammon and Ronen Palan, 'Libidinal Economies and International Political Economy', in Marieke De Goede (ed.), *International Political Economy and Poststructural Politics* (London: Palgrave, 2006). Ashley, however, is arguably one of the few to have applied rigorously the deconstruction method to IR texts. See Richard Ashley, 'The Poverty of Neorealism', in Robert Keohane (ed.), *Neorealism and Its Critics* (New York: Columbia University Press, 1986).

[3] Benjamin J. Cohen, *Building Bridges: The Construction of International Political Economy* (Princeton, NJ: Princeton University Press, forthcoming).

[4] Cohen writes specifically about IPE, but his comments may be applied to IR more broadly.

[5] Ibid.

[6] He continues, theory 'is not pieced together from observed phenomena; it is rather what makes it possible to observe phenomena as being of certain sort, and as related to other phenomena. Theories put phenomena into systems. They are built up "in reverse" – retroductively.' Richard Marsden, *The Nature of Capital: Marx After Foucault* (London: Routledge, 2000), p. 45.

and the many new ideas that are being tried out. They miss the important insight that one can be part of the mainstream and yet not necessarily hold "orthodox" ideas.' The reality, they continue, 'is that at any point in time a successful discipline will have hundreds of new ideas being tried out, as new methods, new technology and new information become available. That is what happens at the edge of economics.'[7]

It is, therefore, the edge of the IR discipline that should interest us, not its centre. And what is happening at the edge? One important development, I argue, is that the core meaning of the term 'inter-national relations', the very boundaries of the discipline, is emerging as a key area of debate. From the early 1970s onwards the discipline had witnessed an inexorable, if wholly understandable, growth in the number of issues, processes and themes under consideration. No longer seen as merely the study of peace and war, the IR discipline has sought to position itself at the heart of great many debates in the social sciences. This trend has been evident in the development of sub-disciplines such as International Political Economy (IPE), normative theory, gender theory and so on. More so, if IR was dominated by the various schools of 'realism' up to say, the early 1990s, a decade or so later the discipline contains a bewildering array of theories and approaches, ranging from – and the list below is by no means not complete – romantic realism, anti-reformation realism, Christian realism, structural realism, neorealism, rational choice realism, legalistic idealism, liberalism, methodological individualism, the interdependence school, structural functionalism, regime theorists, two-level game theory, institution-alists of all variants, post-structuralism, critical theorists, hermeneutics, constructivism (including Weberian constructivism, Wittgensteinian constructivism, symbolic interactionists and few others); Marxism of all sorts and descriptions: Marxists of the world system variants, dependency theorists, Gramscian and neo-Gramscian, derivation school, structural Marxists, Leninists, critical realists, regulationists, Troskyists; gender theorists, feminist theories, queer theorists and speed theorists; Braudelians, Polanyians, Nietschians, Deleuzians, Foucauldians, Zizekians ... Followers of Levinas, Rawls and Schmidt ... and so on and so forth.

The plethora of schools of thoughts, and the alarming rate of expansion in the number of theoretical approaches and methodological and epistemological debates, is characteristic of a discipline in a turmoil, in search of an identity. It is worth asking ourselves why IR scholars display such cravings for change? What is the underlying problem, the unresolved issue (or issues) that drive students of IR with such tenacity to seek alternatives? One popular explanation for the proliferation of theories and approaches in IR can be discounted from the outset. There is little doubt that, as in every other field of the social sciences and the humanities, fashions and fads play a role. Indeed, in the 1960s, every field of the social sciences was touched by structuralism, behaviourism and system theories. By now, even 'hard' disciplines such as law or accounting boast their own variants of post-structuralism, discourse theories, gender theories, constructivisms and game theories, and IR certainly does not wish to fall behind.[8] Nonetheless, it is a mistake to attribute the contemporary proliferation of theories to fads and fashions only. The dissatisfaction in and with IR goes, I believe, deeper, much deeper.

---

[7] David Colander, Richard P. F. Holt and J. Barkley Rosser, 'The Changing Face of Mainstream Economics', *Review of Political Economy*, 16:4 (2004), pp. 485–99, at 487.
[8] And what about 'critical pet studies'? Surely, an IR variant will make its appearance at some point. See Heidi J. Nast, 'Critical Pet Studies?', *Antipode*, 38:5 (2006), pp. 894–906.

At issue is the manner and the way by which the expansion of the International Relations discipline can take place. The principle contribution of the critical IR theory has been to radically resituate the discipline in relation to the other social sciences. It has done this partly by exposing the weaknesses of mainstream approaches, pointing, for instance, to the plain implausibility of the idea of a timeless unitary state. Even realists had to acknowledge, however reluctantly (as the definition by negation clearly demonstrates), the relevance of 'non-state actors', to some degree. The mainstream attempt to expand IR by 'bolting on' ideas like 'interdependence' or 'domestic actors' onto a realist framework was never really going to work. The critical tradition understood that a far more thorough rethinking of the discipline is necessary. It has abandoned, for all intents and purposes, the efforts to constitute IR as a separate, bounded sphere of activity, and sought to locate IR as a component of pan-disciplinary studies of global order and change. The critical tradition also understood early on that IR is unlikely to serve as (what I call) 'first order discipline' within the social sciences, but will remain a derivative discipline, drawing more explicitly on other, more fundamental, theoretical claims. What it does do, though, is address a particular aspect of the human condition, which is omitted by the other social sciences.

While the critical tradition in IR has been off the mark earlier on these matters, the mainstream too is rapidly developing credible pan-disciplinary approaches to the study of processes of order and change. At this point of the game the principle theories of IR have already reconstituted themselves as components of what I call general theories of order and change. As a result the key difference between orthodoxy and heterodoxy lies elsewhere – a development that is always articulated with sufficient precision in recent debates. The crucial different lies between, on the one hand, the rationalism as Helen Milner describes it, of mainstream founded on methodological individualism and a behavioural theory of the subject,[9] and the non-rationalist perspectives which draw at core on the Freudian conception of the subject.[10] For the one, the subject is a rational advantage-seeking individual operating nonetheless under the principles of bounded rationality. For the other, rationality itself is suspect (or considered historically constituted) as the subject appears to desire their own repression. The one is imbued with liberal optimism about human progress, happiness and the control of nature, and the other takes a more pessimistic view of humanity's capacity to achieve emancipation and progress.

The article discusses these developments in the field of IR. I begin by arguing that the meaning of 'inter-national relations', the very boundaries of the discipline, is emerging as the focus of a debate in the field. This follows with a discussion of the differences between methodological individualism and heterodoxy. I will then outline some of the key methodological and analytical issues pertaining to the conceptualis-ation of IR as a component of a general theory of order and change. Drawing on the ideas of Goran Therborn, I argue that what a critical theory needs to do is pursue an

---

[9] On rationalism, see Helen Milner, 'Rationalizing Politics: The Emerging Synthesis Among International, American, and Comparative Politics', *International Organization*, 52:4 (1998), pp. 759–86; Peter J. Katzenstein, Robert O. Keohane and Stephen D. Krasner, 'International Organization and the Study of World Politics', *International Organization*, 52:4 (1998), pp. 645–85; Amanda Dickins, 'The Evolution of International Political Economy', *International Affairs*, 82:3 (2006), pp. 479–92.

[10] See Gammon and Palan, 'Libidinal Economics'.

approach that is: (a) globally encompassing, (b) historically oriented and (c) focused on political institutions. I conclude this article by sketching out a distinct heterodox approach to IR, found in work of Hegel, Marx and the French School of Regulation, that has been largely ignored so far.

I acknowledge from the outset that as an analysis of a very diverse literature, and as an effort to make sense of what I take to be the implicit, sometimes hidden, issues in contemporary debates, a certain degree of subjectivity is inevitable. Furthermore, due to the enormity of the subject-matter, an article of this size can at best only begin to sketch possibilities for new research.

No longer merely the science of peace and war

Not too long ago, IR was conceived as 'the science of peace and war'.[11] The reason being, E. H. Carr famously explained, was that '[w]ar lurks in the background of international politics'.[12] As a science of peace and war, IR was considered a 'policy-oriented' discipline whose task was to advise governments on policy in what is taken to be a perilous and treacherous sphere of international affairs.[13] To achieve these goals, the 'old' IR sought to develop a theory of the determinant of policymaking in what was regarded as an anarchical system of states.[14] The discipline of International Relations centred, unsurprisingly, on the dynamics of the relationships of conflict and cooperation among states, or as it was sometimes described, the *politics of international relations*.[15]

By the 1970s, however, many scholars had begun to question the narrow remits of IR.[16] Susan Strange lent her voice to the growing dissatisfaction when she wrote: 'Contemporary literature with certain rare exceptions has been predominantly directed at far too narrow set of questions'.[17] For Helen Milner, the problem with the old IR lies in the neglect of the interaction between domestic and international factors. Milner finds Robert Putnam's two-level game theory particularly useful.[18] For Robert Cox, in contrast, the problem lies with the 'distinction between state and

---

[11] Raymond Aron, *Peace and War: A Theory of International Relations* (London: Weidenfield and Nicolson, 1966), p. 6.

[12] Edward Hallett Carr, *The Twenty Years' Crisis, 1919–1939: An Introduction to the Study of International Relations* (London: Macmillan Press, 1981), p. 109.

[13] Michael Nicholson, 'What is the Use of International Relations', *Review of International Studies*, 26 (2000), pp. 183–98; William Wallace, 'Truth and Power, Monks and Technocrats: Theory and Practice in International Relations', *Review of International Studies*, 22:3 (1996), pp. 301–22.

[14] Hedley Bull, *The Anarchical Society: A Study of Order In World Politics* (London: Macmillan, 1977).

[15] Northedge, for instance, defines international politics 'as those mutual dealings of governments representing sovereign states'. Fred S. Northedge, *The International Political System* (London: Faber, 1976).

[16] Robert O. Keohane and John S. Nye (eds.), *Transnational Relations and World Politics* (Cambridge, MA: Harvard University Press, 1972).

[17] Susan Strange, *States and Markets: An Introduction To International Political Economy* (New York: Basil, 1988), p. 12.

[18] 'Although many scholars have recognized the interdependence of domestic and international politics, few have developed explicit theories of this interaction'. Helen V. Milner, *Interests, Institutions and Information: Domestic Politics and International Relations* (Princeton, NJ: Princeton University Press, 1997), p. 4.

civil society'.[19] Cox finds inspiration principally in the work of Gramsci. Hendrik Spruyt demonstrates that the question of origins of the units that make up the international system has become a hot topic in IR. He finds inspiration in Douglas North's variant of evolutionary institutionalism.[20] Nicolas Onuf goes further. He believes that 'The way to proceed should now be clear. It is to look for a substantial ensemble of practices, the coherence of which is not reflected in, much less produced by, the constitutive claims of established social sciences disciplines.'[21] Looking beyond 'established' social sciences, Onuf believes that Wolin's notion of 'political society' is the answer.

The expansion of the number of topics and issues under investigation represents a critical phase in the maturing of the IR discipline. It poses, however, two sets of interrelated dilemmas. The first dilemma concerns the relationship between an expanded version of the discipline and existing theories. Is it possible to bolt-on new theories and approaches onto existing theories? Or does an expanded IR imply a reordering of theory itself? The second, and related dilemma, is whether the expansion of the field into new areas and topics may compromise the coherence of the field, perhaps to the point of destroying the possibilities for a credible theory in the first place. There is a danger, in other words, that IR would become a place where everything goes – which is the impression sometimes given by some of the more outlandish new theories.

Let us discuss briefly the first concern. Bolt-on theories are normally advanced in recognition that at least some of the existing theories offer something valuable. Knowledge is supposed to be cumulative and we should resist, as far as possible, the temptation to throw the baby out with the bathwater. Such a bolt-on approach to theory is represented, for instance, by Keohane and Nye's interdependence theory. Interdependence, they say, 'affects world politics and the behaviour of states' but 'governmental actions also influence patterns of interdependence'.[22] Indeed, they acknowledge in another influential book, that 'a good deal of intersocietal inter-course, with significant political importance, takes place without government con-trol'.[23] Although they assure their readers: 'there would be no point in ignoring the nation-state.'[24]

What becomes clear is that for Keohane and Nye interdependence does not challenge the fundamentals of world politics as described by realists. They merely seek to bolt on a new concern upon an existing theoretical framework. But what if interdependence is not a late arrival 'affecting' world politics at later stages of capitalism, but a constant feature of world politics? How should we understand world politics in the age of intensified interdependence, or, as it is now called, globalisation? The interdependence school is unable to provide satisfactory answers to these questions because it placed itself under this epistemological straightjacket.

---

[19] Cox, *Approaches to World Order'*, p. 86.
[20] Hendrik Spruyt, *The Sovereign State and Its Competitors: An Analysis of Systems Change* (Princeton, NJ: Princeton University Press, 1994).
[21] Nicholas Greenwood Onuf, *World of Our Making: Rules and Rule in Social Theory and International Relations* (University of South California Press, 1989).
[22] Keohane and Nye, *Transnational Relations*, p. 5.
[23] R. O. Keohane and Joseph Nye, *Power and Interdependence: World Politics In Transition* (Boston, MA: Little, Brown, 1977), p. x.
[24] Ibid., p. xxiv.

The problem with bolt-on theories, in other words, is that they tend to be historically specific and date very quickly. They encourage the use of theory as a 'toolbox, out of which one can take individual concepts and theorems depending on one's immediate goals, without having to worry about the rest of the theory'.[25] Indeed, quite often bolt-on theories undermine the very theory to which they have been bolted on. Milner, for instance, proposes to 'relax' the unitary state thesis – in reality, she abandons the theory altogether.[26] Milner's treatment of the older theories is not an exception, it is the norm.

Susan Strange represents the opposite trend when she calls for wholesale reordering of theory itself. For her the problem with contemporary IR is not with this or that theory, but with the very orientation of the field towards too narrow questions. International Relations (or IPE, as she calls it),[27] she avers, is not simply a theory of interstate conflict, as many seem to believe, but 'a framework of analysis, a method of diagnosis of the human condition as it is, or as it was, affected by economic, political and social circumstances'.[28] I believe that Strange captures with these words an important undercurrent in contemporary IR scholarship, speaking for the fledgling heterodoxy in IR.

One of the common, justifiable criticisms of Strange was that she intuited, but never spelled out clearly the full implications of her approach. Her words capture, however, in a condensed form *some* of the fundamentals of the emerging tradition. They consist of three ideas:

1. IR is a framework of analysis or a method of diagnosis;
2. IR is concerned, first and foremost, with the 'human condition';
3. In reorienting IR towards the study of the 'human condition', Strange reopens the question of the specificity of IR, in other words, she raises the thorny question of the relationship between IR and other academic disciplines which, after all, are equally concerned with the question of the 'human condition'.

Let us dwell briefly on Strange's proposals. Strange's first point, that IR is a framework of analysis or a method of diagnosis, is arguably the least controversial. Robert Cox, for instance, has something similar in mind when he writes that 'the primary task of theory is ... to enable the mind to come to grips with the reality it confronts'.[29] Katzenstein, Keohane and Krasner advance similar ideas, albeit employing a somewhat different jargon when they point out the differences between what they call general theoretical orientations and specific research programmes.[30] Their notion of a 'general theoretical orientation' is equivalent to Strange's idea of a framework. They suggest that a fundamental reorientation of the field must take place, first and foremost, at the very general level of theoretical orientation.

---

[25] Schimank as quoted in Alex Viskovatoff, Foundations of Niklas Luhmann's Theory of Social Systems, *Philosophy of the Social Sciences*, 29:4 (1999), p. 81.

[26] Milner, *Rationalizing Politics*.

[27] Strange expresses disenchantment with IR and hence she speaks of IPE. Susan Strange, 'International Economics and International Relations: A Case of Mutual Neglect', *International Affairs*, 46:2 (1970), pp. 304–15.

[28] Strange, *States and Markets*, p. 16.

[29] Cox, *Approaches to World Order*, p. 87.

[30] 'General theoretical orientations provide heuristic – they suggest relevant variables and causal patterns that provide guidelines for developing specific research programmes ... and specific research programmes links explanatory variables to a set of outcomes, or dependent variables'. Katzenstein, Keohan and Krasner, 'International Organization', p. 646.

Constitutive and derivative theories in the social sciences

What does 'general theoretical orientation' means? How do we apply these ideas specifically to IR? Somewhat schematically, we may distinguish two types of social sciences disciplines: *first order* disciplines may be described as constitutive disciplines; *second order* disciplines may be described as derivative disciplines. First order disciplines are concerned, among other things, with the essential theories of human behaviour, rationality and causation. Second order disciplines derive their ideas about human behaviour, rationality and causation from one or another first order discipline applying them to a specific time-space or thematic context. By describing some disciplines as derivative, I do not wish to denigrate or diminish the merits of these disciplines. I am simply pointing out that certain disciplines and subject-matters are not directly concerned with the fundamentals of human behaviour, but draw their constitutive concepts from order disciplines.

I am not sure whether my list of first order disciplines is complete, but I would say that moral philosophy, political economy, linguistics and sociology have emerged as first order disciplines in the social sciences and humanities. Political economy, for instance, seeks to provide a constitutive theory of capital as a totalising force of society. Linguistics emerged in the twentieth century as another constitutive discipline, when the work of De Saussure, among others, inspired the development in literature, structural anthropology, psychoanalysis and so on.[31] Such first order disciplines do not provide for comprehensive theories of order and change. That is why first and second order disciplines always relate to second order disciplines within pan-disciplinary *general theoretical frameworks*, each of which, I propose, offers what Katzenstein, Keohane and Krasner call 'general theoretical orientation'.

General theories may be defined as *synthetic efforts aimed at providing a credible link between theories of the subject (or individuality), the collective (state, society, nation) and the international (world-economy, civilisation, the transnational arena)*.[32] While unsurprisingly, IR theories are centred on the third dimension, it can be easily demonstrated that every reasonably developed IR theory draws upon, and in turn, contributes to, a general pan-disciplinary heuristics, which consists of theories of the three dimensions and the relation between them.[33]

Let us take the case of Hobbes as an illustration of a more general proposition.[34] Students of International Relations may be somewhat surprised to learn that Hobbes' great work, *The Leviathan*, begins not with a theory of the state (the commonwealth) or international relations, but with theories of language, thought

---

[31] Ferdinand De Saussure, *Course in General Linguistics* (London: Duckworth, 1983). Broadly conceived, sociology, (including social anthropology), lays the foundations for individualist, structural and systemic theories of society. Sociology, however, can serve as first order and second order discipline concomitantly, as some sociological theories draw their basic insights of human behaviour from other disciplines.

[32] The notion of a general theory does not imply a universally accepted unitary, systematic and comprehensive theory of order and change. Obviously, in contrast to the sciences, the social sciences are unable to agree on one dominant general theory on par with say, the dominance of Newtonian mechanics until the advent of relativity theory, and probably never will. Nevertheless, social sciences theories are not isolated islands of thought, but belong, if often very roughly and unwittingly, to pan-disciplinary general theories, or at the very least, an effort to establish theories whose ultimate aim is the establishment of a unitary theory of order and change.

[33] For a similar point see Cox, *Approaches to World Order*, p. 91.

[34] Thomas Hobbes, *Leviathan*, ed. C. B. Macpherson (Harmondsworth: Penguin, 1951).

and rationality. The Leviathan, literally a whale in Hebrew, represents the commonwealth to Hobbes. The commonwealth is depicted therefore as the largest mammal on earth, as for Hobbes the commonwealth was the equivalent of an artificial organism, a work of art. The concept of art, which is epistemologically at the origins of the notion of 'artificiality', was understood differently at the times of Hobbes. In Hobbes' words, 'For by art is created that great LEVIATHAN called a COMMONWEALTH, or STATE (in Latin, CIVITAS), which is but an artificial man, though of greater stature and strength than the natural, for whose protection and defence it was intended; and in which the sovereignty is an artificial soul'.[35]

Hobbes' Leviathan is narrated in the form of deduction from first principles. Hobbes begins his great work by outlining a theory of subjectivity, rationality and desire. The first chapter is entitled 'of sense', the second, 'the imagination'. From general propositions about the nature of the senses, language and abstract thought, Hobbes develops a theory of discourse, speech, writing, reason and knowledge. These concepts are then employed as the building blocks of a theory of desire, including the desire for power. 'The power of a man, to take it universally, is his present means to obtain some future apparent good, and is either original or instrumental'.[36] From this Hobbes arrives at his famous deduction (interestingly, he understood it as a component of a theory of manners), 'So that in the first place, I put for a general inclination of all mankind a perpetual and restless desire of power after power, that ceaseth only in death.'[37] The Hobbesian theory of the state and inter-state relationship has been developed explicitly within the framework of a general theory of order and change.[38]

In sum, all IR theories establish, whether explicitly or implicitly, a relationship with a general theory in the social sciences and social philosophy. That does not mean, unfortunately, that IR theories do so systematically. Nonetheless, all the familiar concepts we employ in IR such as state, power, actors, rationality, hegemony, interest, balance, equilibrium and so on, as well as the various metaphors and analogies that inform and shape our thinking in IR, are drawn from one or another general theory in the social sciences.

Towards a general theory of order and change

Considering the link between IR and general theoretical frameworks, Strange's second point, concerning nothing less than the human condition itself, provides an important insight. For Strange strives to identify the underlying 'problematique' that

---

[35] Ibid., Introduction, capitalised in the original.
[36] Ibid., ch. x, 'of Power, Worth, Dignity, Honour and Worthiness'.
[37] Ibid., ch. XI, 'Of the Difference of Manners'.
[38] Within the discipline of IR, Hans Morgenthau comes closest to Hobbes when he argues that 'The main signpost that helps political realism to find its way through the landscape of international politics is the concept of interest defined in terms of power. This concept provides the link between reason trying to understand international politics and the facts to be understood. This is reminiscent of Hobbes' theory of desire which translates into a theory of desire for power. Hans J. Morgenthau, *Politics among Nations: The Struggle for Power and Peace*, 4th edn. (New York: Alfred A. Knopf, 1967), p. 5.

links critical and heterodox theory to a general theory of the social. She believes she had found it in the notion of human condition 'as it is, or as it was, affected by economic, political and social circumstances'.[39]

Where does the concept of the human condition come from? The concept of the human condition is reminiscent of Heidegger's description of sociology as 'a general theory of man and his human relations'.[40] Or Weber who identifies two disciplines, history and sociology (or the cultural sciences).[41] For Strange, it appears, IR is part of a pan-disciplinary *sociological* tradition which seeks to investigate the nature of order and change in society. It may be argued that one of the great forces for change in the IR field is motivated by the conviction that the international arena adds a vital, often missing, dimension to the study of the processes of order and change in society. A conviction that implies, in turn, that International Relations as a discipline should be integrated into the broader field of investigation of the nature of order and change in the contemporary world.

This raises a third question. If IR is no longer merely the study of peace and war, but should be oriented towards existential questions such as the human condition, why have a field of study called International Relations in the first place? This is a very good question. In fact, the concept of 'inter-national relations' offers an important clue to a bias in the discipline, alluding to one of the leading heuristics in the field – classical realism. The term 'inter-national' is an historical overhang from a period in the history of state formation, around the late eighteenth century, when the nation began to be considered as an 'actor' in its own right in world politics.[42] Inter-national relations, as it implies, is the study of the relationship between nations or people in the world, constituted as it were, as personalities.[43]

Contemporary thinking, however, considers the nation in very different light. The nation is a constructed identity, a product of historical encounters. The nation, therefore, cannot be considered the primary unit of 'inter-national relations', nor indeed, is the state the primary unit – particularly as some begin to think about a post-state scenarios which they call 'globalisation'. If the nation is not the main 'actor' in world-politics, then the very meaning of inter-national relations becomes problematic. The heterodox tradition, however, may not be satisfied to replace one set of actors with another; it seeks to question the very idea of privileging an 'actor' in the first place. That is exactly what Strange is aiming for with her notion of the 'human condition'.

---

[39] Strange, *States and Markets*, p. 16.

[40] Martin Heidegger, *History of the Concept of Time: Prolegomena*, trans. Theodore J. Kisielime (Bloomington, IN: Indiana University Press, 1992), p. 15.

[41] Max Weber, *Economy and Society: An Outline of Interpretive Sociology*, 2 vols., edited by Guenther Roth and Claus Wittich (Berkeley, CA: University of California, 1978), p. 19.

[42] For discussion of the emergence of the nation as a force in world politics, see Gérard Mairet, *Le Principe de Souveraineté: Histoires et Fondements du Pouvoire Moderne* (Paris: Gallimard, 1997).

[43] A point that was already clear to Heinrich von Treitschke in the nineteenth century: 'Treat the State as a person', says Trietschke in a typical classical realist fashion, 'and the necessary and rational multiplicity of States follows . . . Just as in individual life the ego implies the existence of the non-ego, so it does in the State. The State is power, precisely in order to assert itself as against other equally independent powers. War and the administration of justice are the chief tasks of even the most barbaric States.' Heinrich von Treitschke, *Politics* (London: Constable, 1916), p. 19. The use of the concept of 'ego' in a pre-Freudian manner is exemplary of my point about a general theory. Classical realism evolve out of a general theory of the subject and the collective to arrive at a theory of international relations.

Methodological individualism vs. heterodoxy

We encounter at this point an important dispute in the social sciences between two sets of heuristics, methodological individualism (or rationalism) and heterodoxy. They each yield radically different conceptions of the international. Arguably, the most important exponent of contemporary methodological individualism was Max Weber.[44] Weber was an important contributor to late nineteenth century philosophical debate on the relationship between the sciences and the social sciences.[45] He took from the sciences an important methodological point: scientific advance could be achieved only on the basis of commonly observable phenomena. Some fashionable theories of his time, which attributed cause or volition to unobservables such as God, the nation or the working-classes, were therefore considered by Weber unscientific.

Weber argued that the only possible solid scientific basis for the cultural sciences was meaningful individual action. In his words, '[a]ction in the sense of subjectively understandable orientation of behaviour exists only as the behaviour of one or more individual human beings.'[46] Thus Weberian action-based methodology privileges the notion of the 'actor'. The commonly heard reference to states as 'actors' or, worse, to 'non-state actors', is, therefore, essentially misguided. The notion of actor is reserved by Weber (and other methodological individualists) to the individual. This is why Helen Milner, for instance, prefers to describe states as 'agency', a more appropriate terminology from a methodological individualistic perspective.[47]

There are, however, two significant points of dispute between methodological individualism and the heterodox approach. While methodological individualists presume the rationality of the subject (bounded rationality or not), and hence centre on the concept of preferences and choice, heterodox approaches in the social sciences are founded on a radically different theory of the ego. Rather than assuming that people chose what is best for them, and then puzzle over those cases that patently contradict such assumptions. It was the genius of Deleuze and Guattari to have noticed that the subject of methodological individualism 'presupposes a fantastic repression' – largely self-repression of the subjects ostensibly by they themselves.[48] The key question for heterodoxy, they argue, is 'how could the masses be made to desire their own repression?[49] To be somewhat schematic, orthodoxy asks how people

---

[44] Richard Miller defines methodological individualism as 'the doctrine that social phenomena must be explainable in terms of the psychologies and situations of the participants in those phenomena.' Richard W. Miller, 'Methodological Individualism and Social Explanation', *Philosophy of Science*, 45:3 (1978), pp. 387–414, at 387. Kenneth Arrow credits Menger as the originator of methodological individualism. Kenneth Arrow, 'Methodological Individualism and Social Knowledge', *American Economic Review*, 84:2 (1994), pp. 1–9, at 2. Others believe the methodology goes all the way back to Hobbes. Joseph Agassi, 'Methodological Individualism', *The British Journal of Sociology*, 11:3 (1960), pp. 244–70. For recent criticism of methodological individualism, see Barry Hindess, *Philosophy and Methodology in the Social Sciences* (Hassocks: Harvester Press, 1970); Andrew Sayer, *Method in Social Science: A Realist Approach* (London: Routledge, 1992).

[45] For a good discussion, see Guy Oakes, *Weber and Rickert: Concept Formation in the Cultural Sciences* (Cambridge, MA, MIT, 1988).

[46] Weber, *Economy and Society*, p. 9. The behavioural 'revolution' took a step further and pronounced the idea of meaningful or individual subjective meaning to his or her action redundant.

[47] Milner, 'Rationalizing Politics', p. 4.

[48] Gilles Deleuze and Félix Guattari, *Anti-Oedipus: Capitalism and Schizophrenia* (London: The Athlone Press, 1984), p. 3.

[49] Ibid., p. xiv. They continue '[t]his is a question which the English and Americans are reluctant to deal with directly', p. xiv.

achieve what is good for them; heterodoxy asks why people desire what is bad for them. This starting point leads orthodoxy to a radically different conception of the subject, history, social institutions, causality and indeed rationality. It brings us back and clarifies further Strange's point about the 'human condition' as the core problematic of the social sciences.

One of the ironies of contemporary research is that while orthodoxy assumes a rational subject, and ends up frequently with theories of systemic irrationality; heterodoxy assumes the irrationality of the subject, but often ends up with theories of systemic rationality. Heterodoxy seems to have been attracted to some totalising reductionist theories of world order, in which the entire human experience is reduced to one overwhelming structure aimed at maintaining exploitation, alienation and poverty – in short, we are back to the 'moral' sciences. Growing interest in evolutionary epistemology in the social sciences is aimed precisely at overcoming such normative presumptions. In addition, we should note that heterodoxy does not contradict the theory of the utility-maximising individual, it merely suggests that such subjectivity is historically constituted. There are, not surprisingly, many 'border-crossers' among these two general types of theorising.

My second point concerns the area where the two approaches differ significantly. It is in the way they understand the relationship between different fields of enquiry. Methodological individualists posit different spheres of meaningful action. (Hence, presumably, the approach is considered 'positivist' and even 'empiricist' by IR scholars – although it is often recognised that rationalist methodologies tend to be deductive and hence, strictly speaking, non-empiricist.)[50] From such a perspective the IR discipline is defined as a distinct sphere of activities, interstate relationships. However as John Wilkinson points out, methodologically individualistic approaches have 'no use for interdisciplinary collaboration, since by definition no one actor can influence the behaviour of another and preferences and technology represent an exogenous 'state of the world'.[51] Orthodoxy assumes that similar dynamics prevail in different spheres of action, so that in principle, we can employ neoclassical concepts such as utility, collective choice, transaction costs in sociology, political science and so on.[52] Wilkinson contrasts methodological individualism with heterodoxy in which 'activity is socially constructed and maintained and historically determined by individual and collective actions expressed through organisations and institutions.

[50] I am using 'tend' and 'often' because it is increasingly difficult to make categorical statements. Kathleen Thelen writes about the different schools of institutionalism 'Each of these three schools in fact represents a sprawling literature characterized by tremendous internal diversity, and it is often also difficult to draw hard and fast lines between them. The differences that have been identified amount to tendencies that apply unevenly across particular authors within each school of thought. The walls dividing the three perspectives have also been eroded by 'border crossers' who have resisted the tendencies toward cordoning these schools off from each other and who borrow liberally (and often fruitfully) where they can, in order to answer specific empirical questions.' Kathleen Thelen, 'Historical Institutionalism in Comparative Politics', *Annual Review of Political Science*, 2 (1999), pp. 369–404, at 370. Thelen is correct: 'Border crossers' make it difficult and unnecessary to make such categorical statements.

[51] John Wilkinson 'A New Paradigm for Economic Analysis?', *Economy & Society*, 26:3 (1997), pp. 309.

[52] Gerlad M. Meier, 'Trade Policy, Development, and The New Political Economy', in Ronald W. Jones and Anne O. Krueger (eds.), *The Political Economy of International Trade: Essays In Honor of Robert E. Baldwin* (Oxford: Basil Blackwell, 1990).

The analysis ... becomes a collective endeavour of economics, sociology, history, organisation theory and political philosophy'.[53]

Heterodoxy and the constitution of the field of International Relations

If an analysis is a 'collective endeavour,' as Wilkinson suggests, what is the distinctively international dimension of these pan-disciplinary efforts? Goran Therborn summarises succinctly heterodoxy under what he calls, 'a three-dimensional approach'. An holistic investigation, he says, is 'globally encompassing in a sense meaningful to actors in the world; historically oriented, with an eye both for concrete processes and for broad, connecting, epochal interpretation; and ... having a clear focus on political institutions'.[54] The three-dimensional approach is a good summary of heterodox methodology. And it reads like a theoretician's nightmare, particularly to one who aspires for parsimony! For how can a credible theory come out of this? Let us go over the three points, they are interrelated:

1. Globally encompassing research agenda

The notion of a 'globally encompassing' research agenda implies a number of things.

First, heterodoxy encourages a geographically expansive perspective, and takes, in effect, the entire planet as its subject matter. For Waltz, for instance, small states are nearly 'washed up' as economic entities and 'pose no problem for international-political theory', I have argued, in contrast, that some of the smallest and least powerful countries in the world, the tax havens, played a crucial role in globalisation and forced changes upon larger states.[55] Equally, Cox considers one of the advantages of Marxism to 'add a vertical dimension of power to the horizontal that dimension of rivalry'.[56] While readily acknowledging asymmetries in power and capabilities, heterodoxy sees no particular reason for privileging certain states or regions in the world *a priori*.

Second, in principle, heterodoxy is sympathetic to comparative research. Yet, comparative research is of value up to a point because many mechanisms and processes do not necessarily correspond to the political boundaries of the nation-state. By its very nature, comparative research is incapable of appreciating such mechanisms and processes, and may either exclude them from the outset or misinterpret them. Third, the notion of a globally encompassing research implies an expansion of the number of issues under investigation. The discipline of International Relations should concern itself, according to this view, not only with interstate

---

[53] Wilkinson, 'A New Paradigm', p. 310.

[54] Goran Therborn, 'The Right to Vote and the Four World Routes through Modernity', in Rolf Torstendahl (ed.), *State Theory and State History* (London: Sage, 1992), p. 63.

[55] Kenneth Waltz, *Theory of International Politics* (Reading, MA: Addison-Wesley, 1979), p. 94; Ronen Palan, *The Offshore World: Sovereign Markets, Virtual Places, and Nomad Millionaires* (Ithaca, NY: Cornell University Press, 2003).

[56] Cox, *Approaches to World Order*, p. 95.

relationships and not only with the dynamics and forces of capital, but with the entire range of trans-border communications and exchanges.

2. Historically oriented approach

'Critical theory', writes Robert Cox, 'is theory of history in the sense of being concerned not just with the past but with a continuing process of historic change'.[57] Critical theory takes, in other words, an historical perspective on the present. Roughly speaking, there are three models of historical change: universalistic, cyclical and evolutionary theories. Universalistic theories, associated with orthodoxy, are described by Charles Tilly as 'covering laws': 'In covering law accounts, explanation consists of subjecting robust empirical generalizations to higher- and higher-level generalizations, the most general of all standing as laws. In such accounts, models are invariant – they work the same under all conditions'.[58] Krasner represents such an approach when he says: 'The fundamental problems of international politics and international political economy are enduring, so are the theoretical perspectives that we use to understand them'.[59] Krasner appears to suggest that certain theories are equally applicable to vastly different historical epochs and geographical contexts. Such universalistic or non-historical theories tend to treat the past as if it consisted of a set of isolatable events that may be used to support some general propositions.

Cyclical theories assume recurrence of certain large-scale structural historical patterns. Despite professing to do the opposite,[60] cyclical theories are often non-historical in orientation in the sense that they tend to adopt systemic explanations which 'consist of specifying a place for some event, structure, or process within a larger self-maintaining set of interdependent elements and showing how the event, structure, or process in question serves and/or results from interactions among the larger set of elements'.[61] Wallerstein's theory of hegemonic cycle is a typical cyclical theory of history.[62] Certain variants of dependency theory also adopt a cyclical approach: they take the historical patterns of international division of labour that was typical of the period between 1930 and 1970 as a general theory of capitalism.[63] Cyclical theories are often functionalist, but are not necessarily so.[64]

---

[57] Cox, 'Social Forces', p. 130.

[58] Charles Tilly, 'Mechanisms in Political Processes', *Annual Review of Political Science*, 4 (2001), pp. 421–41, at 423. See also Wilkinson, 'A New Paradigm?'

[59] Stephen Krasner, 'International Political Economy: Abiding Discord', *Review of International Political Economy*, 1:1 (1994), p. 3.

[60] 'Capitalism is first and foremost a historical social system', Immanuel Wallerstein, *The Modern World-System*, vol. I: *Capitalist Agriculture and the Origins of the European World-Economy in the Sixteenth Century* (New York: Academic Press, 1974), p. 13.

[61] Tilly, 'Mechanisms', p. 23.

[62] Immanuel Wallerstein, 'The Three Instances of Hegemony in the History of the Capitalist World-Economy', *International Journal of Comparative Sociology*, 24 (1983), p. 100–8.

[63] Alain Lipietz, *Mirages and Miracles: The Crisis of Global Fordism* (London: Verso, 1987).

[64] 'It is probably in theories of international relations that the tendency to lapse into functionalism or even finalism ... is most obvious, and that it inflicts most damage ... Ricardo and the supporters of the Heckschner–Ohlin–Samuelson theorem seem, for instance, to believe that the international division of labour is the result of some world conference at which brilliant economists explained to an admiring gallery of politicians'. Lipietz, *Mirages and Miracles*, p. 16. See also Tilly, 'Mechanisms'.

Many neo-Gramscians may find it somewhat disconcerting to discover that Robert Cox's theory of hegemony adopts almost word by word what Tilly says about systemic explanation:

For the purpose of the present discussion, the method of historical structures is applied to the three levels, or spheres of activity: (1) organization of production, more particularly with regard to the *social forces* engendered by the production process; (2) *forms of states* as derived from the study of state/society complexes; and (3) *world orders*, that is, the particular configurations of forces with successively defined the problematic of war on peace for the ensemble of states. Each of these levels can be studied as a succession of dominant and emergent rival structures.[65]

Notwithstanding the careful language and caveats employed by Cox ('for the purpose of the present discussion ...' and so on),[66] not only does the Coxian analytical scheme assert a relationship between the three categories, but also emphasises that *the relationship between the three categories is the key to the understanding of human history*. In other words, there are large-scale structural historical patterns which ultimately repeat themselves.[67] The method by which Cox reaches this conclusion, whether through deductive or inductive reasoning, is not entirely clear.[68]

In contrast to systemic and covering laws theories, evolutionary theories adopt the Darwinian principle of cumulative causation. In its pure form, 'Darwinian evolution has no foreordained goal, but a continuity of cause and effect without any trend, any final term, or consummation. It is 'blindly cumulative causation'.[69] Charles Tilly calls such an approach a mechanism – and process-based explanation: 'process-based explanations aim at modest ends – selective explanation of salient features by means of partial causal analogies'.[70] So that, for example, the study of the transition from feudalism to capitalism is important and informative, but generalisations are difficult because transitions are unlikely to repeat themselves.

From an evolutionary perspective concepts such as states, nation, power, are treated as historically specific – a point of agreement between evolutionary thinkers and Gramsicans. However, if for Marxists capitalism is an historical system that undergoes changes and evolution, then for evolutionary economists such as Veblen and Commons, not only capitalism evolves, but capital itself undergoes evolution – a point that Marxists do not take into account.[71] Such deep evolutionary method tends to assume that IR is not only what happens when nation-states have been constituted, but is a field of study that encompasses within itself the evolution and

[65] Cox, *Approaches to World Order*, p. 100, italics in the original.
[66] Indeed, Cox distinguishes between his and the structural Marxist explanation which he regards as ahistorical, ibid., p. 92. It can be argued, however, that Poulantzas' work is far more historicist than Cox has given credit to.
[67] Hence, for instance, Gramsci's theory of hegemony is considered of use to IR. See Cox, p. 100: 'The very notion that Gramsci developed a general theory of hegemony – a very doubtful proposition – is a product of such a structural theory of history'.
[68] This approach is very different to Braudel, who is often confused for a world-system theorist. Braudel adopts an evolutionary approach and says very clearly that he does not believe in the universality of any analytical scheme: 'I do not for instance believe in the permanent and unchallenged superiority of political history and the sacrosanct primacy of the state', he writes, 'sometimes the state is well-nigh all-important, at other times it has little or no influence'. Fernand Braudel, *Civilization and Capitalism 15th–18th Centuries* (New York: Harper, 1979), p. 460.
[69] John Commons, *Institutional Economics* (Madison, WI: University of Wisconsin Press, 1961), p. 128.
[70] Tilly, 'Mechanisms', p. 24.
[71] Commons, *Institutional Economics*.

change in every aspect of life. States, nations, societies, the 'international system' are historically constituted within the very context that IR theory should help explain. Whereas for Cox the evolution of 'state form' is explained primarily in terms of production and world order, for the evolutionary approaches, there could be a much greater variety of explanations.

3. Political institutions

Although it remains one of the most cited articles in IR, a key point in Ruggie's critique of hegemonic stability theory has been somewhat overlooked. 'Efforts to construct international economic regimes in the interwar period' he writes 'failed not because of the lack of a hegemon. They failed because, even had there been a hegemon, they stood in contradiction to the transformation *in the mediating role of the state* between market and society, which altered fundamentally the social purpose of domestic and international authority'.[72] Ruggie alludes here to a third approach, more prevalent in sociology and political science, which regards the state as a key societal institution mediating between different social spheres. The difficulties of the 1930s, he believes, were not due to the failure of hegemony, but rather to the lack of an adequate state form to mediate between market and society. For Ruggie, the state, and other political institutions, serve primarily as mediating institutions between the international arena and domestic politics.

Let us take another example to clarify this notion of mediation. The Marshall plan, typically a key piece of evidence for the hegemony thesis, is significant, argues Michael Hogan, on two counts. There are those – let us call them conventional IR – who view the European recovery programme together with the NATO alliance and other 'instruments' of the Cold War as 'evidence of America's assumption of world leadership after the Second World War'.[73] However more recent works, he notes, 'have portrayed twentieth-century developments as part of a larger historical process by which Americans adjusted their economic and political institutions to the profound transformations brought on by industrialization'.[74]

This is a crucial point that Hogan himself fails to pursue to the full. For he points out two diametrically opposed paradigms of the relationships between IR theories and the broader theories of order and change. The former, associated with the so-called 'realist' approaches (but which could also be subsumed under certain radical approaches), assumes from the outset that leadership and power is a value in itself, and hence, it concludes, once the US found itself in a position of power, it assumed the role of leadership in the world. According to the second position, the 'US' consists of a medley of organisations and institutions, with more or less a degree of coherency between them. The state is less of a volitional 'actor' or a mere arena mediating conflicting interests, it is more of a product of its own institutional arrangement which structures its ways of behaving in the world.

---

[72] John G. Ruggie, 'International Regimes, Transactions and Change: Embedded Liberalism in the Postwar Economic Order', *International Organization*, 36 (1982), pp. 397–415, at 397. Emphasis mine.

[73] Michael J. Hogan, *The Marshall Plan* (Cambridge: Cambridge University Press, 1987), p. 1.

[74] Ibid., p. 2.

Another example of state mediation theory is found in David Lake's work. Lake argues that contemporary efforts at establishing institutions of global governance are:

Reflected in the persistence of the early industrializing model in the United States . . . [and are] premised upon a large private sector that reflected the early American economy, the constitution left large residual rights of control to individuals and the states.[75]

For Lake, contemporary American policy is not the product of some 'national interest', nor can it be reduced to the interplay of competing social forces; the American polity is an inherited complex institutional structure which tends to be to some extent a prisoner of its own evolution.

The two positions may appear the same. They are not. According to the first, states are volitional 'rational actors' that seek to shape their environment to serve their national or vested interests. To the latter, state mediation theory, 'hegemony' is viewed more as a gravitational field, a product of inherited institutional and social forces that shape not only states behaviour in the world, but also their 'structural power', as Susan Strange calls it.[76] The crucial point is that these gravitational forces evolve in processes that are not independent of the state system. States do not undergo transformations independently of the international system, as realist IR has it. Nor are the internal processes of state formation mere reflections of exogenous forces, as world system theorists, for instance, appear to believe. Consequently, what is interpreted as hegemony, leadership, struggle for world hegemony and so on, often considered as an expression and manifestation of the tactics and strategies of states – may have been brought about by 'domestic' realignment of forces, as they seek to cope with circumstances and dynamics that may be beyond their control.[77] Indeed, often under closer scrutiny such 'domestic' forces turn out to be of international origins and vice versa.

But what then, is a better way of conceptualising the complex interaction between the internal and the international? Although this question appears to have arisen in IR only very recently, paradoxically one possible answer can be found in some of the most familiar texts in the social sciences. Only that apparently, we never really paid attention. The rest of this article aims to illustrate how the basis of an alternative, evolutionary approach to world order can be found, among others, in the works of Hegel, Marx and the French School of Regulation.

Hegel's diffusionist theory of world spirit

It may come as a surprise to find that Georg Hegel intuited some of the basic parameters of what is described here as an evolutionary-institutional theory of international orders. Hegel's ambition was to develop a holistic theory of world society, a theory that brings together a theory of subjectivity and rationality with a theory of world history. For Hegel, reason is not an abstract ahistorical set of rules

---

[75] David Lake, 'Global Governance: A Relational Contracting Approach', Aseem Prakash and Jeffery A. Hart (eds.), *Globalization and Governance* (London: Routledge, 1999), p. 345.

[76] Strange, *States and Markets*.

[77] See R. Palan and J. Abbott, *State Strategies In The Global Political Economy* (London: Pinter, 1996).

and norms, 'revealed' to humanity through the grace of God. Reason is evolutionary; it emerges through interaction, and history is the judge of truth. His interest is in what today we consider as IR follows on from his observation that reason matures in world historical conditions, that is, within the context of the international arena.

For Hegel, the emergence of the nation was a critical moment in the evolution of the human spirit. In words that hark back to the origins of the concept of international relations,[78] he writes, 'The nations are the concepts which the spirit has formed itself'.[79] The rational, he believed, 'assumes varying shapes; but in none of them is it more obviously an end than in that whereby the spirit explicates and manifests itself in the endlessly varying forms which we call nations'.[80] But, he warns, 'world history takes account only of nations that constituted themselves into states'.[81]

In light of the momentous significance of the nation-state, Hegel had to consider also the significance of the relationship between states. He notes that:

[i]t is as particular entities that states enter into relations with one another. Hence their relations are on the largest scale a maelstrom of external contingency and the inner particularity of passions, private interests and selfish ends, abilities and virtues, vices, forces, and wrong.[82]

But, he argues, the maelstrom of external contingency and inner particularity can generate from time to time, by sheer accident or otherwise, historical moments whereby some states' internal structure happens to correspond most perfectly to the structural flow of history. Such states emerge at these junctures as the most powerful and successful states in the world. In his words:

If we stop for a moment to consider the political implications – that a state will be well constituted and internally powerful if the private interest of its citizens coincides with the general end of the state, so that the one can be satisfied and realized through the other. . . . But for the state to achieve this unity, numerous institutions must be set up and appropriate mechanisms invented, and the understanding must go through prolonged struggles before it discovers what is in fact appropriate . . . the moment at which the state attains this unity marks the most flourishing period in its history, when its virtue, strength, and prosperity are at their height.[83]

Hegel had the recent experience of revolutionary France in mind. In developing this theory, Hegel expresses the 'problematic' of International Relations for nineteenth century Prussian thinkers: rivalries, wars and competition among states brought the modern world to Prussia. Rivalry and wars are, therefore, not all bad. On the contrary, these are the unwitting processes of history by which states could potentially achieve their coveted unity, the internal harmony of institutions, norms and spirit. Furthermore, rivalry and competition ensured the diffusion of the most recent evolution of the human spirit and rationality in the world – they were positive forces of change in history.

---

[78] See discussion above.
[79] Georg Wilhelm Friedrich Hegel, *Lectures on the Philosophy of World History: Introduction* (Cambridge: Cambridge University Press, 1975), p. 51.
[80] Ibid., p. 28.
[81] Ibid., p. 95.
[82] Georg Wilhelm Friedrich Hegel, *Philosophy of Right*, trans. and notes by T. M. Knox (Oxford: Oxford University Press, 1952), para. 340, p. 215.
[83] Hegel, *Lectures on the Philosophy of World History*, p. 73.

Here we find hints of an alternative conception of the international, and indeed, an alternative conception of the role of hegemony in the international orders, a theory more closely aligned to Hogan's institutionalist interpretation of the Marshall plan. Hegel stresses a view of the state as an historical juncture, a product of contingent confluence of internal and external forces, whereby when a harmony is achieved between ends and means, such a state proves particularly influential. The state is important in Hegel's theory as an institutional framework through which 'the universal which emerges and becomes conscious within the state' manifests itself.[84] But the universal is revealed in the state through the agency of an interactionist order.

Marx, 'primitive accumulation' and succession of hegemonies

Marx famously 'inverted' Hegel's argument to show that what Hegel called 'reason' and 'spirit' were nothing but the spirit of the capitalist world economy. Marx agreed, however, with Hegel on specifics: the role played by international rivalries in the development of capitalism. If for Hegel, the rational emerges and becomes conscious within the state, Marx says capitalism emerges and becomes conscious – that is, a reality, within the state. In his words:

The different moments of primitive accumulation can be assigned in particular to Spain, Portugal, Holland, France and England, in a more or less chronological order. These different moments are systematically combined together at the end of the 17th [century] in England; the combination embraces the colonies, the national debt, the modern tax system, and the system of protection.[85]

According to Marx, each of these 'hegemonies' – a word he did not use – introduced institutional innovations which proved important to future capitalist accumulation. For instance, 'the system of public credit i.e. of national debts, the origins of which are to be found in Genoa and Venice as early as the Middle Ages, took possession of Europe as a whole during the period of manufacture'.[86] Genoa and Venice introduced, therefore, an innovation which was diffused throughout Europe. Once the system of public credit was in place, it was developed further elsewhere: 'the colonial system, with its maritime trade and its commercial wars, served as a forcing-house for the credit system. Thus it first took root in Holland. The national debt – whether despotic, constitutional or republican – marked the capitalist era with its stamp the public debt becomes one of the most powerful levers of primitive accumulation.'[87]

'Thus the villainies of the Venetian system ... formed one of the secret foundations of Holland's wealth in capital? There is a similar relationship between Holland and England? The same thing is going on today between England and the United States'.[88] Capitalism, as it appears in these pages, is not an abstract or universal 'mode of production'; capitalism is a specific institutional form that develops within an interactionist order constituted by the state system. Marx has not

---

[84] Hogan, *The Marshall Plan*, p. 97.
[85] Karl Marx, *Capital*, vol. I (London: Penguin, NLB, 1970), p. 914.
[86] Ibid., p. 919.
[87] Ibid., p. 919.
[88] Ibid., p. 920.

made much of the competition between states as a method of diffusion of the institutional gain. But he clearly adopts Hegel's idea that the hegemonic state is a product of a confluence of forces, some internal, some external. Hegemony, in turn, diffuses its institutional innovation throughout the international system by competition or force. In doing so, hegemony is the product of certain historical circumstances, able to shape the future direction of the world capitalist economy. The world economy as a whole evolves through a succession of hegemonies.

The French regulation theory and evolutionary international political economy

The French School of Regulation is arguably the direct follower of Hegel and Marx. An evolutionary theory of international orders can be teased out in a close reading of some of the texts of this school of thought, particularly once the acknowledged over-structural tendencies of the theory are laid to rest. The French School of Regulation was originally a Marxist approach that emerged in the 1970s partially in order to explain the continuing robustness of the world capitalist economy. The crisis of the 1930s, which according to Marxist theory was the major and potentially cataclysmic crisis predicted by Marx, should have resulted in the collapse of the world capitalist system. Instead, following the twenty years which witnessed a global-spanning great depression, the rise of extreme right movements such as Nazism and Fascism and a major world war, a new order has emerged based on the universalisation of the New Deal principles among the advanced capitalist countries. The regulationist answer to the Marxist conundrum – after all capitalism was supposed to collapse – pointed out the ability of the state to generate systematic, if ultimately contradictory, countervailing conditions to the natural crisis-prone tendencies of capitalism. The new order, known as a Fordist mode of accumulation, which is very similar to Ruggie's idea of 'embedded liberalism', did not only resolve the crisis tendencies, but also contributed to an unprecedented rate of economic growth among the advanced industrialised countries. The question, then, is how and why capitalism is able to regenerate itself and how and why such propitious regimes of accumulation arise.

In answering these questions, Alain Lipietz, who is keenly aware of the structural and (hence functional) tendencies of regulation theory, goes out of his way to soften the edges and dispel any lingering notions of structural inevitability. Regime of accumulation, he says, emerges in an evolutionary process reminiscent of Hegel and Marx' theory.

> The important point, however, is that the emergence of a new regime of accumulation is not a *pre-ordained part of capitalism's destiny, even though it may correspond to certain identifiable 'tendencies'* ... Regimes of accumulation and modes of regulation are *chance discoveries* made in the course of human struggles ... So *the history of capitalism is full of experiments which led nowhere: aborted revolutions, abandoned prototypes and all sorts of monstrosities.*[89]

In a similar fashion, Michel Aglietta argues: '[t]here is no royal road where the most abstract concepts magically command the movement of society. There is rather a

---

[89] Lipietz, *Mirages and Miracles*, p. 15. Emphasis mine.

two-way process marked by frequent mishaps'.[90] Here, Hegel's idea of the maelstrom of internal and external conditions is marshalled in order to explain the appearance of successful states. Like Hegel and Marx before them, the regulationists argue that a system founded on competing sovereignties ensures, to quote Lipietz, that the 'history of capitalism is full of experiments'. State sovereignty makes certain that each state of whatever size and constitution develops a somewhat different combination of institutions and policies in response to changes in the environment of accumulation. Often these changes, 'experiments' in regulation, have led, he notes, to aborted monstrosities. But the sheer diversity of states of varying size, history and location, creates possibilities otherwise absent in the capitalist system as a whole.

Regulation theory suggests, therefore, that wholesale changes in the nature of capitalism impact in a variety of ways upon social formations, producing a plethora of outcomes. Most of these 'outcomes', modes of regulation, prove to be 'aborted revolutions'. But in some cases, and for reasons that are difficult to predict or anticipate, these outcomes prove propitious to capitalist accumulation. Successful experiments pull such states ahead. In the history of capitalism, economically powerful states, particularly if they were sufficiently sizeable and militarily powerful, have tended to serve as models for emulation to others. Considering that historically states have emulated each other by adopting successful techniques of governance and control,[91] the modern state is a product of such systemic emulation and innovation.[92] When that happens, we recognise the emergence of a new regime of accumulation with a corresponding mode of regulation. However, we should not confuse cause with effects: rather than assuming that such regime of accumulation is a necessary historical outcome, 'at best, we can adopt a posterior or almost metaphoric functionalism'.[93]

Regimes of accumulation emerge, therefore, in the interaction between the general capitalist tendencies, which are forces operating at a transnational level, and the specific configuration of institutions and forces within each society. The international realm ensures diversity and experimentation which creates the possibilities for positive outcomes. That is why Aglietta maintains that that '[s]uch a study [i.e. regulationism] demands knowledge of the general tendencies of capitalist development within the different nations, and careful attention to the relations between states'.[94]

In a typical evolutionary manner, Aglietta chose the US example to study the rise of Fordism. But, he warns, there was nothing inevitable about the rise of the US and its place in the world after World War II. On the contrary, the foundations of the US success were laid down in the nineteenth century and were largely internally generated: 'The US experienced a capitalist revolution from the civil war onwards, the extension of the wage relations brought about a unification of the nation by its own internal dynamic alone'.[95] In time, however, the US emerged as a major

---

[90] Michel Aglietta, *A Theory of Capitalist Regulation: The US Experience* (London: NLB, 1979), p. 66.

[91] For discussion, see Jacques Ellul, *The Technological Society*, trans. John Wilkinson (London: Jonathan Cape, 1965).

[92] John U. Nef, *War and Human Progress* (London: Routledge, 1950). C. Tilly (ed.), *The Formation of National States In Western Europe* (Princeton, NJ: Princeton University Press, 1975).

[93] Lipietz, *Mirages and Miracles*, p. 16.

[94] Aglietta, *Capitalist Regulation*, p. 22.

[95] Ibid., p. 22.

capitalist power and began to shape the development of global capitalism. It was only after World War II, that the US government launched a concerted and active policy aimed at the 'universalisation of its structural forms'[96] and adopted hegemonic policies. The hegemon, according to this perspective, is more of a product of historical confluence of the international order than the originator and organiser of an international order.

Conclusion. Towards a heterodox theory of international orders

This article has sought to identify the underlying shared premise, the cluster of conclusions that are currently in search of a premise, that make up critical and heterodox IR. I have argued that the critical tradition in IR is no longer concerned only with the nature of peace and war, but rather has shifted towards a broader conception of IR as a component of a transdisciplinary study of order and change. The shift raises a number of important methodological points.

First, as a derivate discipline, IR scholars should develop greater awareness of first order theories. This suggests, for instance, that we should put greater emphasis on teaching our students the basic sociological theories of power, state, agency as well as first order theories of political economy, linguistics and so on.

Second, as components of general theories of order and change, the different theories and approaches in IR must make clear whether their contribution to the general theories are theoretically plausible. Attempts to 'bolt on' new themes or processes upon an existing theoretical framework are likely to fail. Equally, theory that may appear entirely plausible in IR, such as the realist theory, but which makes extraordinary demands on state theory, is suspect. As indeed, are some of the radical theories that assign an extraordinary degree of unity and purpose to the disparate members of the 'ruling classes', often brushing aside legitimate concerns about the difficulties of 'collective action'.

Third, I have argued that IR should adopt Goran Therborn's ideas for a good research agenda and pursue an approach that is globally encompassing, historically oriented, and focused on political institutions. Lastly, I have tried to demonstrate that an evolutionary-institutionalist theory of global order, founded on these three principles, is already on offer albeit in a rather rudimentary format in the social sciences.

What, then would an international dimension of a critical general theory of order and change be? It appears to me that heterodoxy does not perceive the international sphere as a system constituted in its own right, but tends to view it as a gigantic arena, or a transmission belt, a huge communication device. The international dimension is important, first and foremost, because it facilitates the transmission and diffusion of ideas, practices, rules, norms and institutions throughout the world. It contributes today, as it always has, to the *transmission and diffusion of modernising practices* throughout the world.

The key theoretical question posed by such a perspective is whether the transmission of modernising practices throughout the world amounts to mere stochastic

---

[96] Ibid., p. 22.

processes, or alternatively, operates according to certain patterns. How does a state system – if indeed it is a system – mediate the diffusion of modernising practices in the world? What is the relationship between the sedimented, inherited institutions of our time; primarily state and capital on the one hand, and power and politics, on the other? These are the sort of questions that, it seems to me, should constitute the core occupation of the discipline of International Relations today.

Happy Anniversary! Time and critique in International Relations theory

KIMBERLY HUTCHINGS

Abstract. All critical theories lay claim to some kind of account not only of the present of international politics and its relation to possible futures, but also of the role of critical theory in the present and future in international politics. This article argues that if critical international theory is to have a future that lives up to its revolutionary ambition, then it needs to listen more carefully to the voices of postcolonial and feminist critics and take on board the heterotemporality of international politics.

Introduction

Contributors to this Special Issue have been asked to comment on the fate of critical International Relations theory, twenty-five years after two of its founding texts were published.[1] My particular contribution takes its starting point from the peculiar features of *calendar temporality* that underlie this request. In his 'Theses on the Philosophy of History',[2] Walter Benjamin commented on the distinction between clock time and calendar time:

The great revolution introduced a new calendar. The initial day of a calendar serves as a historical time-lapse camera. And, basically, it is the same day that keeps recurring in the guise of holidays, which are days of remembrance. Thus the calendars do not measure time as clocks do; they are monuments of a historical consciousness of which not the slightest trace has been apparent in the last hundred years. In the July revolution an incident occurred which showed this consciousness still alive. On the first evening of fighting it turned out that the clocks in towers were being fired on simultaneously and independently from several places in Paris.[3]

Benjamin associates clock time with the linear, deterministic, irreversible and indifferent time of historicism, in which political (even revolutionary) action is

---

[1] Robert Cox's 'Social Forces, States and World Orders: Beyond International Relations Theory', *Millenium: Journal of International Studies*, 10:2 (1981), pp. 126–55. An abridged version of this article was reproduced in Robert Cox and Timothy Sinclair, *Approaches to World Order* (Cambridge: Cambridge University Press, 1996), and all page references in this article are to that version. Richard Ashley, 'Political Realism and Human Interests', *International Studies Quarterly*, 25:2 (1981), pp. 204–36. For the purposes of this article I use the label 'critical international theory' to encompass theoretical approaches to international politics that self-identify with the term 'critical' and are influenced by post-Marxist and post-Nietzschean thought.

[2] Walter Benjamin, 'Theses on the Philosophy of History', in *Illuminations*, trans. Harry Zorn (London: Pimlico, 1999), pp. 245–55.

[3] Benjamin, *Theses*, p. 253.

71

explained, in terms borrowed from Newtonian physics, as the product of material determination. Calendar time is different. Calendars require points of origin, and their recurrent dates are not indifferent points on the bland surface of a clock, but opportunities for remembrance and recreation that cut across and reinvent time. In invoking calendar time through the idea of the twenty-fifth anniversary of critical IR theory, the editors of this volume are constructing just such opportunities. Simply in referring to the anniversary they affirm another revolutionary calendar, one that was initiated by heroic intervention twenty-five years ago and may encourage us to (metaphorically speaking) stop the clocks again. However, as another highly distinguished critical theorist reminds us, what plays first as tragedy may replay as farce.[4] There are no guarantees that the inspiration of a revolutionary tradition will have genuinely revolutionary consequences. This is the burden of Marx's analysis of 'The Eighteenth Brumaire of Louis Bonaparte' and also of Derrida's reflections on Marx's own revolutionary legacy, *Specters of Marx*.[5] In both cases, these thinkers draw our attention to the difficulties of theorising the relationship between time, politics and critique. It is with these difficulties that this article is concerned.

Although critical theory takes many different forms, it always distinguishes itself from other forms of theorising in terms of its orientation towards change and the possibility of futures that do not reproduce the patterns of hegemonic power of the present. This means that all critical theories lay claim to some kind of account not only of the present of international politics and its relation to possible futures, but also of the role of critical theory in the present and future in international politics. The argument below falls into three sections. In the first section, 'The Time of Critique', I explore the understanding of time in international politics inherent in Cox's and Ashley's articles from 1981. I argue that this understanding rests on the privileging of a particular relationship between clock and calendar time, in which international politics is comprehended from the perspective of a singular, progressive temporality. In the second section, 'The Critique of Time', I examine ways in which this privileging of a singular, progressive temporality for international politics in critical theory has been put into question, and identify alternative trajectories for thinking critically about the time of international politics. I suggest, however, that predominant ways of thinking about critique and time in critical international theory, of whatever complexion, continue to privilege aspects of the relation between clock and calendar time in Cox's and Ashley's pioneering work. This means that, in spite of its commitment to challenging the international status quo, the temporal assumptions of critical theories tend to reproduce and confirm the hegemonic pattern of international power. In the third section, 'Thinking the Future of Critique', I begin to address the question of how critical theorists might theorise international political time in a way that matches up to their counter-hegemonic aspirations. I use the example of feminist theory as one context in which there are significant political incentives to rethink Cox's and Ashley's revolutionary calendar and pluralise our

---

[4] Karl Marx, '18th Brumaire of Louis Bonaparte', in Karl Marx and Friedrich Engels, *Selected Works in One Volume* (London: Lawrence and Wishart, 1968), p. 96. The temptation to pursue the analogy and map the participants of debates in critical IR theory onto the *dramatis personae* of the French Revolution and the revolutions of 1848 is almost irresistible, but perhaps better left to the imagination of the reader.

[5] Jacques Derrida, *Specters of Marx: The State of Debt, The Work of Mourning and the New International* (New York and London: Routledge, 2006).

understanding of international political time. Following the lead of Chakrabarty and Connolly, I argue that Deleuze's theory of time is particularly useful as a way of conceptualising 'heterotemporality' in international politics. In conclusion, I claim that this means that if critical international theory is to have a future that lives up to the revolutionary ambition of Cox's and Ashley's founding texts, then it needs to listen more carefully to the voices of postcolonial and feminist critics.

The time of critique

For the purposes of this article, I will take the 'time of critique' to refer to the twenty-five years since the publication of Cox's and Ashley's articles. Both of those articles were calls to rethink established modes of theorising in IR, and both refer to issues that preoccupied mainstream and critical voices of the time. This was a world in which questions about US hegemonic decline and how to manage the nuclear arms race between two superpowers were of critical importance to scholars. If we see the time of critique in IR theory as beginning in 1981, we can chronicle it in two different ways: by reference to events and developments in the international realm; and by reference to the history of IR scholarship during this time. In terms of the former, there is no question that the break up of the Soviet Union and the end of the Cold War stand out as events crucial to the changing dynamics of world politics, within, across and between states. Equally obvious is the importance of ongoing and accelerating neoliberal processes of economic globalisation. The world in which Cox and Ashley wrote was still the world of the Cold War, and of alternatives to liberal capitalism. But it is notable that Cox's concerns, with social and economic forces in relation to state power and world order, conjures up a world much more immediately familiar than Ashley's references to Herz's arguments concerning prospective nuclear holocaust. In some ways 1981, as it is invoked in these texts, seems a lot longer ago than in others.[6]

The articles, at least on the surface, also provide a contrast if we interpret them in terms of a project of founding new ways of doing IR theory. Cox's argument, drawing on Marx and Gramsci, is firmly historical and sociological in tone, calling for empirical analysis to identify sources of counter-hegemonic futures immanent within a complex and multi-faceted present.[7] Ashley's argument uses a set of formal theoretical distinctions, drawn from Habermas's early work, between different kinds of knowledge-constitutive interest, to categorise and enable the deconstructive critique of neorealist analysis and suggest alternative possibilities.[8] In spite of their differences, however, both articles exhibit the characteristic that makes a theory 'critical' in Cox's terms, in that both are oriented towards the possibility of alternative futures, rather than to the perpetuation of the *status quo*.[9] Both therefore are making claims about how the time of international politics works, or might work,

---

[6] Ashley, 'Political Realism', pp. 236–331.

[7] Cox, 'Social Forces', pp. 97–101.

[8] Ashley, 'Political Realism', p. 208. I am not using 'deconstruction' in its technical Derridean sense, Ashley's argument is deconstructive insofar as it uses the idea of internal tensions between different aspects of political realism as a critical technique.

[9] Cox, 'Social Forces', pp. 87–91.

and how critique relates to its time. At the heart of these claims is a set of arguments about progress and singularity in international politics and the relationship between them.

Cox's argument deals with the time of international politics in a way that echoes the traditions of enlightenment philosophy of world history, as developed in the work of Kant, Hegel and Marx. According to this tradition, the possibility of critique, and therefore of progress, is immanent within history, and the complexity and plurality of history can be subsumed under either an actual or hypothetical 'as if' unity. This does not mean that Cox treats the history of international politics as a linear, mechanical or teleological process. For Cox, history is dialectical, the product of ongoing contradictory processes, the outcomes of which cannot be predicted with any certainty. Two things, however, are clear from Cox's account. The first is that critical theory is on the side of historical progress, aligned with the historical forces potentially contributing to counter-hegemonic international politics. The second is that the history of international politics can and should be considered holistically, as a complex, fluid but nevertheless singular object of analysis. These two claims are mutually reinforcing. Critique and progress in international politics invoke history in the singular, either as something to be *diagnosed* or something to be *made*. In 'diagnostic' mode, critique identifies the potential for progress immanent in history. In 'making' mode, by acting on the potential for progress immanent in history, critique helps to bring progress about. Theory and practice are mutually reinforcing. Whereas problem-solving is wholly oriented in relation to the hegemonic structure of the present, critical theory is self-consciously partial and political in its orientation towards change.

Critical theory is theory of history in the sense of being concerned not just with the past but with a continuing process of historical change. Problem solving theory is nonhistorical or ahistorical, since it, in effect, posits a continuing present . . .[10]

Cox's critique of realism in effect substitutes time for space as the unifying factor in analysing and judging international politics. In order to do this, Cox utilises both clock and calendar time. Clock time acts as a unifying principle in that it situates all events in a unidirectional and irreversible continuum of past, present and future. In so far as Cox is identifying causal relations between ideas, institutions and material capabilities in his critical theory, he is relying on clock time as their universal condition, and including all events (and their effects, intended or unintended) within the remit of his analysis. But Cox is also relying on calendar time, the idea of founding a new time, as the principle according to which critical theory operates in both diagnostic and 'making' modes. This dual operation of clock time and calendar time is characteristic of the distinction drawn by philosophers of history between the empirical, contingent course of events (Hegel's 'slaughterbench' of history)[11] and their deeper level structure and meaning. But philosophies of history notoriously struggle to explain how these two aspects of temporal organisation relate to one another. There are essentially two possibilities, both of which subsume clock time under calendar time. *Either*, there are certain material forces that ultimately take history in a progressive direction, so that only certain elements *matter* in clock time, *or*, it behoves the critical theorist to work 'as if' this were the case. In either case, the

[10] Ibid., p. 89.
[11] G. W. F. Hegel, *Philosophy of History*, trans J. Sibtree (New York: Collier and Son, 1902), p. 66.

plurality and contingency of events is subsumed under a higher level of unity, in which it becomes possible to talk about progress in international politics as such.

As with Cox's article, Ashley relies on the idea that the relation between present and future could be reconfigured in opposition to the international stasis (and status quo) reproduced by realist analysis. However, Ashley makes no attempt to root his argument for critique in historical-sociological analysis, instead he grounds it in the idea of different temporalities of judgment, deriving from trans-historical truths about human engagement with the world. The argument is based on Habermas's three-fold classification of knowledge-constitutive interests, which Habermas identifies in his early work as the empirical-transcendental conditions of knowledge acquisition: technical; practical; and emancipatory. Technical interests are interests in control, associated by Habermas with the natural sciences. Practical interests are interests in understanding, associated by Habermas with the social sciences. Psychoanalysis and Marxism are examples of knowledges inspired by an interest in emancipation.[12] Ashley argues that political realism in the analysis of international politics was traditionally oriented by practical interests, but has become increasingly harnessed to a technical project of control. He also argues that the interest in control inherent in technical realism (neorealism) dominates and distorts the interpretive range of practical realism (classical realism).

In short, thanks to the constraint imposed by prior technical theory, the very empirical developments that might seem to invalidate the theory's essential impossibility theorem are recorded in practical realism as threatening developments that justify the immediate practical relevance of the theory built upon the theorem.[13]

For Ashley, the once flexible, reflective tradition of practical realism has become dogmatic, because of its links to the axiomatic claims of technical realism, which have reified a reductive version of a 'true tradition' of realism. The result is a vicious circle, in which the requirements of technical realism become built into advice about the practice of statesmanship, so that realism, in its technical form, becomes a self-fulfilling prophecy, most obviously in relation to policies of nuclear deterrence. In contrast to this, Ashley paints Herz's work as a dissident realist voice, in which practical realism is not wholly subsumed under a project of technical control, but is identified instead with a principle of 'reflective reason'. For reflective reason everything is open to question and understandings of interests, for instance in survival, are open to revision, in particular in a world in which nuclear war threatens the human species as such. Ashley identifies Herz's commitment to 'reflective reason' with Habermas's 'emancipatory interest':

Herz's, in short, is an interest in reason as such. It is an interest in exercising reflective reason to dissolve limits on the self-conscious development of life and thereby restore to men and women a true awareness of their place in history and their capacities to make the future.[14]

Ashley's sketch of what a reflective version of realism would look like has strong echoes of Cox's account of critical theory. Firstly, it involves broadening the range of

[12] Jürgen Habermas, *Knowledge and Human Interests* (Boston, MA: Beacon Press, 1971); Ashley, 'Political Realism', p. 208.
[13] Ashley, 'Political Realism', p. 225.
[14] Ibid., p. 227. It should be noted that Herz himself is not convinced by Ashley's reading, see John Herz, 'Comment', *International Studies Quarterly*, 25:2 (1981), pp. 237–41.

phenomena considered relevant to international politics beyond the 'true tradition' of statesmanship.[15] Secondly, it is oriented towards the possibility of progress, in a future in which universal values are potentially embedded. Cox reaches his conclusion via a reading of history, whereas Ashley reaches it by reference to an ethic of freedom, which is rooted in transhistorical human capacities. Nevertheless, not only are their conclusions substantively the same, so too is the way in which time substitutes for space as the key principle through which international politics can be theorised in critical terms. For Ashley, just as much as for Cox, international political time is understood through a story in which progress and singularity are mutually implicated. As with Cox, this doesn't mean that Ashley is predicting the way in which history *will* develop, but it does mean that critical theories of international politics are committed to treating it *as if* such a development were possible. Once more we are taken from the contingencies of the 'slaughterbench' of empirical events in clock time, to the calendar time of freedom, in which history is made rather than suffered.

Later developments in critical international relations theory have followed the trails blazed in Cox's and Ashley's storming of the Bastille of realism in 1981.[16] Some of these developments have followed Cox's historical/sociological path towards highlighting different futures for international politics. We can see this in critical research that has focused on identifying sources of explanation for developments in international politics other than a reified understanding of the Westphalian state system; and also in the massive amount of critical attention paid to the kind of phenomena that 'technical realism' banishes as fundamentally irrelevant to the international sphere, from ecological issues to gender. Others have followed Ashley's ethical path, in particular using the idea of freedom as a vantage point from which to criticise the theory and practice of international politics and indicate alternative ways forward. Much research, of course, has operated with a 'twin track' approach, making links between historical/sociological, ethical and praxeological levels.[17] Such arguments have often taken inspiration from Habermas's work, which latterly revived the philosophy of history through linking the historical shift to modernity to the recognition of moral principles underlying communicative practice, thus embedding the idea of emancipatory interest in historical 'learning' processes.[18] In all of this work, the issues of progress and singularity in international politics have been at the centre of critical theory, in its negative, deconstructive mode as a critique of neorealism and neoliberalism, and in its positive mode as the source of new

[15] Ashley, 'Political Realism', p. 232.

[16] For a recent summary of different pathways taken by critical theory, see Scott Burchill et al., *Theories of International Relations*, 3rd edn. (Basingstoke: Palgrave, 2005), chapters by Linklater, Devetak and True. See also my earlier discussions in *Kant, Critique and Politics* (London: Routledge, 1996) and *International Political Theory: Rethinking Ethics in a Global Era* (London: Sage, 1999); see also Richard Wyn Jones (ed.), *Critical Theory and World Politics* (Boulder, CO: Lynne Rienner, 2001).

[17] See Andrew Linklater, 'The Question of the Next Stage in International Relations Theory', *Millennium: Journal of International Studies*, 21:1 (1992), pp. 77–100; and *The Transformation of Political Community: Ethical Foundations of the Post-Westphalian Era* (Cambridge: Cambridge University Press, 1998). See also Seyla Benhabib, *The Claims of Culture: Equality and Diversity in a Global Era* (Princeton, NJ: Princeton University Press, 2002).

[18] Jürgen Habermas, *Communication and the Evolution of Society* (Boston, MA: Beacon Press, 1979); *The Theory of Communicative Action*, vols I and II (Boston, MA: Beacon Press, 1984 and 1987).

methodological approaches, empirical research and normative theories.[19] These issues have also, from early on, been at the heart of debates *between* different versions of critical international theory. The major fault-line between critical theories, since the late 1980s, has been drawn between theories that are explicitly committed to the legacy of the philosophy of history in the work of Kant, Hegel and Marx on the one hand, and theories that deny the validity of the accounts of progress and singularity inherent in that legacy on the other.[20] The critique of time within these debates raises sociological, ethical and political problems with the temporal assumptions of Cox and Ashley in 1981.

The critique of time

In Cox's and Ashley's original articles, revolutionary (counter-hegemonic) action and emancipatory knowledge-constitutive interests, respectively, are sources of progressive change immanent to history. Similar claims are involved in the work of international critical theorists such as Richard Falk, Andrew Linklater or Seyla Benhabib, and in a broad range of work that identifies economic globalisation, international human rights regimes or transnational social movements with the progressive potential of international politics.[21] Even if the future is not predictable, the mechanisms of progress are known. There is, however, some equivocation as to what kind of mechanisms they are. Critics of Cox et al. suggest that this kind of critical theory hovers between historicist and normative alternatives. When the historicist path is taken technological, political, economic and social features of the history of Western modernity invariably come to the fore. This privileging of the experience of Western modernity, it is argued, commits critical theory to assessing other historical trajectories only in the vocabularies of anachronism or reaction, thus confirming rather than challenging global hierarchies of power.

Analogous problems can be identified with the alternative possibility, in which progress in history is grounded in universal moral values rather than in material factors or social relations. In Cox's case, these universal values are embedded in counter-hegemonic action, in Ashley's case in fundamental human interests, but they are essentially the same values of freedom and reason. These normative standards enable us to discriminate between those political actions that are genuinely progressive and those that essentially preserve the status quo or are more profoundly

---

[19] In an earlier article, I suggested that critical theory works *negatively* when it is being used to undermine alternative theoretical approaches, most often in the critique of realism. The *positive* implementation of critical theory refers to the new kinds of conceptual and empirical work that it inspires. For example, this could include redefining power in Foucauldian or feminist terms, adopting discourse analysis research techniques, engaging in cross-disciplinary work, focusing on non-state actors and movements, et cetera (see Hutchings 'The Nature of Critique in Critical International Relations Theory', in Wyn Jones, *Critical Theory*, pp. 88–9.

[20] I do not intend to repeat here arguments that I have made elsewhere. For my account of the faultlines between different versions of critical theory, see Hutchings, *Kant: Critique*, pp. 146–66 and 'Nature of Critique'.

[21] Linklater, *Transformation*; Benhabib, *Claims of Culture*; Richard Falk, *On Humane Governance* (University Park: Pennsylvania University Press, 1995). See also: David Held, *Democracy and the Global Order: From the Modern State to Cosmopolitan Democracy* (Cambridge: Polity, 1995); Randall D. Germain and Michael Kenny (eds.), *The Idea of Global Civil Society* (London: Routledge, 2005).

reactionary. On this kind of account the values of freedom and reason are universal in two senses: first, in being immanent to history they either are, or ought to become, empirically universalised; second, such values are universal in the sense that they have universal validity regardless of the extent to which they are yet instantiated historically. Critics challenge both of these claims to universality, claiming that both, once again, privilege the particular history and culture of Western modernity.

Critics of Cox et al. complain that critical theory distorts the complexity and plurality of international politics through normatively directed, selective readings of history. They also complain that the grounds of this normatively selective reading are persistently fudged in a mysterious, dialectical relationship between the history of Western modernity and transcendent moral standards. Over and above this, however, they argue that this brand of critique fails to grasp the nature of political action. Cox and Ashley provide measures for the value of political action in the present in terms of a projected future, which is known but not yet achieved, and may never be achieved. In this form, critical theory provides guidance about 'what is to be done' (and therefore also, what should not be done), by both critical theorists and political actors, if a different future for international politics is to be envisaged or is to be possible. But, it is argued, this is to radically underestimate the role of context and contingency in international politics.

In 1981, Cox and Ashley claim to eschew the abstraction of purely rationalistic ethical and political theory (both reject the label of idealism). In spite of this, critics of their arguments counter that they (the arguments) turn out not to be historical enough. This is because, by reading clock time in terms of calendar time, Cox and Ashley have endowed international political time with a unified meaning (principles of freedom and/or reason) that does not match the plurality of political temporality across the realm of international politics. And, as the critics of critique point out, even if the values inherent in freedom and reason were genuinely universal, transcendental moral truths, if the context in which they are being applied is one in which those truths are not recognised, the political effects of their application will be different than in a context in which they are recognised. They are likely to be experienced as coercive and imperialistic rather then emancipatory and progressive, and they may end up meaning something very different than was intended.[22]

The generic 'critics' of critique referred to in the above discussion are most often grouped together under the labels of 'postmodernist' or 'post-structuralist' international relations theory.[23] Ironically, one of the foremost exemplars of this 'turn' in the time of critique has been Ashley himself, who in post-1981 deconstructions of realist analysis turned to the work of Derrida and Foucault, over that of Habermas, for critical inspiration.[24] These are critics who identify themselves as taking the idea

---

[22] See the discussion of transnational feminist politics below for examples of this kind of mismatch between intention and actuality in political practice.

[23] The meaning of these terms is notoriously hard to pin down. Within the context of this article, I will follow the practice of using the term 'postmodernism' to refer to theories that argue for a historical transformation from a 'modern' to a 'postmodern' era in international politics, and the term 'post-structuralism' for theoretical approaches inspired by, in particular, Foucault's and Derrida's critique of structuralist theory.

[24] Ashley, 'Untying the Sovereign State: A Double Reading of the Anarchy Problematique', *Millennium: Journal of International Studies*, 17:2 (1988), pp. 227–62. For other examples of the postmodernist/post-structuralist turn in critical international theory, see James Der Derian and Michael Shapiro (eds.), *International/Intertextual: Postmodern Readings of World Politics*

of critical theory forward, but in a way that does not privilege the calendar of Western modernity in accounts of the present and future of international politics. The claims of such critiques to be 'critical', however, continue to follow Cox's definition in that they are oriented towards the idea of alternative futures for international politics, in theory and practice. As with Cox's and Ashley's founding texts, therefore, postmodernist and post-structuralist critiques require some kind of account of international political time, one which avoids the imperialist moves argued to be inherent in Cox's and Ashley's reliance on Gramsci and Habermas respectively. In general, however, more attention has been paid to the deconstruction of 'modernist' meta-narratives of international political time in critical international theory of this kind than to the articulation and defence of alternatives. Nevertheless, we can discern two possible pathways for a rethinking of time inherent in post-modernist and post-structuralist ideas respectively, both of which have begun to be explored by critical international theorists. The first path takes the post-Marxist, materialist route of thinkers such as Virilio, and builds on the idea that technological developments and economic globalisation are marked by a global shift in temporality, which can provide us with a new perspective for thinking about the relation of present and future in international politics. The second path follows Derrida's idea of the 'untimely' in politics, as a perspective from which to rethink the relation of past, present and future within international politics.

The postmodernist route for rethinking international political time follows from the broader claims of postmodernist theory that during the course of the twentieth century there have been substantial shifts in global social and economic relations and structures, from 'modern' to 'postmodern' forms.[25] The argument is that this transition has involved, amongst other things, a dramatic compression of time and space in the world. Whereas in the past, time was mediated and measured by space (the time it took to deliver the post by horseback or railway), in the postmodern age the spatialisation of time has shrunk to nothing (the instantaneous transmission of an image from the other side of the world, the automation of reactions which might once have had to be humanly mediated, and so on). For postmodernist theorists of international politics and processes of globalisation, this means that at all levels of social life, from everyday communication with others to elite international (military, political and economic) decision-making, the sense of a trajectory from the past through the present to the future, has been replaced by an experience of immediacy, of speed, of the moment.[26]

(Lexington: Lexington Books, 1989); Ashley and R. B. J. Walker, 'Reading Dissidence/Writing the Discipline: Crisis and the Question of Sovereignty in International Studies', *International Studies Quarterly*, 34:3 (1990), pp. 367–416; James Der Derian, *Antidiplomacy: Spies, Terror, Speed and War* (Oxford: Blackwell, 1992); R. B. J. Walker, *Inside/Outside: International Relations as Political Theory* (Cambridge: Cambridge University Press, 1993); David Campbell, *National Deconstruction: Violence, Identity and Justice in Bosnia* (Minneapolis: University of Minneapolis Press, 1998). See also Richard Devetak, 'Postmodernism', in Burchill et al., *Theories*.

[25] See Jean-François Lyotard, *The Postmodern Condition: A Report on Knowledge* (Manchester: Manchester University Press, 1984).

[26] The person best known for taking the arguments of Virilio forward into the theorisation of international politics is James Der Derian, see *Antidiplomacy*; 'The (S)pace of International Relations: Simulation, Surveillance, and Speed', *International Studies Quarterly*, 34:3 (1990), pp. 295–310; *Virtuous War: Mapping the Military–Industrial–Media-Entertainment Network* (Boulder, CO: Westview Press, 2001). See also Der Derian (ed.), *The Virilio Reader* (Oxford: Blackwell, 1998). Other texts by Paul Virilio include: *Open Sky* (London: Verso, 1997); *Desert Screen: Was at the*

This argument takes issue with assumptions about international political time in the work of theorists such as Cox in relation to both clock and calendar time. The work of earlier versions of critical theory relies on the idea of underlying causes and forces giving an intelligible shape to international historical development, which can then be grasped and acted on by revolutionary subjects. In such accounts, clock time is subsumed under calendar time. But in a world of simultaneous cause/effect relations, in which human mediation is becoming minimised, neither clocks nor calendars are able to work in the same way. In critical theories influenced by the philosophy of history time operates as a principle through which international politics is unified, since it is through connecting with the potential for progress immanent in history that progress can be achieved by self-conscious action can be oriented towards emancipation. But in a globalised, postmodern world, time becomes flattened out, there is no room either for the working of deeper level causes and forces or for the kind of self-conscious planning with which counter-hegemonic action is associated. For thinkers such as Virilio, the postmodern world of international politics is one of thorough contingency. The time of this world is better understood through the concept of 'accident' than through the concept of progress. For this reason, there is a distinctly apocalyptic tone in much of the work inspired by the idea of accelerating international political time.[27]

A different kind of counter to the philosophy of history can be found in post-structuralist work that is influenced by Derrida's arguments about critique, politics and the 'untimely'.[28] Derrida elaborates on the implications of his understanding of time for political thought in his meditations on Marx, in which he counterposes an 'ontological' to a 'hauntological' Marx.[29] The ontological Marx is the philosopher of history, who is committed both to the idea of a future materially immanent in the present, and to the idea of the proletarian revolution as a genuine new beginning, the decisive break with an exploitative past. The hauntological Marx is the Marx who, in analysing the '18th Brumaire of Louis Bonaparte', or the commodity form under capitalism, recognises and elucidates the 'untimely' contamination of any given present by an assortment of pasts and futures. The first Marx is interested in exorcising ghosts and using his secular and materially grounded knowledge to control the production of the future. The spectre of this particular Marx, for Derrida, is the one that haunts the gulags and the terrible waste and destruction of state socialist regimes.[30] The second Marx, in contrast, understands the plurality and contingency of political events, and our incapacity to fully grasp or control them. The spectre of this second Marx, for Derrida, is one that haunts revolutionary action, the possibility of critique and aspirations towards justice.

Speed of Light (London: Continuum, 2002); *The Information Bomb* (London: Verso, 2000); *City of Panic* (Oxford: Berg, 2005).

[27] See, for example, Virilio, *Open Sky*, pp. 124–5. Connolly takes exception to this apocalyptic tone, arguing that the pace of globalisation may also open positive opportunities for political change, see William Connolly, 'Speed, Concentric Cultures and Cosmopolitanism', *Political Theory*, 28:5 (2000), pp. 596–618, and also discussion of Connolly on pluralism and time below.

[28] See, for example, Campbell, *National Deconstruction* and 'Time is Broken: The Return of the Past in the Response to September 11', *Theory and Event*, 5:4 (2002); see also Jenny Edkins, 'Forget Trauma? Responses to September 11', *International Relations*, 16:2 (2002), pp. 243–56.

[29] Derrida, *Specters*, pp. 213–14.

[30] Ibid., pp. 130–1.

For critical theories looking for a way of thinking the relation between present and future that is uncontaminated by the assumptions of philosophy of history, Derrida's 'hauntological' Marx provides a possible model for thinking about critique and international political time. On this account it is a mistake to assume that the future can be produced according to a particular pattern or end. The future is always contingent, unpredictable and uncontrollable. We must therefore abandon the idea of the revolutionary calendar, with its promise of progress. Nevertheless, this does not mean that the possibility of critical theory, with its commitment to political progress, is undermined. On Derrida's account the structure of all experience is 'messianic', in the sense that any statement or action in the present is oriented towards the promise of an indeterminate future as a condition for the redemption of its meaning.[31] The task of the critical theorist is to keep this promise open by always acknowledging that even actions inspired by aspirations towards justice will inevitably fail to do justice to the indeterminacy of the future. This acknowledgement of necessary failure operates in Derrida's argument as a 'quasi-transcendental' condition of critique. And it commits the critic, not to any particular political programme or substantive normative value, but to an open and agonistic ethic.

In the case of postmodernist theories, the material (via technology) transcendence of the relevance of clock time to international social and political relations is key to the undermining of the revolutionary calendar. In the case of post-structuralist theories, that calendar is deconstructed through techniques such as Derrida's reading of the two Marx's, in which claims to certainty about past and future are shown to depend on grounds that subvert those claims. Both kinds of critical theory stress the openness and indeterminacy of the future, though this is interpreted more or less bleakly in different cases. They also stress contingency and plurality in their accounts, setting themselves against the idea of revolutionary action as being plugged into the potentially progressive and universalising forces of history. In this respect, postmodernist and post-structuralist arguments appear to have transcended the sociological, ethical and political problems identified with the Cox and Ashley of 1981. However, on reflection there are reasons why this transcendence may not be as radical and complete as it appears. It can be argued that although these arguments do much to undermine the role of the idea of *progress* in accounts of international political time, they are less successful in undermining the notion that a *singular* temporal perspective has a privileged status within international politics.

Postmodernist theories eschew the notion that one can acquire and act on insights into the progressive mechanisms that govern history, but nevertheless time continues to operate in such theories as a unifying principle through which the relation of past and present to future is understood. In such theories one account of time takes on a privileged position for both analysis and normative judgment. The result of this is the overturning of readings of history that rely on determinate notions of progress. At best, international political time is at the mercy of chance, at worst it is presented as verging on apocalypse. At the same time, however, those developments in international politics that can most easily be captured in terms of accelerated temporality come to stand for international political time in general. And this means that the

---

[31] Ibid., pp. 210–11. See also, Derrida 'Force of Law: The "Mystical Foundation of Authority"', in Drucilla Cornell et al. (eds.), *Deconstruction and the Possibility of Justice* (New York: Routledge, 1992).

significance, or even possibility, of alternative temporalities is marginalised. The accelerated time privileged in postmodernist accounts confirms rather than undermines the special significance of the trajectory inherent in Western capitalist modernity.

If postmodernist theories seem in some ways to fall into an historical/sociological trap similar to more obviously historicist versions of critical theory, then post-structuralist theories can be argued to return us to the dilemmas inherent in normatively-driven versions. Just as Ashley used Habermas's notion of knowledge-constitutive interests to open up the possibility of international critical theory, so Derrida relies on the idea of the 'quasi-transcendental' conditions of meaning and experience. These conditions are not specifiable in the form of substantive moral principles or prescriptions and they do not provide a theory of progress. But to the extent that Derrida is able to specify them, these conditions are the inexhaustibility of the possibilities of deconstructive critique, which follow from the necessary inadequacy of any attempt to do justice, to actually do justice. In *Specters of Marx*, this is best expressed in the (doomed) aspiration to capture the spirit, without the spectres, of revolution. In *Philosophy in a Time of Terror*, this is best expressed as commitment to an (unachievable) idea of Europe.[32] In either case it is clear that Derrida's ethical orientation is specific to a particular ethical and political tradition, which is given a universal pertinence, even though it is not identified with a projected universal end of history.

I do not mean to suggest that postmodernist and post-structuralist theories are the same as versions of critical international theory more influenced by the philosophy of history. They are clearly different in their interpretation of the possibility of progress in history. And they bring new and distinctive theoretical and methodological vocabularies to, as well as extending the range of relevant objects of analysis and inquiry of, critical international theory. When it comes to the account of international political time, however, the ways in which time operates as a unifying principle, either materially or in the theorist's ethical orientation, continue to reflect the historicist and normative moves characteristic of Cox's and Ashley's founding critical texts. In spite of the fact that the watchwords of postmodernist and post-structuralist critical approaches are terms such as 'plurality' and 'difference', the legacy of the revolutionary calendar is not completely shaken off, and the account of international politics remains, in Spivak's memorable phrase, 'the willed (auto) biography of the West'.[33]

Thinking the future of critique

The most obvious evidence of the dominance of a singular reading of international temporality within critical international theory is the belated nature of the latter's engagement with post-colonial thinking. It is only in the last decade that critical international relations theory has begun to reckon with the idea of 'provincializing

---

[32] Giovanna Borradori, 'A Dialogue with Jacques Derrida', in Borradori, *Philosophy in a Time of Terror* (Chicago, IL: Chicago University Press, 2003), p. 116.
[33] Gayatri Chakravorty Spivak, *A Critique of Postcolonial Reason: Toward a History of the Vanishing Present* (Cambridge, MA: Harvard University Press, 1999), p. 208.

Europe' either theoretically or empirically.[34] And even now the concept of 'post-colonialism' gets only marginal acknowledgement within standard accounts of what critical international relations theory is all about.[35] And yet it is within this body of thought that the possibility of theorising international political time critically, without privileging the time of Western modernity has received most sustained attention.

> ... I want to raise the question of how we might find a form of social thought that embraces analytical reason in pursuit of social justice but does not allow it to erase the question of heterotemporality from the history of the modern subject.[36]

Given the commitment of all critical theories to debunking global hierarchies and challenging hegemonic power, in theory as well as practice, the neglect of post-colonial theory is quite difficult to explain. One possible explanation is that it is assumed that post-colonial theories are a subset of either Gramscian/Habermasian or postmodernist/post-structuralist theories.[37] But this still doesn't explain why critical international theory has engaged so little with Fanon, Said and Spivak in comparison to its engagement with, for instance, Virilio or Agamben. Alternatively, it could be argued that the reasons for the neglect of post-colonial thinking go deep into the collective unconscious of critical international theorists. Whatever our commitment to critique and pluralism, in the vast majority of cases, and regardless of particular cultural background, our identity is strongly bound up with the hegemony of the West in scholarly as well as in institutional and political terms. But whether this is true or not, what is true is that within the academy there is little incentive to take international temporal plurality seriously, and that even if we wanted to do so, we lack a philosophical vocabulary adequate to the challenge.

> 'Europe' cannot after all be provincialized within the institutional site of the university whose knowledge protocols will always take us back to the terrain where all contours follow that of my hyperreal Europe.[38]

---

[34] The phrase 'provincializing Europe' is taken from Dipesh Chakrabarty, *Provincializing Europe: Postcolonial Thought and Historical Difference* (Princeton, NJ: Princeton University Press, 2000). For examples of work bringing together post-colonial critique with IR theory, see Nayeem Inayatullah and David Blaney, *International Relations and the Problem of Difference* (New York and London: Routledge, 2004); Geeta Chowdhry and Sheila Nair (eds.), *Power, Postcolonialism and International Relations: Reading Race, Gender and Class* (London and New York: Routledge, 2004). Some recent work on the history of international thought has also taken an interesting post-colonial direction, for example, Edward Keene, *Beyond the Anarchical Society: Grotius, Colonialism and Order in World Politics* (Cambridge: Cambridge University Press, 2002).

[35] For example, there is only one reference to post-colonialism, as part of a list of 'identity politics'-related developments in post-Marxist international relations, in Burchill et al., *Theories*. It also seems symbolic of post-colonialism's position in international relations theory that Inayatullah's and Blaney's *International Relations and the Problem of Difference* is catalogued in the library of my institution with anthropology rather than with international relations texts. The post-colonial theory I am referring to here, in addition to the texts by Spivak and Chakrabarty already cited, includes: Frantz Fanon, *The Wretched of the Earth* (London: Penguin Books, 2001); *Black Skin, White Masks* (London: Pluto Press: 1986); Edward Said, *Orientalism: Western Conceptions of the Orient* (Harmondsworth: Penguin Books, 1995); *Culture and Imperialism* (London: Vintage, 1993). For a background text on post-colonial thought, see Robert J. C. Young, *White Mythologies: Writing History and the West* (London and New York: Routledge, 2004).

[36] Chakrabarty, *Provincializing Europe*, p. 239.

[37] It is the case that postcolonial theory is influenced by both post-Marxist and post-Nietzschean ideas, but it is a mistake to see it as derived solely from these sources, See Chakrabarty, *Provincializing Europe*, p. 6.

[38] Chakrabarty, *Provincializing Europe*, p. 45.

There is one area of critical international theory in which the incentive to provincialise Europe has been felt more powerfully than in other areas. For feminists, the relation between critical theory and hegemonic power has been persistently encountered as a problem for the international politics of feminism. For this reason, feminist international theorists have had a long-standing interest in the critique of this relation. Historically, the feminist movement is an archetypal example of a transnational movement with a self-consciously counter-hegemonic, progressive mission. Early feminists and their more recent heirs have identified themselves as carrying forward the task of improving the political conditions and possibilities of women across boundaries of state and nation. In recent years, the most important discourse for this kind of transnational activism has been that of women's human rights.[39] And this language has underpinned, and provided normative force for campaigns around civil, political and economic issues, from female genital mutilation, to women's reproductive rights, to development. For feminist critical theorists of international politics such as Benhabib, this kind of development signals a process of moral learning, in which through a mixture of communicative and coercive encounters, the world as a whole may be improved. Speaking of the Habermasian distinctions between morality, ethics and values, she says:

Increasingly, though, the globalised world we are inhabiting compels cultural traditions that may not have generated these differentiations in the course of their own development to internalise them or to learn to coexist in a political and legal world with other cultures that operate with some form of these differentiations. Many traditional cultures, for example, still consider women's and children's rights as an aspect of their life-world, of the way things are done in that particular culture. However, the international discourse on women's rights, the activism of international development and aid organizations, migration and television programmes are transforming these assumptions.[40]

Benhabib's argument follows in the tradition of Cox and Ashley in 1981 in its mix of historicist and normative claims. However, many feminists involved in transnational activism, in particular 'third world' and post-colonial feminists, have taken issue with the legacy of the philosophy of history within the feminist movement. In terms of practice, it has been pointed out that this kind of discourse has justified 'maternalist' intervention by Western women in the lives of non-Western women of a kind that echoes the history and ideology of Western imperialism, colonialism and neo-colonialism.[41] Moreover, post-colonial feminists argue that this kind of ethical universalism treats all women as in some sense modelled on a Western 'norm' and is therefore insensitive to the significance of specific cultural and social contexts and to differences in the issues that are most politically significant for different women.[42]

---

[39] G. Ashworth, 'The Silencing of Women', in T. Dunne and N. Wheeler (eds.), *Human Rights in Global Politics* (Cambridge: Cambridge University Press, 1999); C. Bunch et al., 'International Networking for Women's Human Rights', in M. Edwards and J. Gaventa (eds.), *Global Citizen Action* (London: Earthscan, 2001).

[40] Benhabib, *Claims of Culture*, p. 40.

[41] C. T. Mohanty, A. Russo and L. Torres (eds.), *Third World Women and the Politics of Feminism* (Bloomington & Indianapolis, IN: Indiana University Press, 1991); C. T. Mohanty, *Feminism without Borders: Decolonising Theory, Practicing Solidarity* (Durham, NC and London: Duke University Press, 2003), pp. 204–31.

[42] So that, for instance, if we look at the debates that have dominated feminist international conferences, there is a pattern in which issues such as reproductive rights, poverty or pornography are given different priorities for different reasons by different categories of women. See A. Basu (ed.), *The Challenge of Local Feminisms: Women's Movements in Global Perspective* (Boulder, CO:

But if one is neither to assume that all women occupy the same time, nor to read temporal plurality in normatively hierarchical terms, then what is the alternative for feminism as a transnational political movement? In practice, one response has been to treat women's human rights, not as being settled in advance according to universal standards, but rather as a kind of 'placeholder', the meaning of which must be negotiated. In order for this negotiation to take place, a first step must be enabling empowerment and voice for those women who are multiplied silenced by the predominant politics of both global civil society and interstate social, political and economic processes. This kind of development in transnational feminist politics reflects Derrida's conception of the ethic of critique as a persistent openness towards, and refusal to subsume, the 'other' in the form of the future. But it also returns us to the question of how to theorise international political time in such a way as to do justice to an ethic of pluralism. The requirement to listen and empower is meaningless unless we have some sense of how it is possible.

Chakrabarty and Connolly both suggest that the way to conceptualise the plurality of political time is to start by thinking of time as double. In Chakrabarty's case, within the context of trying to find appropriate ways of theorising political modernity in South Asia, this means making a distinction between 'History 1' and 'History 2'. The former refers to the universalising narrative of capitalist imperialism, whereas the latter refers to the temporalities inherent in the ways of being in the world with which capitalist imperialism interacts. In Chakrabarty's view, these two modes of temporality cut across and interrupt one another and imply both that there is an inherent undecidability in the nature of historical development, and that plurality (or, 'heterotemporality') is an irreducible feature of history.

Globalization does not mean that History 1, the universal and necessary logic of capital so essential to Marx's critique, has been realized. What interrupts and defers capital's self-realization are the various History 2s that always modify History 1 and thus act as our grounds for claiming historical difference.[43]

At a more general level than Chakrabarty, Connolly argues that critical political theories need to think about the relation of present to future in terms of both a political temporality of 'being' and a political temporality of 'becoming'.[44] The political temporality of being refers to relatively stable contexts for political judgement and action, on the basis of which one extrapolates the meaning of progress in accordance with given, sedimented criteria (such as those inherent in Western modernity). In contrast, the political temporality of becoming refers to shifting and unfamiliar contexts for political judgment and action, where criteria for progress or regress must be negotiated without the certainties embedded in the politics of being. From Connolly's point of view, critical theories have tended to remain within the temporal register of the politics of being, and have therefore been unable to do justice to either plurality or unpredictability in their projects of political transformation. Rather, they have run the risk of imposing a particular political vision in imperialistic

Westview Press, 1995); A. Snyder, *Setting the Agenda for Global Peace: Conflict and Consensus Building* (Aldershot: Ashgate, 2003).

[43] Chakrabarty, *Provincializing Europe*, p. 71. Chakrabarty links History 1 with Marx's theory of history and History 2 with Heidegger's account of human temporality.

[44] William Connolly, *Neuropolitics: Thinking, Culture, Speed* (Minneapolis, MN: University of Minnesota Press, 2002); *Pluralism* (Durham, NC and London: Duke University Press, 2005), pp. 97–130.

fashion, and neglecting resources for change that do not accord with pre-existing criteria of progress.

The touch of paradox is that on my reading, a double-entry orientation to the experience of time must be widely adopted to make it possible to say that ethical progress is being made. To embrace *that* duplicity is to move a distance from, say, Augustine and Kant on the relation between faith, morality and time. What you take from them is the idea that you do project forward from each consolidated interpretation of responsibility to the future. What you subtract from them is the obligation to act *as if* you already know the shape that those dense principles, rights, obligations, and legitimate identities must assume in the future.[45]

Connolly's recommendation that we assume a '*double entry orientation to the experience of political time*'[46] is not purely ethical in nature. It is grounded in an account of the meaning of time, which draws on philosophies of time in the work of thinkers such as Nietzsche, James, Bergson and Deleuze. It is this aspect of his argument that offers critical international theory a way of theorising temporal plurality that does not collapse either into a normative hierarchy of comparison (modern, postmodern, premodern) or into a formal ethical commitment to the inexhaustibility of critique. Of the thinkers he engages with, I want to suggest that Deleuze's philosophy of time is particularly promising for those theorists wanting to de-centre singular accounts of international political time.[47]

Deleuze's account of time is presented in the context of his interpretation of Stoic thought in *The Logic of Sense*. The central argument concerning time in this text is that it is necessary to think in terms of two temporal orders, reflected in Connolly's distinction between the times of being and becoming: *Chronos* and *Aion*.[48] *Chronos* is the temporality internal to particular kinds of entity. On Deleuze's account of Stoic argument, all material entities, from planets to plants to humans, are understood as partial systems that impinge and overlap one another, but are nevertheless distinct. Within the *chronos* of these partial systems, past and future are defined in relation to the present, and each present is peculiar to the system in question. This temporal organisation or lifespan holds the key to the potential of that particular system to flourish or decay. Within the Stoic world-view, there is both 'confidence and mistrust' in *chronos*.[49] On the one hand, it is the ground of measure and conservation, on the other hand there are deep-lying forces within the cosmos whose *chronos* clashes with, and has the potential to destroy, the times internal to the harmonious interplay of

---

[45] Connolly, *Pluralism*, pp. 129–30.

[46] Ibid., p. 129.

[47] Deleuze's work has been drawn on by certain critical international theorists, sometimes in tandem with arguments of thinkers such as Virilio, as a way of capturing the complex, potentially transgressive flows of globalised politics. Particularly significant for this work is Deleuze's and Guattari's emphasis on 'rhizomatic' as opposed to 'arborescent' models for understanding capitalism. 'Rhizomatic' literally means 'root-like', and refers to the ways in which roots spread horizontally and appear unpredictably, rather than developing from a central source, as is the case with 'arborescent' or tree-like growth, see Karen Houle 'Micropolitics', in Charles Stivale (ed.), *Gilles Deleuze: Key Concepts* (Chesham: Acumen, 2005). For a useful discussion of Deleuze and political time, see Paul Patton, 'The World Seen From Within: Deleuze and the Philosophy of Events', *Theory and Event*, 1:1 (1997). The texts on which I am drawing in the brief account that follows are: Gilles Deleuze, *The Logic of Sense* (London: Athlone, 1990); Gilles Deleuze and Félix Guattari, *Anti-Oedipus: Capitalism and Schizophrenia* (New York: Viking Press, 1977); and *A Thousand Plateaus: Capitalism and Schizophrenia* (London: Athlone, 1988).

[48] Deleuze, *Logic of Sense*, p. 5.

[49] Ibid., p. 162.

different systems of being.[50] However, chronological times, whether preservative or destructive, are sharply distinguished from an alternative form of time:

Aion stretches out in a straight line, limitless in either direction. Always already passed and eternally yet to come, Aion is the eternal truth of time: *pure empty form of time*, which has freed itself of its present corporeal content and has thereby unwound its own circle, stretching itself out in a straight line.[51]

Time in the sense of *Aion* is the pure movement of 'becoming' or 'event' in which time perpetually divides itself into past and future, always eluding any form of the present.[52] Time as becoming is opposed to time as *chronos*, since it cuts across the measures internal to specific, organised systems.[53] Where there is no beginning or end then there is also no orientation relative to the present, no measure, no organisation, only the ongoing differential production of past and future. Time as *Aion* is beyond the material forces and normative standards peculiar to particular systems, but it operates as a 'quasi-cause' in the sense that it disrupts all subsistence and perpetually re-orients the relation and conjunction of different systems with each other. Deleuze uses the metaphors of 'depth'/'point' and 'surface'/'line' to capture the distinction between these two modes of time.[54] Worlds which are chronologically organised, which are rule-bound or in which causes produce effects (*chronos*), incorporate successive presents that can be plotted and related like points on a graph. Such worlds are, metaphorically speaking, deep, in that any present will be explicable in terms of a hinterland of previous presents and immanent futures. In contrast, *Aion* operates at a purely 'surface' level, counteracting the vertical pressures inherent in chronological systems with its horizontal sweep, and bifurcating the determinate lines plotted between the successive presents of chronological systems with its own never-ending, indeterminate line.

In Deleuze's and Guattari's critique of psychoanalysis and capitalism, *Anti-Oedipus: Capitalism and Schizophrenia*, the Stoic distinction between *chronos* and *aion* is echoed in the distinctive temporalities of 'machine' on the one hand and 'desire' on the other. Machines are partial systems that regulate the productive flow of desire. Any aspect of organic or social reality, from orchids to brains, and from political institutions to military invasions, can be analysed in terms of a 'machine', insofar as it can be understood as an organised, partial system, and all such systems, either actually or potentially, may impinge upon and overlap with one another.[55] Desire is the 'flow' of becoming, not a causal driver of effects as such (which would require a common chronology) but, as sheer contingency, the condition of possibility for the production of novelty in the interactions between different machines.[56]

Deleuze argues that the mistake of the philosophy of history is to assume that the present is fully present in relation to both being (*chronos*/machine) and becoming (*aion*/desire). This is a mistake because it misrepresents both the diverse presents inherent in the chronological temporalities of plural machines, and because it misrepresents the unpredictability of desire. In relation to the time of being in

[50] Ibid., p. 165.
[51] Ibid., p. 165.
[52] Ibid., p. 5.
[53] Ibid., p. 77.
[54] Ibid., p. 165.
[55] Deleuze and Guattari, *Anti-Oedipus*, p. 340.
[56] Ibid., p. 350.

international politics, no present is fully present because international politics is made up of a plurality of diverse partial systems, with their own immanent temporality. There is no synthetic unifying principle that works either immanently within, or transcendentally without, to create a larger pattern through which to make sense of these multiple presents. The temporality of becoming refers not to some external force that governs the time of being but to the contingencies through which different temporal orders come to cut across, impinge on and mutual transform each other. For Deleuze there is no 'beyond' of time, but there is a temporal order of becoming that is always at cross-purposes with the temporality inherent in causally organised or rule-based system.

> The actualisation of a revolutionary potentiality is explained less by the preconscious state of causality in which it is nonetheless included, than by the efficacy of a libidinal break at a precise moment, a schiz whose sole cause is desire – which is to say the rupture with causality that forces a rewriting of history on a level with the real, and produces this strange polyvocal moment when everything is possible.[57]

It's a long way from Deleuze's speculations about the nature of time to the difficulties encountered by feminist theorists in detaching the politics of critique from hegemonic power in international politics. The reason that I find his argument promising is that it is fundamentally opposed to identifying temporal difference with a normative hierarchy, in which Western modernity carries the burden and privilege of judgment. Unlike certain modes of cultural relativism, however, Deleuze's approach still permits a lateral kind of theorising in which multiple, parallel and interacting presents may be understood in relation to one another, in this sense it is systemic as well as pluralist. It seems to me that it is this kind of thinking that both Connolly and Chakrabarty are pointing towards in their doublings of our orientation to political time. And it is also this kind of thinking that speaks to the requirement of feminist international theory to avoid two temptations that have bedevilled critical international theory since 1981. The first of these temptations is for engagement between different political presents to become subsumed under a singular master narrative of history. The second temptation is for this engagement to be articulated only in terms of a formal ethical commitment to a mysterious 'difference' that conditions time, but cannot be temporally (in its dual sense of 'in time' and 'this worldly') understood.

Deleuze's approach to time makes temporal plurality a characteristic of being and experience, rather than a mysterious 'otherness'. Individual human beings and social practices and institutions participate in a variety of chronologies, and the mutual incompatibility of the 'presents' inherent in, for example my middle age and the globalisation of capitalism, does not make them either wholly unconnected or mutually unintelligible. When time is understood in this way, it becomes perfectly possible for the critical theorist to engage with diverse temporalities without reference to a higher level principle of historical organisation. In this sense, it takes us back to Cox's original call for a critical theory sensitive to the immanent structures and forces of international politics, but this time in the light of the call of feminist and post-colonial critics to attend fully to the voices silenced by the hegemony of Western power.

---

[57] Ibid., p. 378.

Conclusion

In Chakrabarty's terms, Cox's and Ashley's 1981 articles depended on History 1 and neglected History 2; in Connolly's terms, they remained too bound up in the political temporality of being as opposed to the temporality of becoming. In other words, Cox and Ashley were only able to stop the clocks of mainstream international theory by importing into the clock time of international politics a certain, progressive and singular, calendar. Postmodernist and post-structuralist developments in critical international theory have been particularly concerned with undermining the narrative of progress in this calendar. However, it is in postcolonial and feminist work that the revolutionary calendar has been put most fundamentally into question. All critical theories seek to challenge hierarchies of power within international politics, and in doing this they are obliged to reckon with theorising the relation between present(s) and future(s). But what postcolonial and feminist critics tell us is that to ask the question of the future of international politics in the temporal register of History 1 or the political temporality of being alone, is to make unwarranted and dangerous assumptions about both the unified nature of the future and our capacity to know it. These assumptions are unwarranted because they rest on partial and particular accounts of the temporal patternings of clock time, and because they rest on a misunderstanding of the complexity and unpredictability of the ways in which these patternings interact and mutually transform each other. These assumptions are dangerous because they distract attention from political plurality, and thereby risk repeating the hubris of Western political imaginaries. To think in the double temporal register ensures that critical international theorists approach questions about the future and the meaning of progress with a certain humility. More positively, such double thinking releases our critical political imagination by multiplying the possibilities for stopping clocks and inaugurating new calendars.

Is critical theory always for the white West and for Western imperialism? Beyond Westphilian towards a post-racist critical IR

JOHN M. HOBSON*

Abstract. In appraising critical IR theory after twenty-five years, this article begins by asking whether critical theory implicitly reinforces the 'superiority' of Western civilisation and naturalises Western imperialism. In revealing the Eurocentrism of much of critical IR theory the article proceeds to reconstruct it by steering it in fresh non-Eurocentric directions. This is not to say that extant critical theory is moribund since it undoubtedly has much to offer. But it is to say that until the problem of Eurocentrism is exorcised from its body theoretique, critical theory inadvertently lies in danger of joining the ranks of problem-solving theories. The first two sections deconstruct the leading schools of critical IR theory – Gramscianism, postmodernism and feminism – to reveal their frequent lapsing into Eurocentrism, while the final section seeks to decolonise 'Westphilian' critical IR by reconstructing a 'post-racist IR'. And this in turn leads on to the conclusion, which sketches out a post-racist emancipatory political project that can help begin the urgent task of effecting global reconciliation between East and West.

Introduction

The short answer to the question posed above in the main title is 'by no means always, but surprisingly far more often than might be expected'. Of course, it might be thought that it would be a standard critical IR theory refrain to debunk those generations of 'scientific' theories which proclaim the positivist fact/value distinction as a means to hide their underlying meta-narrative that ultimately glorifies Western civilisation. But the acute irony is that Gramscian IR and other versions of critical theory often, albeit inadvertently, reproduce the very Eurocentrism that so-called objective mainstream IR scholars all too frequently slip into.

Still, critical IR theory (CIRT) has achieved a great deal since Robert Cox's seminal article was published in 1981,[1] not least in breathing fresh life into a discipline that was in danger of becoming stranded in a 'neo–neo' *cul-de-sac*, with the more recent emergence of constructivism so far offering disappointingly few prospects for escape. Cox's mantra, that 'theory is always *for* someone and *for* some purpose',[2]

---

* Though in no way implicating them, I want to sincerely thank Adam Morton, Craig Murphy, and Nicola Phillips for their extremely helpful and extensive suggestions.
[1] Robert W. Cox, 'Social Forces, States and World Orders: Beyond International Relations Theory', in R. O. Keohane (ed.), *Neorealism and Its Critics* (New York: Columbia University Press, 1986 [1981]), pp. 204–54.
[2] Cox, 'Social Forces', p. 207.

helped spur on the rise of feminism, postmodernism, post-structuralism, and historical sociology. And this idiom was, of course, harnessed to the proposition that theory is always the product of the theorist's position in time and place such that the fact/value distinction becomes impossible to maintain. This in turn flows directly into the distinction between *problem-solving theory* and *critical theory.* CIRT is differentiated from problem-solving theory on a number of grounds. Specifically, it is (allegedly) self-reflexive in that it is aware of its own values and biases, and it (supposedly) rejects problem-solving theory's ahistoricism that eternalises and naturalises the present, in favour of a historicism, which reveals the social forces that issue change in world-historical time. This in turn (supposedly) enables the identification of emergent emancipatory processes that are working to create a new world order.

But this is as good as any place to ask whether CIRT has always remained true to 'its' critical foundations,[3] and whether it has been as self-reflexive as it claims. Cox's framework issues from his claim that: 'There is . . . no such thing as theory in itself, divorced from a standpoint in time and space. When any theory so represents itself, it is the more important to examine it as ideology, and to lay bare its concealed perspective';[4] a point that immediately follows on from the previously stated mantra that 'theory is always *for* someone and *for* some purpose'. It is in this context that I return the gaze to interrogate CIRT by asking whether it is always *for* the White West and *for* Western imperialism? I respond to this rhetorical question by revealing the concealed Eurocentric perspective that underpins so much of CIRT. However this begs the obvious response: that whatever else CIRT is, it has surely always been critical of the West and Western imperialism. And indeed it has. But in the first section I reveal how this very response is embedded in Eurocentrism before fleshing out the hallmarks of Orientalism/Eurocentrism. In the second section I reveal the Eurocentric foundations of much of Gramscianism before turning in the third to critically reflect on two of the leading variants of CIRT–Western feminism and postmodernism. The fourth section simultaneously critiques Eurocentrism and sketches out my own 'post-racist IR', while the conclusion considers how this might be used to issue an emancipatory politics that can begin the long march to global reconciliation.

What is Eurocentrism?

To get to grips with answering the question 'how can critical IR theory be seen as *for* the White West and *for* Western imperialism?' it is noteworthy that much confusion surrounds the definition of Eurocentrism. Some assume that it refers to analyses that focus only on the West. But it is perfectly possible to write a Eurocentric book that focuses only on the East, since what matters here is the ideological lens through which the analysis is framed. Others assume that Eurocentrism is an explicit celebration of all things Western.[5] But one can be Eurocentric at the same time as

---

[3] For we should be aware that CIRT is not a monolith but is a highly complex and heterogeneous body of work; see especially Chris Brown, 'Turtles All the Way Down: Anti-Foundationalism, Critical Theory and International Relations', *Millennium*, 23:2 (1994), pp. 213–36.

[4] Cox, 'Social Forces', p. 207.

[5] As in the works of: Francis Fukuyama, *The End of History and the Last Man* (London: Hamish Hamilton, 1992); Samuel P. Huntington, *The Clash of Civilizations and the Remaking of World*

being critical of the West. To resolve this confusion I differentiate 'conscious' from 'subliminal' Eurocentrism. 'Conscious Eurocentrism', as referenced above, is found in those writers who explicitly celebrate all things Western while consciously or explicitly denigrating all things Eastern. 'Subliminal Eurocentrism' is much more subtle, though no less Orientalist. It does not celebrate the West but is highly critical of it. But what makes it Eurocentric is the assumption that the West lies at the centre of all things in the world and that the West self-generates through its own endogenous 'logic of immanence', before projecting its global will-to-power outwards through a one-way diffusionism so as to remake the world in its own image. I call this pervading white mythology of IR the *Westphilian narrative* (twinned with its accompanying *Eastphobian narrative*). Indeed, the main problem with IR is not simply that it is constrained within a '*Westphalian* straitjacket',[6] but more that it is contained within a '*Westphilian* straitjacket' that at once renders racist hierarchy and racism invisible in the world while simultaneously issuing racist Eurocentric explanatory models of the world.

Most significantly, the uncomfortable implication of this is that the extent to which many critical IR theorists reiterate the Westphilian narrative means that their analyses are *for* the White West and *for* Western imperialism in various senses. First is the assumption that self-generating Western agency and power in the world is 'the only game in town' which, when coupled with the dismissal of Eastern agency, unwittingly naturalises Western civilisation and Western imperialism. Second, it deserves emphasising that the *representational leitmotif* of British imperialism was the very notion of White Western supremacy and Black Eastern inferiority, which served to demoralise the colonised Other in order to portray resistance as futile. Of course, Gramscian IR prides itself on its ability to locate counter-hegemonic resistance. But by elevating world politics/economics into a panopticonesque Western fetish the prospects for Eastern resistance are unwittingly demoted. Moreover, when one scans Cox's major writings, there is surprisingly little discussion of counter-movements and, where there is, the prospect for counter-hegemony is portrayed as very poor given the general representation of the (Western) working class as overwhelmed by the power of global capital.[7] And though there are some notable exceptions,[8] this problem is repeated across most of Gramscian IR.[9] It is for these reasons, then, that much of Gramscian and other forms of CIRT turn out to be (unwittingly) *for* the White West and *for* Western imperialism.

But to understand this claim it is worth briefly outlining the essence of Eurocentrism. As is well-known, Eurocentrism or Orientalism is a discourse that was invented in the eighteenth and nineteenth centuries by European thinkers as they

---

Order (London: Touchstone, 1996); David S. Landes, *The Wealth and Poverty of Nations* (London: Little, Brown, 1998).

[6] Barry Buzan and Richard Little, 'Why International Relations has Failed as an Intellectual Project and What to Do about it', *Millennium*, 30:1 (2001), pp. 19–39.

[7] Robert W. Cox, *Approaches to World Order* (Cambridge: Cambridge University Press, 1996), esp. pp. 191–207, 364–6, 471–90; R. W. Cox, *Production, Power and World Order* (New York: Columbia University Press, 1987), esp. pp. 368–91.

[8] For example, Mark Rupert, *Ideologies of Globalization* (New York: Routledge, 2000); Adam David Morton, ' "La Resurrección del Maíz": Globalisation, Resistance and the Zapatistas', *Millennium*, 31:1 (2002), pp. 27–54.

[9] For example, Stephen Gill, *American Hegemony and the Trilateral Commission* (Cambridge: Cambridge University Press, 1990), esp. pp. 50–2.

went about constructing European identity.[10] Prior to, and even during much of, the eighteenth century, Europeans often recognised that East and West were interlinked. But the emergence of Eurocentrism and the concomitant 'production of alterity' led to the construction of an imaginary *line of civilisational apartheid* that fundamentally separated or split East from West. Having split these mutual civilisations into 'distinct entities', Eurocentric thinkers then elevated the Western Self and demoted the Eastern Other. The West was imbued with exclusively progressive characteristics – including rationality and liberalism – which ensured that the West would not only make political and economic modernity single-handedly but would also be the torch-bearer of political/economic development in the world. By contrast, the Eastern Other was imbued with all manner of regressive and antithetical properties – including Oriental despotism and irrationality – which ensured that slavery and stagnation would be its lot. This culminated in Max Weber's famous distinction between the Western 'ethic of world mastery' and the fatalistic Eastern 'ethic of passive conformity' to the world. Thus Western man was elevated to the permanent 'proactive subject' of global politics/economics – past, present and future – standing at the centre of all things. Conversely, Eastern 'man' was relegated to the peripheral status of global politics' 'passive object', languishing on the Other side of an imaginary civilisational frontier, stripped of history and dignity. In this Eurocentric imaginary, then, the line of civilisational apartheid separates the Western heart of light from the Eastern heart of darkness.

Having constructed Europe as superior and *exceptional*, by the early nineteenth century Romantic thinkers then extrapolated this conception back in time to Ancient Greece, thereby painting an ahistorical picture of permanent Aryan Western supremacy.[11] It was, of course, round about this time when the Social Sciences were emerging. But rather than critique this racist (meta)narrative, social scientists unreflexively endogenised this discourse into their theories. Accordingly they explain Europe's rise by excavating causal variables that allegedly exist only within Europe. This presupposes the Eurocentric endogenous *logic of immanence* through which Europe's rise is self-generated before it subsequently projects its global will-to-power in order to remake the world in its own image. Thus having extrapolated European supremacy back in time to Ancient Greece, they then trace forwards world political and economic development through an immanent journey of the Western 'Oriental Express'. On the way the Western train passes through an imaginary linear series of pristine European/Western way-stations. The journey begins in Ancient Greece and then, having passed through Ancient Rome and European feudalism, steams on to the Italian commercial-financial revolution, through the Renaissance and the Iberian Voyages of Discovery, and then tracks northwards via Dutch hegemony to Westphalia and on through the Enlightenment before finally sweeping westwards, passing through British hegemony/industrialisation to arrive at the global terminus of history – the Pax Americana for liberals and communism for Marxists. Conversely, such a progressive linearity was absent on the Other side of the 'civilisational frontier'. In the process the West is granted an 'iron law of development' while the East suffers an 'iron law of non-development'. Accordingly, the Easterners could

---

[10] Edward W. Said, *Orientalism* (Harmondsworth: Penguin, [1978] 2003).
[11] Martin Bernal, *Black Athena* (London: Vintage, 1991); Samir Amin, *Eurocentrism* (London: Zed Books, 1989).

only passively await the arrival of the Oriental (imperial) Express which, fuelled by an *Occidental/Eurocentric Messianism*, steamed across to pick them up in order to either graciously deliver them to the emancipatory terminus of history (as for liberals and classical Marxists) or to relentlessly hold them down through exploitation (as for most neo-Marxists). How then is this Eurocentric discourse imbricated in CIRT?

Eurocentrism in Gramscian IR

There are various themes that are central to Gramscian IR/IPE, all of which are linked by the Eurocentric predisposition to reify the West as the self-generating, proactive subject of world politics – past and present (and future?). I shall take each in turn. But before doing so, it is noteworthy that some Gramscian IR/IPE scholars have variously challenged Eurocentrism, including Cox in his analysis of civilisations. Moreover, beyond IR/IPE, Gramscianism has gone a very long way in this regard. However, I choose not to consider this line of research in the immediate discussion given that it is not part of the familiar Gramscian canon in IR/IPE – though I shall return to it in the Conclusion. Nevertheless, to the extent that Cox's recent work on civilisations breaks with certain Eurocentric assumptions means that this contradicts the Eurocentrism of Cox's major works for which he is justifiably famous. So let me now turn to revealing this (though I shall supplement this with other prominent Gramscian references where relevant).

World hegemony as an exclusively Western phenomenon

While the Gramscian conception of hegemony was first imported into IR by Robert Cox in his seminal 1981 article in order to counter the conservative, ahistorical and structuralist approach of neorealism, paradoxically his conception serves to make Gramcianism and neorealist hegemonic stability theory (HST) appear as but mere variants on a common Eurocentric theme. How so?

For neorealist HST, American hegemony is viewed as a form of Western universalism, just as British hegemony was in the nineteenth century.[12] Here we learn of the hegemons' 'far-sightedness' to stand above the competitive fray of world politics and guide all other states to pursue progressive policies that they would otherwise not have followed had they been left to their own devices. Above all, it assumes that it has been the selfless generosity of both the US and Britain to make sacrifices for the greater global good that is solely responsible for bringing the light of economic development/order to the (implicitly dark) world. Is it a coincidence that both these powers are Anglo-Saxon?[13] Either way, this vision is highly reminiscent of Rudyard Kipling's notion of 'the White Man's Burden'. And recall that an important aspect of the Burden lies in Kipling's warning (issued to the Americans in 1899) that

---

[12] For example, Robert Gilpin, *The Political Economy of International Relations* (Princeton, NJ: Princeton University Press, 1987).

[13] Isabelle Grunberg, 'Exploring the "Myth" of Hegemonic Stability Theory', *International Organization*, 44 (1990), pp. 431–78.

the 'civiliser' should expect to incur the 'blame of those ye better, the hate of those ye guard'. Likewise, for HST, hegemony is represented as the proactive civilising subject of world politics/economics, with all other states – especially Eastern – cast in the role of ungrateful 'free-riders' (think of Japan and, no doubt, China in the coming years).[14] Thus following this logic, students may be forgiven for thinking that they can learn everything they need to know about IPE by studying Anglo-Saxon hegemony in the last 200 years. How then does Eurocentrism infect the Gramscian concept of hegemony?

First, a line of Gramscians echo HST in that they see the rise and decline of various Western hegemons, ranging from The Netherlands (mid-seventeenth century) through Britain in the nineteenth century and on to the Pax Americana after 1945, as *the* lens through which the world political economy must be viewed.[15] Of course, they signal two major differences: first, hegemony is ushered in by the exigencies of domestic class forces; and second, hegemony is predatory in an imperialist sense, functioning to maximise the profits of the hegemonic capitalist class at the expense of the rest of the world. But the considerable emphasis that is placed on domestic class forces within the hegemon returns us to the Eurocentric notion that the West self-generates through an endogenous logic of immanence. The predatory/imperialist aspect of hegemony as opposed to the benign formulation of HST echoes the key difference between neo-Marxist and classical Marxist conceptions of imperialism. Thus while Marx, Lenin and Trotsky saw in capitalist imperialism a civilising vehicle to spread Western capitalism around the world to thereby hasten the socialist day of reckoning, so neo-Marxists of most persuasions have abandoned this conception in favour of one that emphasises the exploitative relations between North and South.[16] But does this break with classical Marxism imply a break with Eurocentrism?

Apart from the point that Gramscians and classical Marxists share in the Eurocentric assumption of a Western 'logic of immanence', the critical overlap here lies in the shared point that they deny the possibility of autonomous development in the East (that is, the Eurocentric 'Eastern iron law of non-development'). Moreover, in reifying Western hegemony and consigning the East to the irrelevant periphery, so we return full circle to the Eurocentrism of Karl Marx. In this context, a revealing comparison can be made between Cox and Immanuel Wallerstein. Cox is critical of world-systems theory on the grounds that its excessive structuralist ontology precludes the agency of classes in the making of history, thereby rendering it a problem-solving theory insofar as it stands outside of history.[17] But the lowest common Eurocentric denominator is that for both these scholars Eastern states/ societies are represented as little more than *Träger* – as 'passive bearers' of anthropomorphic Western structural forces. Notable here is Stephen Gill's analysis in which the exceptional power of the US is seen as exceptional even for a hegemon.[18] And when coupled with the passivity of the East so he reinforces the 'west-as-norm

---

[14] See also Kim Richard Nossal, 'Tales That Textbooks Tell: Ethnocentricity and Diversity in American Introductions to International Relations', in R. A. Crawford and D. S. L. Jarvis (eds.), *International Relations – Still an American Social Science?* (New York: SUNY Press, 2001), pp. 172–5.

[15] For example, Cox, *Production, Power and World Order*; Giovanni Arrighi, *The Long Twentieth Century* (London: Verso, 1994).

[16] But see Bill Warren, *Imperialism, Pioneer of Capitalism* (London: New Left Books, 1980).

[17] Cox, 'Social Forces', pp. 214–15.

[18] Gill, *American Hegemony*, esp. pp. 75–7, 86–7, 93–5, 102–6, 222ff.

ideology'.[19] But this notion of Western hegemonic supremacy is perhaps not so surprising given that in Gramsci's writings hegemony is represented as 'supremacy'.[20] Ironically, then, Gill's portrayal of the ubiquity of US power in the world is such that it might well prove reassuring to an American hawk.

Globalisation as Western provincialism writ large

While Gramscianism allegedly replaces inter-*national* relations with global-relations and globalisation as a core analytical focus, this is at best mitigated and at worst contradicted by an underlying Eurocentrism. First, Cox reiterates the Eurocentric logic of immanence treating the rise of globalisation as a pure product of endogenous Western developments. Thus a uniquely Western path is traced that leads at first very slowly from Westphalia and Dutch hegemony, through British hegemony and industrialisation, on to the era of rival European imperialisms before culminating very rapidly with the Pax Americana.[21] As he puts it, 'the new [global] economy grew very largely as the consequence of the US hegemonic role and the global expansion of US-based corporations'.[22] Thus the West (specifically the US) is represented as the subject of globalisation while the East is viewed as its passive object.

This is imbricated in the Gramscian accounts of states under globalisation, which are portrayed as having no choice but to conform to Western neoliberalism. Here we encounter two major aspects found in Eurocentric globalisation theory – what Ulf Hannerz calls the 'global homogenisation scenario' and the 'peripheral corruption scenario'. In the former, the West remakes the East in its own image by casting a Western blanket of domination over the East through globalisation – or, put differently, the East is forced to don a Western neo-colonial straitjacket. By contrast, the peripheral corruption scenario is one where the peripheral states adopt Western practices but then corrupt or pervert them to morally regressive ends.[23]

At first in Cox's analysis, Southern states corrupt and pervert incoming Western influences. Thus in his words, internationalised Third World states in the 'early' phase of globalisation were until recently *military-bureaucratic regimes*

that sought to encourage export-oriented development together with the enforcement as necessary of domestic austerity upon the politically excluded elements of society. Physical repression, ranging from widespread violations of human rights to open civil wars, generates the 'refugee problem'. In part, it may be explained by a political psychology of authoritarianism but in its broadest terms, the refugee problem has to be understood as a systematic consequence of the globalization trend.[24]

Here there are clear shades of the old Eurocentric Oriental Despotism argument, for it is the political irrationality/immaturity of Third World state forms that blunts the

---

[19] L. H. M. Ling, *Postcolonial International Relations* (Houndmills: Palgrave, 2002), p. 56.
[20] See the excellent discussion in Enrico Augelli and Craig N. Murphy, *America's Quest for Supremacy* (London: Pinter, 1988), ch. 6.
[21] Cox, *Production, Power and World Order*, pp. 111–267.
[22] Ibid., p. 216.
[23] Ulf Hannerz, 'Scenarios for Peripheral Cultures', in Anthony D. King (ed.), *Culture, Globalization and the World-System* (London: Macmillan, 1991), p. 108.
[24] Cox, *Approaches to World Order*, pp. 195–6.

pure Westernisation thrust, perverting and morally degenerating it in the process. Of such a portrayal, Hannerz's description is worth quoting:

The peripheral corruption scenario . . . is deeply ethnocentric, in that it posits a very uneven distribution of virtue, and in that it denies the validity and worth of any transformations at the periphery of what was originally drawn from the center. There is little question of cultural difference here, but rather of a difference between culture and non-culture, between civilization and savagery.[25]

Nevertheless, over time this 'corruption scenario' increasingly becomes replaced by the master-process of globalisation: what Cox calls the hyperliberal 'internationalisation of the state', or what Stephen Gill calls the neoliberal 'transnationalisation of the state'.[26] This is where the globalisation-as-homogenisation process becomes apparent. Thus while the previous liberal state (that is, the Keynesian welfare state) acted 'as a buffer protecting the national economy from disruptive external forces', now the hyperliberal state adapts 'domestic economies to the perceived exigencies of the world economy'.[27] In short, the latent Eurocentrism here is reflected in the fact that the hyperliberal internationalised state acts as a passive conveyor belt or valve, through which dominant Western capitalist practices and norms are transmitted from the Western core into the non-Western periphery. For as Cox puts it:

The domestic-oriented agencies of the state are now more and more to be seen as transmission belts from world-economy trends and decision making into the domestic economy, as agencies to promote the carrying out of tasks they had no part in deciding.[28]

And this links up with Cox's Westphilian narrative of Western hegemony where he asserts that:

A world hegemony is . . . in its beginnings an outward expansion of the internal (national) hegemony established by a dominant social class. The economic and social institutions, the culture, the technology associated with this national hegemony *become patterns for emulation abroad.*[29]

Thus, in sum, for all the talk of global relations that supersedes the 'thin' conception of mainstream theory's emphasis on inter-*national* relations, Gramscianism generally produces an equally thin, Eurocentric conception of the global – as the realm of *Western provincialism writ large.* And coupled with the extremely poor prospects for a radical challenge to this scenario, so globalisation is implicitly represented as the 'triumph of the West', if not the closure of history by the West.

Gramscian historicism as ahistorical Eurocentrism written backwards

This discussion culminates with the problem of Gramscian IR's historicity insofar as its basing in Eurocentrism renders it an ahistorical approach. Most Orientalist

[25] Hannerz, 'Scenarios for Peripheral Cultures', p. 109.
[26] For example, Cox, *Production, Power and World Order*, pp. 253–65; Gill, *American Hegemony*, p. 94.
[27] Cox, *Approaches to World Order*, p. 193.
[28] Ibid., p. 193. But for an alternative neo-Marxist conception see Andreas Bieler, Werner Bonefeld, Peter Burnham, and Adam D. Morton, *Global Restructuring, State, Capital and Labour* (London: Palgrave, 2006).
[29] Ibid., p. 137, my emphasis; and Gill, *American Hegemony*, p. 76.

history takes the form of subliminal Eurocentrism. That is, such historians do not go out explicitly to make the West central to world history/politics. But the logic of their approaches and methodology leads directly into Eurocentrism. As Janet Abu-Lughod explains, 'The usual [Eurocentric] approach is to examine *ex post facto* the outcome – that is, the economic and political hegemony of the West in modern times – and then reason backward, to rationalize why this supremacy *had* to be'.[30] In this way, theorists end up by imputing an inevitability to the rise of the West as it endogenously self-generates through the logic of immanence before its power is universalised through imperialism/hegemony/globalisation, as is found in much of Gramscian IR.[31]

The acute irony, then, is that in reproducing Eurocentrism, Gramscian IR necessarily draws close to the very neorealist 'Other' against which it defines itself. Interestingly, in the 1986 Postscript to his famous 1981 article, Cox states that:

I accept that my own thought is grounded in a particular perspective . . . The troublesome part comes when scientific enterprise claims to transcend history and to propound some universally valid form of knowledge. Positivism, by its pretensions to escape from history, runs the greater risk of falling into the trap of unconscious ideology.[32]

But as should be apparent by now, the troublesome part of much Gramscian IR is that it has effectively transcended history by propounding an ahistorical Eurocentric universalism written backwards, thereby leading it into 'the trap of unconscious ideology' (that is, subliminal Eurocentrism). In the process, then, this structuralist ahistoricism that creeps in through the Eurocentric back-door ultimately transforms critical Gramscianism into a problem-solving theory.

But this interpretation should not be read as one that applies only to Gramscianism since I believe that most Marxist analyses of IR suffer from a Eurocentric bias. This exists particularly within Marxist historical sociology of IR,[33] as well as in classical world-systems and early dependency theory,[34] even if there are some Marxist exceptions to this (as I shall also note in the Conclusion).[35] Moreover, Eurocentrism infects, albeit to varying degrees, other non-Marxist variants of CIRT, to a discussion of which I now turn.

Eurocentrism beyond Gramscianism: postmodernism and feminism?

A range of postcolonial scholars have claimed that postmodernism (as opposed to poststructuralism) and feminism often end up by slipping, albeit in different ways to Gramscianism, into Eurocentrism. Regarding postmodernism the problem is not so

---

[30] Janet L. Abu-Lughod, *Before European Hegemony* (Oxford: Oxford University Press, 1989), p. 12.
[31] For example, Cox, *Production, Power and World Order*, pp. 105–50.
[32] Cox, 'Social Forces', p. 247.
[33] For example, Benno Teschke, *The Myth of 1648* (London: Verso, 2003).
[34] For example, Immanuel Wallerstein, *The Modern World-System*, vol. I (London: Academic Press, 1974); Arghiri Emmanuel, *Unequal Exchange* (New York: Monthly Review Press, 1972).
[35] Cf. R. A. Denemark, J. Friedman, B. K. Gills and G. Modelski (eds.), *World System History* (New York: Routledge, 2000); A. G. Frank and B. K. Gills (eds.), *The World System: Five Hundred Years or Five Thousand?* (London: Routledge, 1996); Abu-Lughod, *Before European Hegemony*; Robbie Shilliam, 'Marcus Garvey, Race and Sovereignty', *Review of International Studies*, 32:3 (2006), pp. 379–400. See also notes 110 and 111 below.

much the reification of the West as we find in Gramscianism and Marxism. Rather, postmodernists seek to deconstruct the West and disturb its own self-selective narrative of power, which is undeniably an implicit vehicle to undermine Eurocentrism. Or as Robert Young puts it, 'Postmodernism can best be defined as European culture's awareness that it is no longer the unquestioned and dominant center of the world'.[36] But I want to raise a number of points that I feel serve to compromise postmodernism's implicit anti-Eurocentrism.

First and foremost, postmodernism refuses to entertain either the possibility of Eastern subjectivity/agency on the one hand, or the possibility of reconstructing an alternative non-Eurocentric narrative on the other. Accordingly, Lily Ling suggests that:

> postmodernism cannot accommodate an interactive, articulating . . . Other. Its exclusive focus on the Western Self ensured, instead (neo)realism's sovereignty by relegating the Other to a familiar, subordinate identity: that is, as a mute, passive reflection of the West or utopian projection of the West's dissatisfaction with itself.[37]

Sankaran Krishna issues a similar complaint.[38] Here the problem is that rejecting the notions of foundationalist reconstruction and subjectivity means that the Eastern agent is robbed of the agential capacity to resist the West, thus eradicating the possibility of emancipatory change. Krishna in particular argues for some notion of enabling essentiality – a 'strategic essentialism' or 'tactical essentialism' – that can enable activist subjectivity.[39] Deconstruction without reconstruction is targeted for harsh treatment by Edward Said, who complains that refusal to 'take the further step and exempt the interpreter from *any* moral, political, cultural or psychological commitments. . . . and to say that we are against theory . . . is to be blind or trivial'.[40]

Second, these problems are reinforced by the point that for postmodernism the identity-formation process through which the Self constructs an Other is seen as an unavoidable or inevitable fact of social existence. This means that we are presented with an ahistorical picture of eternal conflict with no hope of transcending it (thereby transforming postmodernism and neorealism into strange bedfellows). Only if the logocentric identity-formation process can be reimagined out of this impasse can we properly entertain the prospect of an emancipatory politics.[41]

Ultimately, though, a growing number of postcolonialists single out the works of Baudrillard, Lyotard, Mouffe, Deleuze and Foucault for their reification of the West as self-contained and for failing to recognise the interactive relationship between East and West. Moreover, Foucault's exclusive focus on the micro-politics of the local irresistibly precludes such a picture from emerging. And it is noteworthy that even Edward Said – supposedly an erstwhile Foucauldian – turned in his later writings to criticise Foucault for ignoring the role of Eastern resistance in the making of global politics.[42]

---

[36] Robert J. C. Young, *White Mythologies* (London: Routledge, 2004), p. 51.

[37] Ling, *Postcolonial International Relations*, p. 50.

[38] Sankaran Krishna, 'The Importance of Being Ironic: A Postcolonial View on Critical International Relations Theory', *Alternatives*, 18 (1993), p. 402.

[39] Krishna, 'Importance of Being Ironic', p. 405 and n. 36, p. 415.

[40] Edward W. Said, 'The Politics of Knowledge', *Raritan*, 11:1 (1991), p. 29.

[41] See especially, Vanita Seth, 'Self and Similitude: Translating Difference', *Postcolonial Studies*, 4:3 (2001), pp. 297–309.

[42] Edward W. Said, *Culture and Imperialism* (London: Vintage, 1994), pp. 29–30, 335–6; and *Power, Politics, and Culture* (London: Bloomsbury, 2004), p. 53.

All in all, I think it fair to say that postmodernism presents an ambivalent critique of Eurocentrism, effectively stripping the self-designated sense of the West's sovereign subjectivity but simultaneously closing off the avenue into retrieving a global politics in which Eastern subjectivity/agency is accorded significance. And in turn, this connects up with the ensuing discussion of Western feminism, insofar as a growing number of feminists are seeking to go beyond postmodern scepticism which, as Ann Tickner points out, 'could lead to an abandonment of the political project of reducing women's subordination that has motivated feminism since its earliest beginnings'.[43]

Turning, therefore, to feminism and feminist IR theory, it is now some two decades since Chandra Talpade Mohanty chastised much of critical Western feminism for its Eurocentrism,[44] and a quarter of a century since bell hooks chastised white feminist movements for their racism.[45] But while some progress has been made to overcome this problem in the social sciences, the gap between much of feminist IR and non-Eurocentrism remains. In developing Mohanty's argument further, there are a number of strands to note here. First, pioneering critical IR feminists such as Ann Tickner have located the specificity of gender by revealing how the world economy works to disadvantage women in relation to men, especially within the Third World.[46] This is an undeniably important project and I in no way wish to denigrate it. But the problem here is that revealing gender *exclusively in this way* runs the risk of returning us back into the Eurocentric *cul-de-sac* of rendering Eastern women as but passive victims of Western power, thereby stripping them of agency.

Second, much critical Western feminism presupposes a great divide between First and Third World women. The former are portrayed as educated, modern, having (relatively greater) control over their own bodies and the freedom to make their own decisions, while Third World women are (re)presented as ignorant, traditional/religious-oriented, passive, pathetic and victimised. In returning us back into the *cul-de-sac* of patriarchal and Eurocentric discourse, this tendency leads many Western feminists to construct themselves as the higher normative referent in a binary schema.[47] That is, Western women are represented as subjects while Eastern women are granted only object status, with Eastern women/societies consequently being judged negatively against the White Western female experience. And this problem is exacerbated even further given that women within the West are usually portrayed by feminists as having little or no agency.

Not surprisingly, this flows into the advocation of yet another Western civilising mission and the idea of the White Woman's Burden. This occurs in two principal ways. First, socialist feminists view Eastern women's backwardness as a function of Eastern pre-capitalist social relations. Addressing this point Valerie Amos and Pratibha Parmar cite Maxine Molyneux's argument that:

There can be little doubt that on balance the position of women in imperialist, i.e. advanced capitalist societies is, for all its implications more advanced than in the less

---

[43] J. Ann Tickner, *Gendering World Politics* (New York: Columbia University Press, 2001), p. 20.
[44] C. T. Mohanty, 'Under Western Eyes: Feminist Scholarship and Colonial Discourses', *Boundary 2*, 12:3 (1986), pp. 333–58.
[45] bell hooks, *Ain't I a Woman?* (Cambridge, MA: South End Press, 1981).
[46] Tickner, *Gendering World Politics*, ch. 4.
[47] Gayatri Chakravorty Spivak, 'Three Women's Texts and a Critique of Imperialism', *Critical Inquiry*, 12 (1985), p. 243.

developed capitalist and non-capitalist societies. In this sense the changes brought by imperialism to Third World societies may, in some circumstances have been historically progressive.[48]

No less surprisingly, this reiteration of Marx's conception of imperialism as a civilising mission issued a hostile response by Black feminists. Amos and Parmar, for example, replied by stating that:

[W]hen Black and Third World women are being told that imperialism is good for us, it should be of no great surprise to anyone when we reject a feminism which uses Western social and economic systems to judge and make pronouncements about how Third World women can become emancipated. Feminist theories which examine our cultural practices as 'feudal residues' or label us 'traditional', also portray us as politically immature women who need to be versed and schooled in the ethos of Western feminism.[49]

In a second version of the Western feminist civilising mission, it is Western woman who is portrayed as the dashing saviour who comes to the rescue of the uncivilised, enslaved Eastern woman. Martha Nussbaum is one of the more outspoken representatives of this genre advocating an emancipatory Western universalism against a relativism that in her eyes is complicit with the exploitation of Eastern women.[50] As she boldly put it, taking on the cultural relativists, 'we would rather risk charges of imperialism . . . than to stand around . . . waiting for a time when everyone will like what we are going to say'.[51] In this genre, oppressive practices such as 'female genital mutilation', 'honour killings' and 'dowry deaths' are deemed to be so barbaric that they require female Western (humanitarian) intervention – though equally, the same logic was deployed by British male imperialists in the nineteenth century when confronting the Hindu practice of *Sati* (widow burning). While Nussbaum's claims are undeniably motivated by a profoundly empathic humanism that cannot be dismissed out of hand, the fact remains that her's is very much a white Western humanism.

Still, the critical issue at stake is where we draw the line. The extremely emotive issues that are often mentioned in this context should not be (ab)used as the basis to call for an eradication of *all* Eastern cultural practices regarding the treatment of women. Do we, for example, include the Asian arranged marriage system or the *nekab* (Islamic veil) as signs of repression that must be done away with – as advocated by many Western feminists? Significantly, Lily Ling points out that many Muslim women *choose* to wear the veil, and that it can be worn as a sign of resistance to the West (as happened after the 1979 revolution in Iran). She concludes that 'nowhere did Nussbaum . . . consider that Others could [draw hope] from their own traditions'.[52] Clearly, then, there is a very thin (if not permeable) line between a genuine humanitarian feminist concern and a female imperial civilising mission. And paradoxically, this position joins hands with the very postmodern cultural relativist Other against which Nussbaum defines her project, since both ultimately deny

---

[48] Maxine Molyneux cited in Valerie Amos and Pratibha Parmar, 'Challenging Imperial Feminism', *Feminist Review*, 17 (1984), p. 6.

[49] Amos and Parmar, 'Challenging Imperial Feminism', p. 7.

[50] Martha C. Nussbaum, 'Human Capabilities, Female Human Beings', in M. C. Nussbaum and Jonathan Glover (eds.), *Women, Culture and Development* (Oxford: Clarendon, 1995), pp. 61–104.

[51] Martha C. Nussbaum, 'Introduction', in Nussbaum and Glover (eds.), *Women, Culture and Development*, p. 2.

[52] Ling, *Postcolonial International Relations*, p. 52.

Eastern women agency and the possibility for their own emancipatory politics.[53] For as Parita Trivedi notes here, this portrayal of a submissive Eastern woman who is repressed by the arranged marriage system (and other practices) is a figment of 'racist imaginings which have taken strands from oppressive Hindu practices . . . and welded these into an inhumane whole which shackles us down. Your [ie., white women's] task is to un-learn and re-learn. Our task is to create new imaginings'.[54] How then might we begin to imagine an alternative to Westphilian CIRT?

Decolonising Westphilian international relations: reconstructing a post-racist IR

Why post-racism?

Of course, that much of CIRT turns out to be Eurocentric means that it is not necessarily 'wrong' or without some merit. Indeed, Eurocentric CIRT constitutes a powerful challenge to a non-Eurocentric IR. Accordingly, in this section I provide a critique of Eurocentrism while simultaneously outlining my own alternative perspective. In essence I seek to return the Eurocentric fetish of Western supremacy back down to earth by 'decolonising Westphilian IR' through reconstructing a 'post-racist IR'. But choosing this label requires me in the first instance to justify its usage. Just as postcolonialism refers to the point that since decolonisation neo-colonial structures of power and meaning continue to characterise global politics, so post-racism reveals the point that since the receding of scientific racism after 1945 cultural racism continues to infuse the global realm. Of course, this is a similar point to that made by most postcolonialists, which will elicit the obvious response: 'why not just go with the term *postcolonial*?' I am, however, unhappy with the term for a variety of reasons, a few of which are as follows.

First and foremost, the term 'postcolonial' seems increasingly to be straining at its seams, incorporating a proliferating series of theories with varying ontologies and epistemologies many of which are incommensurable, as even some postcolonialists recognise.[55] This is one, though not the only, reason why postcolonialism appears bewildering, if not incomprehensible, to 'outsiders'. At one extreme are postmodern postcolonialists who, like all postcolonialists, seek to disrupt the singularity and centrality of the West. But they refuse to grant subjectivity to Eastern actors and thereby deny them agency, which returns us to the problems of postmodernism discussed earlier.[56] Moreover, they also treat history as inherently Eurocentric – which is precisely why they refuse to reconstruct an alternative historical narrative (past and present).[57] But as ironically postmodernists readily point out, everyday people consume, and live through, narratives. This is how they make sense of their place in the world – something that derives from the quest for meaning and the need

[53] Cf. C. T. Mohanty, ' "Under Western Eyes" Revisited: Feminist Solidarity through Anticapitalist Struggles', *Signs*, 28:2 (2003), pp. 518–21.

[54] Parita Trivedi, 'To Deny Our Fullness: Asian Women in the Making of History', *Feminist Review*, 17 (1984), p. 38; see also Mohanty, ' "Under Western Eyes" Revisited', p. 519.

[55] Ania Loomba, *Colonialism/Postcolonialism* (New York: Routledge, 1998).

[56] See the excellent discussion in Phillip Darby, 'Pursuing the Political: A Postcolonial Rethinking of Relations International', *Millennium*, 33:1 (2004), pp. 1–32.

[57] For example, Homi Bhabha, *The Location of Culture* (London: Routledge, 1994).

to feel good about themselves. Not just everyday people, though, but politicians too. Given this, the clear and present danger of 'reconstructionist refusal' is that in the absence of an alternative non-Eurocentric narrative, Eurocentrism will remain by default rather like the USA after the demise of the Soviet Union – as the only one left standing. I do not, however, believe that we have to give up either on history or in producing an alternative narrative, since empathy and imaginative thinking – which *inter alia* draws on many of the insightful ideas from postcolonialism's postmodern wing – can produce a post-racist IR that avoids the pitfalls of either a pure Orientalism or Occidentalism; a task that I set myself in the following pages.

Nevertheless, the main reason why I label my approach 'post-racist' lies in the point that for many postcolonial-inspired scholars the assumption is that the antidote to Eurocentrism lies in 'retrieving the imperial' (to quote the title of one of Barkawi and Laffey's important articles).[58] But this can be done while retaining Eurocentrism – as in, for example, world-systems theory and neo-Marxism more generally. Moreover, East–West relations have for the majority of word-historical time existed *outside* the orbit of empire, thus rendering a central focus on imperialism as inadequate to the task of revealing Eastern agency. And even today Eastern agency is frequently enacted in the interstices of the neo-colonial net behind the backs of the neo-colonialists (of which more later). Above all, the deafening silence that rings out in critical and mainstream IR is not the 'E-word' (empire) as Niall Ferguson argues in a different context,[59] but the 'R-word' (racism). Modern IR's *weltanschauung* has worked, usually subconsciously, to render not so much neo-colonialism but above all racism as all but invisible. This may take the form of representing world politics in terms of West–West relations that revolve around bipolar great-power rivalry (as in neorealism); or characterising North–South relations in predominantly economic terms (as in neo-Marxism); or through the frequent assumption that the rise of the UN and the end of the legal standard of civilisation broke fundamentally with the racism of the old imperial period (as in much of Constructivism and the English School).[60] Accordingly we need to deconstruct this intellectual containment strategy in order to reveal how post-racist hierarchy has marked the post-1945 era of world politics/economics.

Post-racism is in its purest form 'racism without racialism', or more specifically, cultural racism (Eurocentrism) without scientific/genetic racism'. This is what Etienne Balibar usefully calls 'neo-racism'.[61] Except that the whiff of explicit racism still very much lingers, and has become more poignant in the West since the end of the Cold War.[62] In essence, cultural racism, in locating difference in terms of culture and institutions, elevates the West to exceptional status. Nevertheless, it is the association of genetic/explicit racism with European imperialism that reinforces the myth of the end of contemporary racism (given the assumption that decolonisation sounded scientific racism's death-knell and that racism is generally conflated with its scientific

---

[58] Tarak Barkawi and Mark Laffey, 'Retrieving the Imperial: *Empire* and International Relations', *Millennium*, 31:1 (2002), pp. 109–27.

[59] Niall Ferguson, 'Hegemony or Empire?', *Foreign Affairs* (September/October, 2003).

[60] But see Edward Keene, *Beyond the Anarchical Society* (Cambridge: Cambridge University Press, 2002).

[61] Etienne Balibar, 'Is There a Neo-Racism?', in Etienne Balibar and Immanuel Wallerstein, *Race, Nation, Class* (London: Verso, 1991), p. 21.

[62] Kenan Malik, *The Meaning of Race* (Houndmills: Palgrave, 1996).

variant). But while scientific racism did indeed mark European imperialism, so cultural racism also played its part.

This argument links directly into a further reason why race has been rendered invisible today. In his pioneering book, *Colonial Desire*,[63] Robert Young argues that in our rush to celebrate the rise of contemporary 'multiculturalism' (though certainly not everyone is complicit in this project!) we have exaggerated the racist aspect of Western thinking in the eighteenth and nineteenth centuries. That is, an (a)historical temporal great divide or binary schemata has been constructed in which the eighteenth and nineteenth centuries are (re)presented as more racist than they were so that the post-1945 era can be portrayed as less racist than it is. Ironically, the postcolonial mantra – that the Enlightenment was fundamentally racist – must share some of the blame. A fairer picture of the Enlightenment reveals it as schizophrenic – or better still, ambivalent – oscillating between the two faces of racism and non-racism. For while Eurocentrism emerged during the Enlightenment we should not forget that many Enlightenment thinkers reached out in a genuinely positive way to Eastern cultures, as did the Romantic thinkers of the nineteenth century.[64]

Nevertheless, while scientific racism was not important to the Enlightenment, many philosophers emphasised the role of climate in shaping civilisations, which, of course, opened the door to the idea of 'polygenesis' and the rise of explicit or scientific/genetic racism that took off in the nineteenth century. But even the rise of scientific racism, which flourished in Britain only after 1840, had an ambivalent relationship to colonialism. Not all 'racialist theorists' called for imperialism. Some such as Robert Knox and Comte de Gobineau explicitly rejected colonialism. Colonialism would either fail because it would lead to a degeneration of the superior race, or it was pointless because the inferior races were incapable of being civilised. Thus European thinking in the eighteenth and nineteenth centuries was neither purely racist (in a genetic sense), nor did all of it reject other cultures, and nor was scientific racism always imperialist.

Significantly, the discourse of imperialism flourished under cultural racism though with a significant injection of scientific racism into its discursive corpus. Since 1945 scientific racism has receded (though not disappeared) with cultural racism forming the mainstay of contemporary Eurocentrism, or what I call post-racism. And today's Western civilising missions – whether via US hegemony/neo-imperialism or human rights regimes and humanitarian wars – echo the themes of British imperialism. In sum, despite various differences there are also crucial continuities in the discursive contexts between the earlier and contemporary periods under review. Thus I choose ultimately to use the label of post-racist IR in order to highlight the very point that racism and 'racist hierarchy' continues as a major constitutive force in contemporary global politics/economics. Or as Robert Young asserts: 'the question becomes not colonial discourse or even neo-colonialism [*per se*] but racism. Colonial discourse shows the enactment of racism in its colonial moment. Analysis needs to be extended now to the discursive forms, representations and practices of contemporary racism'.[65] How, then, might this be achieved?

---

[63] Robert J. C. Young, *Colonial Desire* (London: Routledge, 1995).
[64] Young, *Colonial Desire*; J. J. Clarke, *Oriental Enlightenment* (London: Routledge, 1997).
[65] Young, *White Mythologies*, p. 218.

Key concepts and analytical focus of post-racist IR

First, because I use the terms 'East' and 'West' it requires me to explain why, since this might convey the false impression that I adhere to the conventional Eurocentric meta-geography.[66] Congruent with Eurocentrism, I (somewhat controversially) locate everything that is not in the West in the East. This includes Africa and Latin America – which are conventionally portrayed in Orientalist terms – even though they are located in the same lines of longitude as Europe and the USA respectively. But *contra* Eurocentrism, I see neither African nor Latin American peoples as passive victims of the West and accord them certain amounts of agency. Moreover, this broad categorisation enables me to show in a simple and direct way how an exclusive focus on the West as the only agent of global politics/economics is inadequate. And, of course, if not East and West, then what? This is a massive question that I cannot solve in this article. Accordingly, I continue to deploy the terms 'East' and 'West' only as a convenient heuristic device; one that unlike the more familiar 'North/South Divide' brings racism to the fore. What then of the major concepts of my post-racist IR?

As Lily Ling recently argues, Eurocentric IR theory works within a *monological* perspective, which produces a reductive narrative in which only the West talks and acts.[67] It is essentially a 'winner/loser' paradigm that proclaims the East as the loser thereby ensuring that central analytical focus is accorded to the West. But when we grant agency to the East (as well as the West) we shift towards *dialogical* thinking that transcends the either/or, winner/loser logic. For one does not have to equate winners with everything that goes on in the world economy. This entails revealing first, the manifold ways in which the East shapes and retracks the West as well as *vice versa*; and second, how East and West interact to produce global politics/economics. In the process this elevates *hybridity* to analytical centre stage. Thus as the East shapes the constitution of the West (and *vice versa*) so new hybrid civilisational entities are formed, which reveals the Other in the Self and the Self in the Other;[68] something that lies at base of my post-racist emancipatory politics (see the Conclusion below). And in turn, this points up the process of 'hybridised mimicry' (to adapt Bhabha's concept of mimicry),[69] or 'inflections',[70] wherein imported Western influences are not passively received and absorbed but are negotiated and refracted into specific Eastern cultural contexts (and *vice versa*) to produce new hybrid civilisational forms. All in all, recognising this co-constitutive process means that we can no longer talk of East and West as if they are separate and pure or pristine entities.

In turn, going beyond the winner/loser framework brings to light what Ling calls 'interstitiality' or what Michael Mann calls 'interstitial surprise'.[71] In contrast to the Eurocentric depiction of civilisations as billiard balls that meet only in direct head-on conflict where the West wins and the East loses, civilisations promiscuously entwine

---

[66] The best discussion of this issue is in Martin Lewis and Kären E. Wigen, *The Myth of Continents* (Berkeley, CA: University of California Press, 1997).
[67] Ling, *Postcolonial International Relations*, ch. 1.
[68] Ibid., pp. 20–2. Also, Arlene B. Tickner, 'Seeing IR Differently: Notes from the Third World', *Millennium*, 32:2 (2003), esp. pp. 305–7.
[69] Bhabha, *Location of Culture*, ch. 4.
[70] Pal Ahluwalia, *Politics and Post-Colonial Theory* (London: Routledge, 2001), pp. 124–30.
[71] Michael Mann, *The Sources of Social Power*, vol. I (Cambridge: Cambridge University Press, 1986), pp. 15–19.

through what Mustpaha Pasha usefully calls 'chains of elective affinities',[72] thereby shaping each other in complex ways. But the major aspect here lies in the point that although the East is (currently) subordinate to the West in general terms, the West cannot be likened to a machine that locks the East within a vice-like grip of tightly linked cogs or plugs (whether this be in the forms of international institutions, US/British hegemony or globalisation more generally). It is more akin to a poorly constructed net wherein Eastern agents slip through its many interstices in all manner of ways so as to shape the world in manifold ways. In turn, this attention to interstitiality overcomes the monological assumption that we can only entertain the prospect of Eastern agency should it successfully challenge the West and win. Moreover, interstitiality is vital to understanding a post-racist emancipatory politics where Eastern agents work within the interstices of Western discourse to reveal its contradictions and double standards (see Conclusion).

More generally, an emphasis on post-racism emphasises the importance of identity and culture in the making of IR; something which is surprisingly underdeveloped in most Gramscian IR.[73] Nevertheless, I do not advocate a *pure* post-structuralism since materialist forces also require ontological weighting. So, for example, in analysing great power politics/economics, we would begin by bracketing culture/identity and trace the materialist origins of the power base upon which great power rests. We then bracket material power and move to identity, which inscribes power with moral purpose and thereby channels great power in specific directions. Thus, for example, while China was the leading power between 1450 and c.1800 its specific identity led it to construct an international system in which imperialism was largely absent. By contrast, British identity channelled its great power in a specifically imperialist direction.[74] Pure materialist analysis cannot adequately reveal these different *expressions* of great power without falling into teleological functionalism, while pure post-structuralism is ill-equipped to reveal why it was China and Britain and not Russia or the US that rose to the top in the period before the twentieth century. Nevertheless, it should be noted that identity/culture and material power are ontologically inseparable since they are at once co-constitutive.

I can now introduce the final series of concepts by considering the key analytical focus of my approach – the dialogues and dialectics of civilisations. First, the *dialogues of civilisations* refers to the manifold ways in which each civilisation develops through the borrowing and assimilation of 'resource portfolios' (ideas, technologies and institutions) that emanate from other civilisations. This process has been going on since at least 500 CE and embodies a non-conflictual relationship. Here I suggest that in the dialogue, the meeting point of civilisations is a two-way 'dialogical zone' that generates poly-civilisational hybridity through what Pratt calls 'transculturation',[75] in what amounts to a form of 'dialogical negotiation' (as opposed to a monologic one-way passive receptivity).

---

[72] Mustapha Kamal Pasha, 'Islam, "Soft" Orientalism and Hegemony: A Gramscian Rereading', in Andreas Bieler and Adam David Morton (eds.), *Images of Gramsci* (London: Routledge, 2006), p. 153.

[73] See the excellent discussion in Pasha, 'Islam,' pp. 149–64. But see Augelli and Murphy, *America's Quest*.

[74] For a full discussion see J. M. Hobson, *The Eastern Origins of Western Civilisation* (Cambridge: Cambridge University Press, 2004), esp. pp. 305–12 and 50–70, 219–42.

[75] Mary Louise Pratt, *Imperial Eyes* (London: Routledge, 1992).

But the 'edges' of civilisations can simultaneously be conceptualised as *imperial dialectical frontiers*. This emerges in the *dialectics of civilisations* where Western imperialism/neo-imperialism and Eastern resistance dialectically engage and entwine. At first sight this might seem reminiscent of Huntington's 'clash of civilisations' thesis. Huntington's civilisational edges are likened to volatile 'fault lines' where self-constituting, monolithic civilisations meet and clash. In his conception there is no possibility for a two-way transcultural socialisation process since civilisations retain their autonomous and 'natural cultural essences' after social interaction. But in my alternative formulation, which I adapt from the pioneering analysis in Jan Nederveen Pieterse's book, *Empire and Emancipation*,[76] these 'edges' can better be imagined as *permeable two-way dialectical frontiers* where civilisations once again shape and retrack each other, thereby coming to constitute and guide each other's internal social constitutions and developmental trajectories. In contrast to Eurocentric monologism, this process of 'dialectical negotiation' reveals, as Nederveen Pieterse emphasises, a bottom-up logic of emancipation/resistance entwined with a top-down logic of imperial domination. Indeed, the Eastern peoples never simply lay passively underneath the (neo)empire thinking of England as the British and Americans went about doing their thing, as we shall see below – a point that connects with the 'dialogical dialectic of civilisations', which lies at the very heart of post-racism's emancipatory politics, as I explain in the Conclusion.

All in all, this framework enables us to reveal what Edward Said calls 'the voyage in' through which the 'empire writes back'.[77] This is a vital emancipatory strategy, wherein resistance is viewed as writing back to the Occident in an attempt to break down the very discourse that splits the Self and Other into separate, self-constituting entities. As Said puts it, 'The conscious effort to enter into the discourse of Europe and the West, to mix with it, transform it, to make it acknowledge marginalized or suppressed or forgotten histories . . . I call this effort the voyage in'.[78] How, then, might this be achieved?

The first voyage in: revealing the dialogues between East and West in the making of globalisation

The familiar Westphilian narrative represents globalisation as a Western relay race, in which in the aftermath of the Voyages of Discovery the Iberians passed the global batôn to the Dutch, who then passed it to the British before culminating with the American anchor-man, who ran the final leg in record time. But this obscures globalisation's emergence during the era of what I call the 'Eastern Age of Discovery' after c.500 CE.[79] The creation of a global economy (and the process of 'Oriental globalisation') owes much to the West Asian Muslims after about 650 CE. With the exception of the Americas and possibly Australasia, the rest of the world was drawn together into a complex trading and capitalist network that was initially reproduced mainly by the Muslims but also by the Japanese, Jews, Indians, Chinese and Africans.

[76] Jan P. Nederveen Pieterse, *Empire and Emancipation* (London: Pluto, 1990), ch. 15.
[77] For an excellent discussion, see Ahluwalia, *Politics and Post-Colonial Theory*, ch. 2.
[78] Said, *Culture and Imperialism*, pp. 260–1.
[79] For a full discussion of Oriental globalisation see Hobson, *Eastern Origins*, chs. 2–4.

According to Janet Abu-Lughod this global economy reached its nadir in the thirteenth/fourteenth centuries before it was taken over by the Europeans.[80] But this obscures the important role provided by the Chinese after 1450; a role that is traditionally dismissed by Eurocentrism on the grounds that China withdrew from the international trading system with the pronouncement of the official ban on foreign trade in 1434. However, between 1450 and c.1800 China stood at or near the centre of the global economy,[81] which simultaneously gives the lie to Eurocentrism's assumption that all great powers in the last millennium have been Western. Crucially though, having recently converted onto a silver standard and, given the point that China's economy was the strongest in the world, China effectively *sucked the Europeans directly into the global economy.* How so?

Europe's trade deficit with Asia and China was only paid for by sending across the majority of the plundered bullion from the Americas. This was partly carried eastward by European ships round the Cape as well as westward from Acapulco to China via the Philippines aboard the Spanish Manila galleons. And it was the gold/silver arbitrage system which centred on China that provided the Portuguese, Dutch and English with the majority of their profits (in addition to their role in the so-called Asian country-trade). Nevertheless, while this granted the Europeans a direct presence in the global economy, they remained only bit players in the Indian Ocean trading system right down to about 1800.[82] It was only really during the nineteenth century that the Europeans began to colonise – formally and informally – Asia and Africa. But it would be misplaced to assume that from the early nineteenth century on the Western story is the only one that matters. For the fact is that Eastern agents carried on their everyday economic intercourse often in the interstices of so-called Western imperial control. One such example lies in the developmental role that the Chinese business diaspora has played throughout much of East and South-east Asia during the nineteenth and twentieth centuries.

Still, this discussion should not be read as an ahistorical projection of globalisation back in time, since Oriental globalisation differed in many profound ways from modern globalisation. But the key point is that the presence of Oriental globalisation fundamentally disrupts the Westphilian narrative of globalisation.

The second voyage in: revealing the dialogues of civilisations in the making of the West

While the Westphilian narrative portrays the rise of the West as a self-generating process, this obscures the civilisational dialogues that propelled the West forwards. Because I have laid out these arguments elsewhere in detail, I shall merely skim over some of the key claims.[83] To counter the Westphilian narrative of a self-generating West, I note that at every major turning point in the rise of the West, Eastern 'resource portfolios' were assimilated as they diffused across through Oriental

---

[80] Abu-Lughod, *Before European Hegemony.*
[81] A. G. Frank, *ReOrient* (Berkeley, CA: University of California Press, 1998); Hobson, *Eastern Origins*, ch. 3.
[82] Hobson, *Eastern Origins*, ch. 7.
[83] Ibid., chs. 5–9.

globalisation. Beginning with the crucial economic revolutions of the post-1000 era, I note that almost all of the financial institutions for which the Italians unjustly became famous, originated in, and diffused across from, Islamic West Asia. Moreover, there would in all likelihood have been no Italian/European commercial revolution without the Eastern trade that flowed into Europe via West Asia and Egypt. Nor might there have been a Renaissance without the assimilation of Chinese, Indian, Jewish, African, but above all, Islamic ideas. Nor might there have been a European Age of Discovery, given that the critical trans-oceanic nautical and navigational techniques/technologies that made the voyages possible diffused across from Islamic West Asia and China. Nor would the European military revolution (1550–1660) have occurred in the absence of the Chinese military revolution (850–1290). In turn, all these Eastern impulses fed directly into the rise of the sovereign European state.[84] And while the European Enlightenment was heavily influenced by Chinese ideas, so these ideas, coupled with Chinese technologies and methods, in turn spurred on the British agricultural and industrial revolutions. Moreover, all the aforementioned Eastern portfolios diffused across through Oriental globalisation.

None of this is to say that the Europeans were the passive beneficiaries of an Eastern diffusion process, since they put all the assimilated resource portfolios together through hybridised mimicry, while their agency was also apparent in their colonial policies that proved vital in stimulating industrialisation in Europe.[85] But either way, the conclusion must be that without the Rest there would be no West (certainly not the one that actually emerged).

·

The third voyage in: the dialectics of civilisations at the imperial dialectical frontier

As noted earlier, here I draw from and build upon Nederveen Pieterse's discussion.[86] In this conception civilisations also entwine through imperialism/neo-imperialism and resistance, thereby remaking and retracking each other continuously across the imperial dialectical frontier. Thus, for example, in the Haitian revolution of the 1790s Toussaint L'Ouverture claimed for the Black Haitians the founding principles of the French Revolution – *liberté*, *egalité* and *fraternité*.[87] And with the declaration of Haitian independence in 1804 it soon became clear that this was a seminal event that marked a turning point for those on both 'sides' of the imperial frontier. This then ricocheted back and forth, inspiring new Black resistance movements that in turn issued new defensive strategies by the West. Black resistance to American slavery was then responded to by the Emancipation Proclamation in 1863, which in turn led on to new modes of oppression such as the Jim Crow Laws, and the establishment of the Ku Klux Klan in 1866. Attitudes hardened because of emancipation 'as evidence that black people were beginning to count. Some forms of racism are premised on the threat of equality rather than on the simple assumption

---

[84] J. M. Hobson, 'Provincialising Westphalia: Eastern Origins of Sovereignty in the Oriental Global Age' (forthcoming).

[85] Hobson, *Eastern Origins*, chs. 10–11.

[86] Nederveen Pieterse, *Empire and Emancipation*, ch. 14.

[87] C. L. R. James, *The Black Jacobins* (Harmondsworth: Penguin [1938] 2001).

of inequality'.[88] Significant too were Christian ideas that were appropriated and converted into Black emancipatory ideas (which Nederveen Pieterse aptly dubs 'strange opium'), and which guided many Black resistance movements throughout the twentieth century.

Within the British Empire, colonial resistance emerged in the 1857 Indian 'Mutiny' and the revolt in Morant Bay, Jamaica in 1865, which in turn led to a rapid hardening of English attitudes thereby furnishing a permissive context for the flourishing of scientific racism in Britain. This led not just to a more repressive colonial policy but prepared the way for the 'Scramble for Africa'. Simultaneously this occurred at the time when KKK brutality heightened to such a point that 'the bloody era of the new imperialism advertised the affinity of expansionist conscious-ness and racism'.[89] This consciousness led to the creation of many radical African movements including Pan Africanism (associated with W. E. B. Du Bois), the Back-to-Africa idea of Marcus Garvey, and the Négritude movement (associated with Aimé Césaire and Leopold Senghor).[90] In turn, I argue that these movements fed into the decolonisation wave after 1945, which in turn led on to major changes in the international sphere. Standard analyses of globalisation – critical and liberal – assume that the Pax Americana was vital in stimulating modern globalisation. But this obscures the resistance agency of Eastern nationalist movements that ultimately secured decolonisation, which in turn directly expanded the reach of the global economy beyond the islets of formal empire within which it had previously been contained. Moreover, these dialectical relations have continued on throughout the period down to the War on Terror, with even the latter revealing mutual intercon-nections. Indeed, Osama Bin Laden's thinking reveals a 'long history of intercon-nections and mutual constitution . . . [which draws on] currents of Western, Arab and Islamic cultures and histories [and] modern technologies and communications'.[91]

In sum, the dialectics of civilisations reveal how efforts at imperial control are resisted and negotiated and how in the process East and West co-constitute and retrack each other in highly complex ways. Moreover, this process is enhanced much further through the civilisational dialogues and dialogical negotiations that have occurred at the same time. Thus these multiple forms of inter-civilisational negotia-tive relations have constituted the driver of world politics/economics throughout the last millennium. And in turn, this means that contemporary globalisation cannot be conflated with Westernisation/Americanisation precisely because the global is the product of continuous negotiative interactions between Western and Eastern agency. In recognising this we can secure what Nicola Phillips calls the 'globalising of globalisation studies'.[92] And so we might conclude our discussion of these three voyages in by posing Nederveen Pieterse's important rhetorical question: 'is not part of the meaning of "globalization" that already the East is in the West and the West is in the East?'[93]

---

[88] Nederveen Pieterse, *Empire and Emancipation*, p. 338.

[89] Ibid., p. 345.

[90] See especially Shilliam, 'Marcus Garvey, Race and Sovereignty'.

[91] Tarak Barkawi and Mark Laffey, 'The Postcolonial Moment in Security Studies', *Review of International Studies*, 32:2 (2006), p. 347.

[92] Nicola Phillips, 'Globalization Studies in International Political Economy', in N. Phillips (ed.), *Globalizing International Political Economy* (Houndmills: Palgrave Macmillan, 2005), pp. 20–54.

[93] Nederveen Pieterse, *Empire and Emancipation*, p. 374.

Racist double standards and the contradictions of Western hegemony/imperialism

Finally, one of the most important aspects of post-racist IR that leads directly into an emancipatory politics lies in revealing the manifold racist double standards and contradictions that underpin British and American hegemony/imperialism. There are three fundamental contradictions that have marked these civilisational projects. First, hegemony/imperialism is sold as a benign policy of 'cultural conversion' through which Eastern societies can be raised up or civilised. But this is a strategy of 'ethnocide' through which the imperial powers *attempt* to eradicate Eastern cultures/ identities in order that Western supremacist identity be shored up. Second, the strategy of 'cultural conversion' has gone hand-in-hand with 'containment' in which Eastern societies are 'helped up' but contained at a point where they could not pose an economic challenge to the West. And third, despite the proclamation of helping through civilising, the Western hegemons and empires have exploited Eastern economies on the basis that because Eastern peoples/cultures are deemed to be inferior so they are axiomatically considered as 'ripe for exploitation'. What then of double standards? Gramscianism's materialist focus on capitalism as the motor of hegemonic discourse brings to light the issue of hypocrisy.[94] But locating racism/ post-racism at the core of hegemonic discourse definitively places the issue of double standards at the analytical centre.

Turning to British 'hegemony' in the nineteenth century, a litany of racist double standards emerges through its free trade policy. Cox, implicitly echoing Friedrich List, argues that despite public pronouncements to the contrary, British free trade maximised the economic power of the British economy at the expense of her Continental European counterparts and the Third World.[95] But British free trade policy could not have been designed to maintain Britain's lead over Continental Europe, given that the British did very little to promote free trade in Europe in the first place nor did they take any action to prevent the return to continental protectionism after 1877–79.[96] This passive stance that the British adopted *vis-à-vis* their 'civilised' White neighbours contrasted strikingly with their aggressive imperial free trading policy. Thus while the British negotiated 'reciprocity treaties' with their European 'contracting partners', they unilaterally imposed 'unequal treaties' throughout the East. Moreover, while the European powers industrialised through tariff protectionism free of British military intervention, many Eastern economies were held down by virtual free trade backed up by the British threat of, and frequent resort to, violence. And there were many other racist double standards too numerous to report here.[97]

Turning now to US hegemony, I begin by noting that American identity, which significantly informs US foreign policy, has been defined through a sense of exceptionalism, endangerment and paranoia that issues the need to maintain eternal vigilance against the non-Western Other.[98] Notably, while American and British

---

[94] But see Augelli and Murphy, *America's Quest*.
[95] Cox, 'Social Forces', pp. 219–23.
[96] J. M. Hobson, 'Two Hegemonies or One? A Historical Sociological Critique of Hegemonic Stability Theory', in P. O'Brien and A. Clesse (eds.), *Two Hegemonies* (London: Ashgate, 2002), pp. 305–25.
[97] See Hobson, *Eastern Origins*, pp. 258–77.
[98] David Campbell, *Writing Security* (Manchester: University of Manchester Press, 1992), chs. 5–6; Richard Slotkin, *Regeneration Through Violence* (Middleton: Wesleyan University Press, 1973).

identities in their respective hegemonic phases have shared many similarities, the American differs in that its fear of the Other is yet more pronounced which, in turn – in an ever-moving show – constantly feeds the US desire for manufacturing new enemies and then containing them in order to maintain American identity. The racist double standards of the US civilising mission abound, whether these be in its uneven-handed free trade policy (as the recent breakdown of the Doha Round talks reveals); or through its wielding of the IMF as a vehicle to help indebted countries but in fact imposing cultural conversion and containment of the East in the debt crisis after 1982 and the Asian financial crisis of 1997; or again in its policies that were imposed on Japan in the 1980s.[99] Moreover, the War on Terror opens up a Pandora's box of racist double standards where, *inter alia*, indiscriminate American bombing and the killing of tens, if not hundreds, of thousands of non-Whites differentiates US foreign policy from 'Islamic terrorism' only in terms of the many more innocent lives that are taken by the former. When will this global nightmare end?

Conclusion. Bringing the world to heal: post-racist emancipatory politics and the dialogical dialectics of civilisations

If Eurocentrism portrays the West as bringing the world to heel, post-racist emancipatory politics seeks to bring the world to heal. How, then, might we begin to imagine this? Post-racist IR singles out analyses of identity-formation and civilis-ational dialogues/dialectics as the first port of call for a global emancipatory politics. The centre-piece of racism as it has been constructed in the West is a repressing of the Other in the Self. It is precisely this that underpins the Eurocentric construction of a line of civilisational apartheid, which creates the illusion of a pure, self-generating, supremacist White Western Self. Accepting the Other in the Self and recognising that the Self is therefore hybrid must be central to the process of global reconciliation.

The second step is, however, much more fraught but all the more pressing nevertheless – namely the creation of a political dialogue between East and West.[100] This can take the form of a counter-hegemonic bloc comprising a rainbow coalition of groups from the West though mainly from the East, which can articulate an alternative discourse to challenge Eurocentric post-racism. Still, there are undoubt-edly many hurdles that stand in its way. These include the not inconsiderable spiritual capital that Westerners have invested in their Eurocentric identity; the economic interests of capital in maintaining post-racist neo-colonialism; and, ironically, those Eastern political elites who embrace Eurocentrism in order to hold on to power. But global reconciliation need not be portrayed as an impossible dawn, for there *is* historical precedent here in the shape of the Eastern nationalist movements that successfully challenged the discourse of empire. And while decolonisation has been succeeded by the imposition of post-racist policies this should not detract from the success of Eastern resistance agency in terminating formal empire. Decolonisation

---

[99] See J. M. Hobson, 'Civilizing the Global Economy: Racism and the Continuity of Anglo-Saxon Imperialism', in Brett Bowden and Leonard Seabrooke (eds.), *Global Standards of Market Civilization* (New York: Routledge, 2006), pp. 60–76.

[100] Mohammed Khatami, *Islam, Liberty, and Development* (Binghamton, NY: Institute of Global Cultural Studies, Binghamton University, 1998).

also provides a crucial precedent given that 'the setting of the sun on the British empire' was always portrayed by the British elites as an impossible dusk. Salutary too is that Nelson Mandela's long walk to freedom would also have appeared prior to its success as a feat too far.

Naeem Inayatullah and David Blaney argue that this political dialogue needs to work on an empathic approach in which both sides appeal to their own experiences of suffering.[101] This needs to be coupled with a major injection of humility in the West, which can be enabled by revealing, and facing up to, the massive moral debt that it owes the East (given that the East did so much to enable the West's rise through both dialogue and sacrifice). In any case, failure to do this is to be complicit with that which went on not just in the past but also in the last fifty years. But alongside these rhetorical manoeuvres, the Eastern and Western spokespersons need to emphasise the contradictions and double standards that underpin contemporary post-racist Western foreign policy. Here they need to engage not simply in dialogue but a *dialogical dialectic* wherein the East prosecutes the unfair and hypocritical practices of the post-racist West in what might be called the 'global court of social justice'. This is not a legal entity, though it is governed like any (formal) court by a certain set of (social) norms that adjudicate over what is right and wrong. The nationalist movements effectively prosecuted the West in the global court of social justice through 'mimetic challenge',[102] or 'rhetorical entrapment',[103] where they rendered empire illegitimate by appealing to Western social norms of justice, since there was no other way of revealing the racist double standards that the West committed in its imperial policies (much as the Black Jacobins had done in the earlier Haitian revolution).[104]

Crucially, if revealing the racism of empire had such powerful import in effecting decolonisation, then why cannot the strategy of revealing post-racism today equally be used to decolonise contemporary neo-colonialism? Thus a counter-hegemonic bloc needs to work within the interstices of Western discourse to reveal the post-racist contradictions and double standards that it consciously and subconsciously smoothes over, in order to demonstrate how the West currently fails to uphold its own self-referential norms of human justice. Appealing only to Eastern norms would most likely be rejected out of hand by the West with no progress forward possible. Indeed, '[f]or the oppressed it is a strategic necessity to address the oppressor in its own language, the language which it knows and understands: indeed the point is to manipulate the self-understanding of the oppressor'.[105] Besides, no court can operate according to conflicting norms. And it is to the West that the East must turn if only because it currently holds disproportionate (though not anthropomorphic) power.

---

[101] Naeem Inayatullah and David L. Blaney, *International Relations and the Problem of Difference* (London: Routledge, 2004).

[102] J. M. Hobson and Leonard Seabrooke, 'Everyday IPE: Decentering the Discipline – Revitalising the Margins', in Hobson and Seabrooke (eds.), *Everyday Politics of the World Economy* (Cambridge: Cambridge University Press, 2007), ch. 1.

[103] Frank Schimmelfennig, 'The Community Trap: Liberal Norms, Rhetorical Action, and the Eastern Enlargement of the European Union', *International Organization*, 55:1 (2001), pp. 47–80.

[104] Daniel Philpott, *Revolutions in Sovereignty* (Princeton, NJ: Princeton University Press, 2001).

[105] Nederveen Pieterse, *Empire and Emancipation*, p. 368; also Said, 'Politics of Knowledge', pp. 30–1.

Still, this dialogical project is one that can simultaneously benefit the West.[106] For as noted, Eurocentrism leads to the repression and sublimation of the Other in the Self. Thus doing away with Eurocentrism can end the sociopsychological angst and alienation that necessarily occurs through such sublimation. Indeed, the ultimate irony is that racist/post-racist Western imperialism has *underdeveloped* the Western Self. And so, hopes for Western emancipation must to an important extent lie with the 'Eastern civilising mission' and the associated 'Black Human's Burden', which can launch the Western peoples on an ethnographic maiden Voyage of Self-Discovery that, with humility, empathy and above all sincerity, steers around the icebergs of tragic self-deception to return fully humanised. In the process, we take one giant leap towards a global dream that exorcises the global nightmare of cycles of war and Western civilising missions – a dream in which the dusk of post-racism brings in its wake the dawn of a new era wherein the peoples of the world can finally sit down at the table of global humanity and communicate together as equal partners.

But in the end none of this is possible until we begin the task of reconstructing world politics – past and present – through alternative critical post-racist imaginings. And at the most fundamental of levels, post-racist IR is founded on two core principles. First, IR's obsession with anarchy/sovereignty, hegemony, or capitalist globalisation serves to obscure the presence of a *post-racial hierarchy* which, entwined with inter-civilisational dialectics and dialogues, forms the racial sinews of power and agency that bind together and generate contemporary global politics/economics. Accordingly, I hope that we can begin the urgent task of breaking the 'norm against noticing' the presence of racism,[107] so as to reveal the operation of the 'invisible colour line' in both IR theory and the practice of world politics, past and present. And second, both Self and Other are not merely interconnected, rather than separate and exclusive, but are intimately entwined. Thus, to critically reflect on Marx's eleventh thesis on Feuerbach, the point is *not* to dispense with interpreting the world *in favour* of changing it, as if the two are mutually exclusive. Rather, the point is to (re)interpret the world *in order* to change it.

In closing, however, I want to counsel against one possible interpretation of this article in which my approach is offered as a 'remedy' to other forms of 'flawed' critical theory, especially Gramscianism and Marxism. For as I signalled earlier, especially outside of IR, Gramscianism and Marxism have undoubtedly gone some way towards producing non-Eurocentric enquiries that speak to many of the themes of my own preferred perspective.[108] Indeed it is not hard to recall the influence of Gramsci on Edward Said, or on the likes of Partha Chatterjee and the Subaltern Studies group.[109] And though within IR Gramscianism has further to go in this

---

[106] See more generally: Ashis Nandy, *The Intimate Enemy* (Delhi: Oxford University Press, 1983); Tzvetan Todorov, *The Conquest of America* (New York: Harper and Row, 1984); Inayatullah and Blaney, *International Relations and the Problem of Difference*.

[107] Robert Vitalis, 'The Graceful and Generous Liberal Gesture: Making Racism Invisible in American International Relations', *Millennium*, 29:2 (2000), pp. 331–56.

[108] For example, Eric Williams, *Capitalism and Slavery* (London: Andre Deutsch, 1944); James, *Black Jacobins*; Eric R. Wolf, *Europe and the People Without History* (Berkeley, CA: University of California Press, 1982); Peter Gran, *Beyond Eurocentrism: A New View of Modern World History* (Syracuse, NY: Syracuse University Press, 1996); S. Hall, 'The Work of Representation', in S. Hall (ed.), *Representation* (London: Sage, 1997), pp. 15–74; Amin, *Eurocentrism*; Malik, *Meaning of Race*.

[109] Partha Chatterjee, *Nationalist Thought and the Colonial World* (London: Zed, 1986); Ranajit Guha, *Subaltern Studies*, vol. I (New Delhi: Oxford University Press, 1982).

regard,[110] nevertheless the recent Gramscian turn towards civilisational analysis – particularly in the works of Cox and Mustapha Pasha for example – speaks to an intensifying common-ground.[111] Moreover, by no means is all feminist CIRT Eurocentric, and the growing affiliations between feminism and postcolonialism are surely to be welcomed even if this thrust has occurred largely outside, or on the margins, of IR.[112] Thus I very much hope that the dialogues that I have spoken about above might be extended further to bridge all these perspectives within and without IR, wherein a collective reinterpretation of the world can enable us to discover a better future for all.

[110] But see Randolph B. Persaud, *Counter-Hegemony and Foreign Policy* (New York: SUNY Press, 2001); David Slater, *Geopolitics and the Post-Colonial* (Oxford: Blackwell, 2004); Adam D. Morton, *Unravelling Gramsci* (London: Pluto, 2007), ch. 3.

[111] Robert W. Cox, 'Civilizations and the Twenty-First Century: Some Theoretical Considerations', *International Relations of the Asia-Pacific*, vol. 1 (2001), pp. 105–30; cf. Pasha, 'Islam'.

[112] Loomba, *Colonialism/Postcolonialism*; Mohanty, ' "Under Western Eyes" Revisited'; Sandra Harding, *Is Science Multicultural?* (Bloomington, IN: Indiana University Press, 1998); but in IR see, for example, Geeta Chowdhry and Sheila Nair (eds.), *Power, Postcolonialism and International Relations* (London: Routledge, 2002); Ling, *Postcolonial International Relations*.

The promise of critical IR, partially kept

CRAIG N. MURPHY

Abstract. The critical turn in IR promised a continuous archeology of the field, an empathetic understanding of those we study, and a social science unwedded to the pursuit of universally valid laws. In the United States, this movement was rooted more in a critique of peace research, than in a critique of the 'NeoNeo' mainstream, to which it became sort of 'official opposition'. The promise has not been fulfilled because the research strategies of critical theorists have rarely given them direct access to the understandings of those outside the privileged core of world society. Other research programmes, including that of the Human Development Reports and of some feminists and ethnographic scholars in IR, have been more successful.

The light through a high stained glass window in Helsinki's National Museum (a masterpiece of the early twentieth-century National Romantic Style) draws eyes upward to three allegorical figures: 'Arkeologi', 'Ethnografi', 'Historia'. They could be images of what the twenty-five year old critical turn in International Relations (IR) promised, and of what has only partially been fulfilled: a continuous archeology *of the field* of IR (a constant critical reflection on how we have built our knowledge, aimed at offering reasonable hypotheses about the interests that we have served), a commitment to a detailed, empathetic understanding of those we study (a methodological commitment that was going out of fashion in the early 1980s), and the willing embrace of a 'social science [that] does not envisage any general or universally valid laws which can be explained by the development of appropriate generally applicable theories', for, as Robert W. Cox reminded us, 'both human nature and the structures of human interaction change, if only very slowly. History is the process of their changing.'[1]

If the stained glass images suggest one part of the promise of critical IR. Their context – part of the superstructure of a building that was a revolutionary act, the work of the organic intellectuals of a colonised people (the Finns, nearing the end of 700 years of foreign rule) – suggests another. This article is about the partial fulfilment of both kinds of promises. It offers one interpretation of what those promises were, and one explanation of why they have been fulfilled only to the extent that they have. I make the argument from a particular perspective, as a critical scholar from the United States, someone who was a graduate student in the late 1970s, trained in the behaviourist tradition of the consciously emancipatory field of peace research.

From that perspective, the key argument that linked Cox and Ashley affirmed the necessity and value of the interpretive or hermeneutic sciences and (for Ashley

---

[1] Robert W. Cox, 'Realism, Positivism, and Historicism (1985)', in Robert W. Cox with Timothy J. Sinclair, *Approaches to World Order* (Cambridge: Cambridge University Press, 1996), p. 53.

117

explicitly, for Cox more implicitly) the possibility of an emancipatory science, one that was 'critical' in Jürgen Habermas's sense.[2] Creating space for that kind of IR knowledge-making in US institutions of higher education quickly became one of the goals for many of us who were convinced by Ashley, Cox, and other pioneers. In this we were, perhaps surprisingly, successful, even if, in the US – unlike in many other parts of the world – critical IR remained on the margin for fifteen or twenty years, a kind of 'official opposition' in the IR canon, while, more recently, it has begun to lose even that status.

Yet, the larger emancipatory goals of critical IR could not be fulfilled just by maintaining a comfortable home within the academy. At our most ambitious, critical IR scholars imagined ourselves becoming organic intellectuals of movements among those victimised or marginalised around the world. Few of us did. Feminist scholars – nurtured within the academic spaces created, in part, by early critical IR – were much more successful. Their greater success should give us pause. So should the even more impressive record of another global intellectual project that began in the early 1980s, the study of 'human development' that originated within the North–South Roundtable and was institutionalised in the United Nations Development Programme (UNDP) through the Human Development Reports (HDRs). Most of the more than 500 such reports have involved the collaboration of a panel of local scholar-activists with progressive non-governmental organisations.

The history of the HDRs and the experience of those critical scholars who have become centrally involved with egalitarian movements suggest the same lesson: students of critical IR who wish to have political impact need to be more loyal to the methodology that defined the movement in the first place. We need to develop greater skills with language, greater understanding of culture and cultural difference, and greater attention to the self-understanding of the world's least advantaged.

Empathetic understanding: linking Ashley and Cox

My hunch is that, in recent years, most students have been taught to see Cox's 1981 article, 'Social Forces, States, and World Orders', and his subsequent (1983) article on Antonio Gramsci's method, as the beginning of contemporary IR's critical tradition.[3] At the time, in many US universities at least, Ashley's 1981 'Political Realism and Human Interests' and his 'Gramscian' 'Three Modes of Economism' (1983) were even more important.[4] They resonated with the works of other scholars who were turning from a positivist approach to understanding the structure of world

[2] Jürgen Habermas, *Knowledge and Human Interests*, trans. Jeremy J. Shapiro (Boston, MA: Beacon Press, 1971).

[3] Robert W. Cox, 'Social Forces, States, and World Orders: Beyond International Relations Theory (1981)' and 'Gramsci, Hegemony, and International Relations: An Essay in Method (1983)', in Cox with Sinclair, *Approaches to World Order*, pp. 85–123. See the account given in Stephen Hobden and Richard Wyn Jones's excellent textbook chapter, 'Marxist Theories of International Relations', in John Baylis and Steve Smith (eds.), *The Globalization of World Politics*, 3rd edn. (Oxford: Oxford University Press, 2005), pp. 235–41.

[4] Richard K. Ashley, 'Political Realism and Human Interests', *International Studies Quarterly*, 25:2 (March 1981), Symposium in Honor of Hans J. Morgenthau, pp. 204–36; Richard K. Ashley, 'Three Modes of Economism', *International Studies Quarterly*, 27:4 (1983), Special Issue: The Economic Foundations of War, pp. 463–96.

politics to one more reliant on the method of empathetic understanding, *Verstehen*, long associated with history, anthropology, and sociology. Some of those moving in Ashley's direction were leading IR scholars from the developing world, including the rational-choice theorist, Partha Chatterjee (now better known for his later, Gramscian studies of nationalism) and Edward E. Azar, one of the leaders in the construction and use of large events datasets.[5] In fact, a *samizdat* edition of Ashley's MIT dissertation,[6] in which he gave preliminary versions of his arguments, circulated among graduate students in a number of the most 'rigorously scientific' of the US graduate departments.

The reasons for this attention to Ashley's arguments were simple. Many of the leading US quantitative IR scholars of the 1970s were involved in an explicitly normative project, peace research, a field that, in the waning years of the US war in Vietnam, had attracted politically committed students to the leading 'scientific' departments. Few in the field would disagree with Ashley's (wordy) statement of our goals:

[T]here exists an enormous but possibly closable gap between two visions of the human condition on a global scale. On the one hand, there is the human condition as it has long existed, now exists, and in all probability, will for long persist ... violence-prone, exploitative, unequal in the distribution of valuables, and environmentally destructive ... [and] the preferred condition ... equality, justice, reproductive social norms interiorizing the actualization of humanity's potential within concepts of individual fulfillment, the free flow of information, and shared consciousness of the intimate interconnections of humanity and nature ... the goal of peace research is to contribute to the closing of the gap between the two visions of the human condition, the actual and the preferred.[7]

To most of us, the contrast with the IR taught in places such as Henry Kissinger's Harvard was clear. The fate of one celebrated article, an empirical analysis by the University of Michigan's J. David Singer of the assertions made about international politics in the Kissinger/Nixon 'State of the World Messages' exemplified all that was wrong with traditional scholarship and its cosy relationship to the powers that be. Although Singer's lucid essay had been written to require no special understanding of mathematics, it was rejected by *Foreign Affairs* as too technical for its readership of policymakers and their Ivy League advisers, a decision that also kept the journal's readers from seeing the wide range of inanities that the government served up as 'expert knowledge.'[8] While, in retrospect, it may seem that Singer's students (and Azar's or Chatterjee's) may have had too little interest in the new theories being promulgated in the late 1970s by likes of Waltz, Nye, or Keohane (some of whom we considered to be scientists *manqué*, even if their politics were not as objectionable as Kissinger's), we were ready to listen to someone like Ashley. He was one of our own – even when he pointed out the contradictions at the centre of our scientific practice. Peace researchers already accepted half of Habermas's critique of positivism

[5] See Partha Chatterjee, *Arms, Alliances, and Stability* (New York: John Wiley, 1975); Edward E. Azar and Thomas N. Havener, 'Discontinuities in the Symbolic Environment: A Problem in Scaling Events', *International Interactions*, 2:4 (1976), pp. 231–46.

[6] Later revised and published as Richard K. Ashley, *The Political Economy of War and Peace: The Sino–Soviet–American Triangle and the Modern Security Problematique* (London: Frances Pinter, 1980).

[7] Ibid., p. 310.

[8] J. David Singer and Melvin Small, 'Foreign Policy Indicators: Predictor of War in History and the State of the World Message', *Policy Sciences*, 5:3 (1975), pp. 271–96.

that Ashley (and other, now less well-remembered) US scholars brought to IR.[9] We recognised that the 'theoretical attitude' of disinterest in our objects of study – justified by the chimera of a clear gap between 'facts' and 'values' – took social science 'into the service of the internalization of norms and thus estranged it from its legitimate task.'[10] We knew that 'theory was always for someone and for some purpose'.[11]

The other part of Habermas's critique was a little more difficult. Recall that he offered the image of a positivist science that transformed the original meaning of 'theory'. The original Greek *theoros* was a foreign representative at the public celebrations of the death and rebirth of a city's gods. By dispassionately looking on, letting the sacred events take hold of him, the theorist allowed his internal *kosmos* to be reordered in harmony with the greater world and gained, through that *mimesis*, a new ethical compass. When he returned home, that *ethos* made his *praxis* unusually valuable to his fellow citizens. Habermas averred:

> ... although the sciences share the concept of theory with the major tradition of philosophy, they destroy its classical claim. They borrow two elements from the philosophical heritage: the methodological meaning of the theoretical attitude and the basic ontological assumption of a structure of the world independent of the knower. On the other hand, however, they have abandoned the connection of *theoria* and *kosmos*, of *mimesis* and the *bios theoretikos* that was assumed from Plato through Husserl. What was once supposed to comprise the practical efficacy of theory has now fallen prey to methodological prohibitions. The concept of theory as a process of cultivation of the person has become apocryphal. Today it appears that the mimetic conformity of the soul to the proportions of the universe, which seemed accessible to contemplation, had only taken theoretical knowledge into the service of the internalization of norms [and so on, as above].[12]

Peace researchers had abandoned the theoretical attitude of purely disinterested contemplation. We also, Ashley argued, needed to abandon the strictest version of the ontological assumption of a world independent of the knower. We needed to accept, as the pre-scientific or 'classical' realists understood, that we shape the world through our understanding.

Some cutting-edge positivist peace research pointed to the same conclusion. 'Peaceful international relations' could not be defined *a priori* in a way that allowed the unproblematic measurement of international events. 'Peace' differed from context to context, from relationship to relationship, and it changed as relationships changed, as Azar's experiments in scaling international events had revealed.[13] Even human attention to self-interest – the assumption that allowed rationalist theorists like Chatterjee to build powerful models rooted in the simple Prisoners' Dilemma (PD) game – turned out to be something that was learned, and could be radically unlearned or reshaped even in the course of playing that simple game, as experiments by MIT's Hayward Alker had demonstrated.[14] To understand the learning that took

---

[9] Craig N. Murphy, 'Understanding IR: Understanding Gramsci', *Review of International Studies*, 24:3 (1998), pp. 417–25 mentions some of these scholars.

[10] Habermas, 'Knowledge and Human Interests: A General Perspective', in his *Knowledge and Human Interests*, p. 304.

[11] Cox, 'Social Forces, States, and World Orders', p. 87.

[12] Ibid.

[13] Azar and Havener, 'Discontinuities in the Symbolic Environment'.

[14] Hayward R. Alker, 'Beneath Tit-for-Tat: The Contest of Political Economy within SPD Protocols', in Hayward R. Alker, *Rediscoveries and Reformulations: Humanistic Methodologies for International Studies* (Cambridge: Cambridge University Press, 1996), pp. 303–31.

place even in one of the simple PD games studied by Alker, or to appreciate the range of 'peaceful international relations' understood by those Azar consulted in attempting to scale international events, required attention to the self-understandings of the participants. We needed to understand the 'fairly tales' (Alker's words) or Gramscian 'myths' deployed by those involved. Moreover, those stories had histories; they changed as the parties interacted.

To serve its emancipatory ends, peace research would have to end its sole reliance on the methods of the sciences 'oriented toward control'. It would have to learn the tools of the second of Habermas's three kinds of science: the historical-hermeneutic sciences, those oriented toward our human interest in 'the preservation and expansion of the intersubjectivity of possible action-orienting mutual understanding.'[15] Our job was to recognise that another kind of *mimesis* – the feeling-with or empathetic understanding of those we studied – was essential both in order to be able to construct full accounts of the reality of global politics and to have any opportunity to work with others to remake our world.

Thus, the first resting point on the march toward critical IR for those who began in Ashley's camp was with the methods of another (older) kind of social science: ethnography, history, the method of *Verstehen*. And, at that point, Ashley met Cox. 'Critical theory', Cox wrote, 'is theory of history in the sense of being concerned not just with the past but with a continuing process of historical change'.[16] The 'historical mode of thought' had generated 'the realist theory of international relations',[17] and it was a mode of thought that Cox, unlike the peace researchers, had never left behind. Michael Brecher, the celebrated positivist analyst of interstate crises and war, recalls that he marched right before Cox at their graduation from McGill, the alphabet putting the university's top student in politics before its top student in history. Cox simply had become more and more sophisticated as he added Ibn Khaldun, to Vico, to Gramsci and Sorel, to the Collingwood he had learned as an undergraduate.[18]

Opening space in the academy

Ironically (and perhaps to Ashley, Cox, and their early admirers, somewhat unexpectedly), the major opponents of critical IR were not found among the peace researchers, including Brecher and Singer, who refused to modify their positivist practice in the wake of the devastating critique. Instead, the challenge was taken up by people who many peace researchers considered Johnny-come-latelies to the idea of a positivist science of International Relations, those on the two sides of the 'Neo–Neo' debate that has dominated IR for almost two decades. *Neorealism and Its Critics*, the 1986 edited volume compiled by the neoliberal champion, Robert O. Keohane,[19] was at the same time an act of remarkable intellectual generosity (promoting Kenneth Waltz's neorealist theory and honouring Ashley's and Cox's

[15] Habermas, 'Knowledge and Human Interests: A General Perspective', p. 310.
[16] Cox, 'Social Forces, States, and World Orders', p. 89.
[17] Ibid., p. 91.
[18] Brecher, personal communication. The first section of Cox with Sinclair, *Approaches to World Order*, explains Cox's trajectory.
[19] Robert O. Keohane (ed.), *Neorealism and Its Critics* (New York: Columbia University Press, 1986).

critiques) as well as a bit of brilliant academic strategy. It defined the (arguably, minor) disagreements between neoliberals and neorealists as the main conflict in the scholarly field, to which Ashley's and Cox's critiques just provided some useful (but, not essential) insight. Meanwhile, the older generation of classical realists and liberal functionalists (whose 'traditional' historical methods often had, Cox argued, the capacity to generate critical theory) were treated as hopelessly *passé*. At the same time, by appearing to 'hold the line' against Ashley's and Cox's critiques of positivism, the Neo–Neos came to don the mantle of 'science' without actually having been granted a right to wear it by the IR scholars who had fashioned it in the first place.

The newly forming band of critical IR scholars recognised the power of the Neo–Neo rhetorical framings, as well as their purpose: the Neo–Neos hoped to eliminate the place in the US academy for the non-positivist research methods embraced by the critical scholars as well by the older generation of realists and liberals. Equally, the Neos were threatening the kind of emancipatory scholarship that critical IR and, before it, peace research, hoped to be.

In the early 1980s, the resulting battles looked like ones that critical IR scholars in the US would lose. The baby-bust cohort had entered college and, unlike in parts of Western Europe, there would be no rapid extension of university education to a larger part of the population to keep enrolments high. There was no Vietnam War and no series of oil crises to spur interest in IR. The undergraduates who today worry about the effect of globalisation on their own job prospects had yet to be born and the *student* interest generated by Reagan's massive military build-up was not that great. For many years, the US IR job market would be tight, and the generally conservative hiring practices of most departments of political science – dominated, as they were, by scholars of American politics who are often a bit confused by the semi-separate world of IR – meant that 'safe' candidates from 'top' departments would be likely to get the few jobs that appeared.

Not surprisingly then, if you look at the top ranked US graduate departments in IR today, you will find few scholars associated with critical IR. (We are more likely to be found in schools that regularly rank as the country's best undergraduate colleges and professional schools of public affairs.) Nevertheless, even if no academic graduate department dominated by critical scholars emerged in the United States, and even if many US IR scholars who received their doctorates in the 1980s found better opportunities in other countries, critical IR did maintain a place in the US academy. It continued as a kind of 'official opposition' to the Neo–Neo mainstream, the role that had been assigned in *Neorealism and Its Critics*. One indicator of this role was the positioning of some critical scholars as part of the 'globalist' approach (as distinct from 'realist' and 'liberal' approaches) in the 1990s editions of Paul Viotti and Mark Kauppi's widely used international relations theory reader.[20] There, as in other places, the heirs of Ashley and Cox (and, more indirectly, of Habermas and Collingwood) were treated as part of a larger group that included Immanuel Wallerstein and that was traced back to Lenin and to J. A. Hobson. This reflected an only slightly more sophisticated version of the 'realist–liberal–Marxist' division that some of us remember from undergraduate IR courses offered at the height of the Cold War.

---

[20] Most recently in Paul R. Viotti and Mark V. Kauppi (eds.), *International Relations Theory*, 3rd edn. (Boston, MA: Allyn and Bacon, 1999).

The space that critical IR maintained in the US academy reflected the success of a number of quite conscious strategies. One was for critical scholars in positions of influence to reach out beyond the methodologies and political issues that defined the original group in order to include other 'dissident' forms of scholarship whose practitioners could make connections to other allies, both intellectual and practical – world-systems scholars, feminists, post-structuralists, postmodernists, and others. 'Dissident' was the label Ashley and R. B. J. Walker gave to wide range of scholarly traditions represented in their 1990 special issue of the International Studies Association's (ISA) lead journal.[21] Other critical scholars came up with different ways to label such aggregates within and across IR's many subfields, for example, 'the New International Political Economy'[22] and 'the New Realism.'[23] The scholars united under such names tended to cooperate within ISA and other organisations to institutionalise new groups of critical scholars by creating new research sections, sponsoring new journals, and supporting each other's members for professional offices and prizes.

Yet, it would be naïve to assume that the maintenance of space for critical IR in the US was solely or even largely a matter of our own agency or that of our closest allies. One especially crucial factor in the US has been the support of our colleagues across the whole range of other IR traditions. IR in the United States is a notoriously provincial field. For example, the largest recent survey of US scholars suggests that only about one in seven of the readings we assign to our beginning students are written by colleagues from outside the US, even though there is some evidence that this is a significant *improvement* over the situation just a decade ago.[24] The same survey indicates that, despite the rise of 'constructivism' to the position of 'official opposition' to the Neo–Neo mainstream in many US textbooks, a kind of undifferentiated 'Marxism' remains in that position on most US syllabi.

Nonetheless, when our US colleagues are asked to name the scholars who have had the greatest impact on the field in the last two decades, only one of the top 25 mentioned (and the only one on the list who is not a US citizen), is a scholar regularly connected to critical IR, Robert W. Cox. When asked about the most interesting work in the field, a feminist, Cynthia Enloe, appears as well. But a much larger group of self-identified US 'constructivists' appear on these lists: Alexander Wendt, Peter Katzenstein, John Ruggie, Michael Barnett, and Martha Finnemore, and their perspective appears poised to move into the position that critical IR once enjoyed.[25]

---

[21] Richard K. Ashley and R. B. J. Walker, 'Speaking the Language of Exile: Dissident Thought in International Studies', *International Studies Quarterly*, 34:2 (1990), pp. 259–68.

[22] The term Roger Tooze and I used to name the traditions represented in Craig N. Murphy and Roger Tooze (eds.), *The New International Political Economy* (Boulder, CO: Lynne Rienner, 1991).

[23] Cox's term, Robert W. Cox (ed.), *The New Realism: Perspectives on Multilateralism and World Order* (London: Macmillan for the United Nations University, 1997).

[24] Calculated from Susan Peterson and Michael J. Tierney with Daniel Maliniak, 'Teaching and Research Practices, Views on the Discipline, and Policy Attitudes of International Relations Faculty in US Colleges and Universities', unpublished paper, College of William and Mary, Williamsburg, VA, August 2005, p. 9. A summary appeared as Susan Peterson and Michael J. Tierney with Daniel Maliniak, 'Inside the Ivory Tower', *Foreign Policy* (November/December 2005), ⟨http://www.foreignpolicy.com/story/cms.php?story_id=3299⟩, accessed 31 August 2006. Compare Alfredo C. Robles, 'How 'International' are International Relations Syllabi?', *PS: Political Science and Politics*, 26:3 (1993), pp. 526–8.

[25] Peterson and Tierney, 'Teaching and Research Practices', pp. 19–21.

Are the critics still relevant to IR?

The same survey reports that most of my US IR colleagues began teaching in the post-baby-bust, post-Cold War, and post-First Gulf War years of the last decade. They are, the results report, deeply influenced by the end of the Cold War and by the events of 11 September 2001 and their aftermath. More anecdotally, many of their aging colleagues worry that so few IR scholars trained in the US over the last decade have much knowledge of, or sympathy with, the ethnographic and historical methods that are an essential part of critical IR. So much of our younger colleagues' time in graduate school appears to have been taken up with learning the relatively simple rationalist models deployed in the Neo–Neo debates, while the elegant mathematics of the most complex applications of game theory required a even greater commitment. In such a milieu, the insights of the most simplistic version of constructivism may appear radical and refreshing: we are social and conscious beings whose intersubjective agreements are accessible, and they matter.

Yet, it is easy to remain satisfied with only that relatively simple insight, and, in doing so, to miss the politics involved in so many human attempts to build shared understanding. As Maja Zehfuss argues, this simplistic

constructivism limits the space for critical thinking. It operates on the possibility of secure origin. If we start with 'reality as it is', we need not worry about the politics of asserting a particular reality. We need not, and indeed cannot, ask about what has already been foreclosed, who has already lost when we claim the authority to speak about reality as if it were obvious.[26]

The original goal of critical IR – and of those from whom it learned, Habermas, Gramsci, and so on – was something different, something that remains valuable. IR was also to be available to those who, at this moment, 'have already lost', those who lack secure origin. It was to be able to understand the political act of *making* something like that as-yet-unknown 'Finland' that the architects of Helsinki's National Museum began to construct in stone and stained glass. It is ironic, confusing, and important that they used the Swedish of the coloniser rather than the vernacular of the Suomi people, a language that few of the elite nationalists spoke. The goal of critical IR was to understand such contradictions, to understand the struggle to work with others to construct a different world through words as well as deeds.

We might expect that the tools needed to do that would be even more cherished today than they were a quarter century ago. They might help us understand the worlds that have had to be reconstructed since the fall of the Soviet Union and to know something of the complexity, the uncertainty, and the pain involved in the cascading, as yet incoherent rejection of neoliberal and US hegemony in the wake of Washington's 'War on Terrorism'.

Yet, it is unclear whether critical IR scholars have done all we could to create space in the US academy for that kind of work, even if our doing so might be exactly what our colleagues would welcome. Back in 1981, Cox wrote about critical theorists being committed to understanding social structures 'from the bottom or from outside in terms of the conflicts which arise within it and open the possibility of its

---

[26] Maja Zehfuss, *Constructivism and International Relations: The Politics of Reality* (Cambridge: Cambridge University Press, 2002), p. 262.

transformation'. Yet, we often attempt to do that without placing ourselves in the life worlds of those who are, indeed, at 'the bottom' or 'outside'. We do not attempt to understand the global political economy in the ways that they do. When students come and ask me for readings that will help them understand and evaluate some of the most prominent manifestations of opposition to hegemonic neoliberalism – the religious movements in every continent that are attempting to build a new world, I have to point them to scholars of development and to comparativists. (Some of my 'critical' students get upset when they realise that some of the most insightful work of that sort has come from conferences sponsored by the World Bank).[27] There is even been very limited attention by critical IR scholars to the details of concrete, *secular* movements in different parts of the world. That limited attention, in part, may have to do with the limited way in which many us have developed our historical and ethnographic skills.

Perhaps this is forgivable. Even if we do not have the skills, we often try to find ways to work with those who do. For example, consider Stephen Gill, one of the most perceptive and creative scholars associated with the critical turn. His early study of Trilateral elites and the contested structure of US-led globalisation relied upon developing his own deep understanding of the intricacies of the worldviews of the hundreds of political and economic leaders that he interviewed. His more recent collaboration with Isabella Bakker on the contested reproduction of the current global order enlisted scholars with the necessary linguistic and cultural skills to help paint a picture from below.[28] Other critical scholars have followed a similar 'UN strategy' of bringing together the work of different area experts,[29] perhaps after being inspired by Cox's complex project on multilateralism conducted for the UN University.[30]

Yet, there is a problem with the strategy. The analyses of those who have direct access to the understandings of those 'at the bottom' or 'outside' get filtered through the worldview of the project leader, almost invariably a privileged, if 'critical', scholar from the North, white, wealthy, Anglophone, and so on. For example, at one point, in a project that I organised on recent egalitarian social movements around the world, one exasperated comparativist complained that my framework was relevant to only one of the many cases, labour in South Korea. Even there, it obscured the nuance of the case, the real contestation that made South Korea's recent history unique.[31]

The alternative, of course, is to place those with the ethnographic skills and the ability to contextualise history in the drivers' seat. So, for example, the 'critical IR'

---

[27] A good summary of the literature appears in Sabina Alkire, 'Religion and Development', in David Alexander Clark, *The Elgar Companion to Development Studies* (Cheltenham: Edward Elgar, 2006), forthcoming. An exemplary article, based on ethnographic work in four countries, is Christopher Candland, 'Faith as Social Capital: Religion and Community Development in Southern Asia', *Policy Sciences*, 33 (Winter 2001), pp. 355–74.

[28] Compare, Stephen Gill, *American Hegemony and the Trilateral Commission* (Cambridge: Cambridge University Press, 1990) and Isabella Bakker and Stephen Gill (eds.), *Power, Reproduction, and Social Reproduction* (Houndmills, Basingstoke: Palgrave Macmillan, 2003).

[29] I tried this strategy in Craig N. Murphy (ed.), *Egalitarian Politics in the Age of Globalization* (Houndmills, Basingstoke: Palgrave Macmillan, 2002).

[30] Its publications included Cox (ed.), *The New Realism*; Stephen Gill (ed.), *Globalization, Democratization, and Multilateralism* (London: Macmillan for United Nations University, 1999), and Michael G. Schechter (ed.), *Future Multilateralism: The Political and Social Framework* (London: Macmillan for United Nations University, 1999).

[31] That experience prepared me to be sympathetic to the critique offered by J. M. Hobson in this issue.

reading list on contemporary East Asia might include William Callahan's *Contingent States*,[32] Christine Chin's *In Service and Servitude*,[33] Dong-Sook Gills and Nicola Piper's *Women and Work in Globalizing Asia*,[34] Lily Ling's *Postcolonial International Relations*,[35] and Katharine Moon's *Sex Among Allies*.[36]

It should be a little disquieting to those who identify with the critical turn in IR that few of the books on that list present themselves as contributing to that tradition despite the connections to critical IR that exist in the intellectual biographies of every one of the authors. The similarly situated authors in Kevin Dunn's *Africa's Challenge to International Relations Theory* tend to be just as silent about their connection to critical IR.[37] Ling sees it as much of a piece with the rest of Western IR theory in its aim to construct a grand narrative that is focused on a self-conscious, active (largely white, largely male) West that operates in a passive, relatively silent (non-white, female) world. Chin, in contrast, sets out a Gramscian framework and uses it discuss the class, ethnic, and gender bases of the state, but she place the analysis provided by the working women she interviewed at the centre of her interpretation of the specific structure of the Malaysian state. Callahan embraces the label 'critical international relations theory' and provides a critique of constructivism that is similar to Zehfuss's, but he is at pains to emphasise the importance of attention to ethnography, to the tools that let us see the multiplicity of actors and the contestation over identity that is at the centre of world politics.[38] Callahan points to the work of two of critical IR's pioneers, Michael J. Shapiro and R. B. J. Walker, as being particularly exemplary in their demonstration of the power of 'ethnographic international relations'.[39]

Similarly, Larry Swatuk, in *Africa's Challenge*, suggests that Cox might understand one of the main lessons that Africa can teach international relations theorists. The lesson is this:

Given Africa's relative economic and military weakness . . . the continent is least capable of withstanding US pressures for adoption of *laissez-faire* style capitalism and liberal democracy . . . [which will produce neither economic growth, political stability, nor justice.] Moreover, America *needs* African failure. To 'know' itself, America must be constructed against an 'other'. Africa's myriad failures, and state-centered explanations of them, help deflect attention from America's own failed [global neoliberal] project.[40]

Yet, in this instance at least, Swatuk's nod to Cox seems a bit ritualised, a sort of critical IR version of the obeisances to Neo–Neo bigwigs that one sometimes finds in

---

[32] William A. Callahan, *Contingent States: Greater China and Transnational Relations* (Minneapolis, MN: University of Minnesota Press, 2004).

[33] Christine B. N. Chin, *In Service and Servitude: Foreign Female Domestic Workers and the Malaysian 'Modernity' Project* (New York: Columbia University Press, 1998).

[34] Dong-Sook S. Gills and Nicola Piper, *Women and Work in Globalizing Asia* (London: Routledge, 2002).

[35] L. H. M. Ling, *Postcolonial International Relations: Conquest and Desire between Asia and the West* (Houndmills, Basingstoke: Palgrave Macmillan, 2001).

[36] Katharine H. S. Moon, *Sex Among Allies: Military Prostitution in US–Korean Relations* (New York: Columbia University Press, 1997).

[37] Kevin C. Dunn and Timothy M. Shaw (eds.), *Africa's Challenge to International Relations Theory* (Houndmills, Basingstoke: Palgrave Macmillan, 2002).

[38] Callahan, *Contingent States*, pp. xxiv–xxv.

[39] Ibid. He highlights Michael J. Shapiro, *Violent Cartographies: Mapping the Cultures of War* (Minneapolis, MN: University of Minnesota Press, 1997), and R. B. J. Walker, *Inside/Outside: International Relations as Political Theory* (Cambridge: Cambridge University Press, 1993).

[40] Larry A. Swatuk, 'The Brothers Grim: Modernity and 'International' Relations in Southern Africa', in Dunn and Shaw, *Africa's Challenge*, p. 175.

the first few paragraphs of articles in *International Organization*. It is possible that holding space in the academy is the *only* thing that critical IR scholars really did for these new practitioners of ethnographic international relations.

Moreover, it is not a coincidence that most of the scholars on the East Asia list are identified with IR's feminists. J. Ann Tickner (correctly) treats Moon and Chin as exemplars of how feminist research practice has answered Robert O. Keohane's challenge to 'feminists to come up with a research program using "scientific methods in the broadest sense".[41] Chin's and Moon's work is rooted in the lived experience of women, addresses concrete problems that their subjects face, and involved a kind of interactive knowledge-making that Tickner sees as emancipatory. Tickner argues that Moon's study of women from prostitution camps near US bases in Korea gave, 'voice to people who were not considered as having anything worthwhile to say ... [giving one opportunity for] them to construct their own identities rather than having them imposed on them by societal norms and taken-for-granted definitions.' Moon and Chin each have helped create space for marginalised women to define themselves in ways that differed from the ways they were being defined by state officials.[42] Tickner's description of recent exemplary feminist research sounds like the fulfillment of the promise that critical IR made in 1981, but Tickner's account suggests that feminist commitments, not the insights of critical IR, are what have allowed that promise to be kept.

Knowledge that contributes to change

Tickner also points to a number of situations in which feminist IR scholars have been directly involved in the egalitarian politics of the last two decades,[43] situations in which they have acted very much like the 'organic intellectuals' that appear in Gramsci's accounts of the politics of his day. No doubt, many in the Neo–Neo mainstream would dismiss most of the cases that Tickner cites, and that could be cited, as the stuff of 'low politics'. Yet, over the last two decades, the targets of successful feminist scholar-activists have ranged from village elders all the way up to members of the UN Security Council. Many accounts of the passage of Resolution 1325, on 'Women, Peace, and Security', include a roster of feminist scholars from around the world. The resolution has had significant impact on UN peace operations and has become an agenda used by women in many countries (including Iraq) to shift the policies of armed groups and occupying powers.[44] That feminist work is, in a sense, the radical parallel to the activities of mainstream Neo–Neo 'ins-and-outers', the scholars who temporarily serve in government, for example, Stephen Krasner heading Policy Planning at the US State Department under George W. Bush or Joseph Nye chairing the National Intelligence Council under Bill Clinton.

[41] J. Ann Tickner, 'What is Your Research Program? Some Feminist Answers to International Relations Methodological Questions', *International Studies Quarterly*, 49:1 (2005), pp. 1–21, at p. 1.
[42] Ibid., p. 12.
[43] Ibid., p. 10.
[44] Carol Cohn, one of the most widely recognised of the first generation of feminist IR scholars, is conducting a major study of the development and impact of 1325. Some preliminary observations appeared in Carol Cohn, 'Feminist Peacemaking', *The Women's Review of Books*, 21:5 (2005), pp. 8–9.

Surprisingly, except for the feminists, few critical scholars seem to play such roles. Cox explains that, in his case:

My life experience does not fit me well for the role of what Gramsci called an 'organic intellectual'. There is no social group with which I feel a special solidarity or identity and to which I owe a preferential consideration ... Yet I am not content merely to analyse the historical process. I also want to put that analysis to service of historical change.[45]

Cox has chosen to make his impact through his writing and his teaching, and, in that sense, his readers and his students make up a group that do receive preferential consideration. In his *Prison Notebooks*, Gramsci sometimes worked back from a periodical to its readership and then to the class, regional, and other characteristics that defined a particular political tendency and linked the journal's authors to a particular group. I am sure it would be possible to do that with any of the scholars associated with critical IR, but that would not be necessary to make the point that many of us have not chosen to pursue life experiences that might link us more closely to the world's least advantaged and, therefore, to their politics.

There are exceptions. William I. Robinson, the Gramscian who is noted for his work on global class formation and the US strategy of promoting limited democracy, has been deeply connected with a various parts of what he calls 'the global justice movement'. He was, for example, the one scholar invited to an unprecedented international congress of trade unions and social movements in Bangkok in 2001 and was active at the 2006 World Social Forum (WSF) in Caracas. Robinson's political engagements predated his academic career by at least a decade, beginning with his undergraduate training in Africa and Central America and his work as a journalist in revolutionary Nicaragua.[46] Similarly, Teivo Teivainen, who has also spent much of his career in the region, works as the director of a virtual institute that aims to become the intellectual centre of the WSF.[47] In addition, there are, of course, other people with comfortable academic positions in the North who have developed a range of organic connections with egalitarian movements around the world, but, like Robinson, Teivainen, Moon, or Chin, most of them have long personal involvement and well-developed ethnographic and linguistic skills.

Perhaps, given the limited skills that any one scholar can develop, critical IR could have done no better at building connections with political movements of those 'outside' or 'at the bottom'. Yet, Teivainen's current project – and scores of conversations with colleagues over half a lifetime, suggests a longing, albeit perhaps a naïve longing, for something more.

A recent paper by Des Gasper suggests that such a hope may not be totally naïve. Gasper focuses on the work of the celebrated economist, Mahbub ul Haq, in

[45] Robert W. Cox, 'Reflections and Transitions', in Cox with Michael G. Schechter, *The Political Economy of a Plural World: Critical Reflections on Power, Morals, and Civilization* (London: Routledge, 2002), p. 37.

[46] William I. Robinson, personal communication, and see his photo website, ⟨http://www.flickr.com/photo/wirobinson⟩, accessed 30 August 2006. Robinson's major books include *Promoting Polyarchy: Globalization, US Intervention, and Hegemony* (Cambridge: Cambridge University Press, 1996) and *A Theory of Global Capitalism: Production, Class, and State in a Transnational World* (Baltimore, MD: The Johns Hopkins University Press, 2004).

[47] The Network Institute for Global Democratization, ⟨http://www.nigd.org⟩, accessed 30 August 2006. Teivainen's contributions to critical IR include: Teivo Teivainen, *Enter Economism, Exit Politics* (London: Zed Books, 2002).

establishing and propagating the complex network that produces the UN-sponsored, but largely independent, *Human Development Reports* (HDRs).[48] The 'human development' concept grew out of the discussions in the 1980s within the North–South Roundtable, an elite intellectual group that was both a bit more global and more prominent, but certainly no larger, than the early community involved with critical IR.[49] Gasper writes that the concept of 'human development' was powerful because it embodied a value-oriented 'way of seeing, a vision, rather than only isolated observations.'[50] Much of the vision originated in the work of the Roundtable's Barbara Ward, one of Haq's teachers.

Perhaps due to my own parochial background, I think that one of the most inspiring versions of the vision appeared in a speech by Bobby Kennedy (someone else Ward inspired) given shortly before his assassination in 1968:

Too much and too long, we seem to have surrendered community excellence and community values in the mere accumulation of material things. Our gross national product . . . if we should judge America by that – counts air pollution and cigarette advertising, and ambulances to clear our highways of carnage. It counts special locks for our doors and the jails for those who break them. It counts the destruction of our redwoods and the loss of our natural wonder in chaotic sprawl. It counts napalm and the cost of a nuclear warhead, and armored cars for police who fight riots in our streets . . . Yet, the gross national product does not allow for the health of our children, the quality of their education, or the joy of their play. It does not include the beauty of our poetry or the strength of our marriages, the intelligence of our public debate or the integrity of our public officials. It measures neither our wit nor our courage; neither our wisdom nor our learning; neither our compassion nor our devotion to our country. It measures everything, in short, except that which makes life worthwhile.[51]

Amartya Sen notes that that this concept is inherently open-ended and that when Haq was able to institutionalise the human development research programme within the UN, he used this open-ended concept to invite collaboration. The concept seemed to demand an ever-expanding network of HDRs, new reports to focus on one or another new dimension, a new side, of the wealth of relationships and current policy choices that determine the degree to which every human being can enjoy a full life – for example, income inequality, poor governance, restrictive gender relations, and over- and under-consumption. This refraction of the core concept into an entire spectrum of relevant policy realms has required the HDR central office constantly to expand the range of experts involved in their production. Each of the new dimensions explored have, in turn, helped maintain the vitality of the larger human development research programme and of the concept itself. Sen summarises Haq's justification for this methodology:

He wanted to build on agreement (what Cass Sunstein, the Chicago legal theorist, calls 'an incompletely theorized agreement'). Such agreements may emerge pragmatically, on quite diverse grounds, after a general recognition that many things are important. Mahbub . . .

[48] Des Gasper, 'Values, Vision, Proposals and Networks: Using Ideas in Leadership for Human Development, The Approach of Mahbub ul Haq', Paper presented at the IDEA Conference, Makerere University, 19–22 July 2006.

[49] Craig N. Murphy, *The United Nations Development Programme: A Better Way?* (Cambridge: Cambridge University Press, 2006), pp. 229, 244.

[50] Gasper, 'Values, Vision, Proposals and Networks', p. 6.

[51] Robert F. Kennedy, speech at the University of Kansas, Lawrence, KS, 18 March 1968. A recording of the excerpt can be found at: ⟨http://www.angelfire.com/pa4/kennedy4/gross.html⟩, accessed 30 August 2006.

told the world: 'Here we have a broad framework; you want something to be included in the list . . . tell us *what*, and explain *why*. We *will* listen.'[52]

An early result of that listening was a decision to support hundreds of local reports – covering continental regions down to neighbourhoods – and not just the annual global report, which was first published in 1990.

Gasper suggests that moving the reports down to the levels at which most concrete political decisions take place had the effect of incorporating the research programme into the practical work of politics, and making it of interest to many different audiences throughout the world.[53] There have also been effective efforts to make the ideas widely accessible: a beloved East African cartoonist-activist, Terry Hirst, put together a widely circulated comic book on the basic theory,[54] secondary school teachers in Argentina sponsored a high-school version of the national report that focused on the social fragmentation after the most recent financial crisis,[55] and the state-level reports in India have become a major tool of opposition politics.[56]

The reports maintain their critical edge partially because Haq originally demanded, and received, scholarly independence for their authors. That arrangement has been maintained by the successive heads of the UN Development Programme. Moreover, most of the reports themselves are written by teams of local experts, often social scientists connected to reformist – and, occasionally, quite radical – social movements, labour unions, or associations of community development organisations. At any one time, than 10,000 analysts, most with organic connections to concrete movements for social change, are working on the reports.[57]

It would be easy to argue that this is a reformist network, ultimately tied into one of the institutional structures of global capitalism, and, therefore, not a model for critical IR scholars concerned with change that is more fundamental. Yet, to do so would miss some of the relevant lessons of the HDR community. They include Gasper's lessons that change-generating knowledge must provide an inspiring vision, but it must also be incorporated into, and come to inform, real struggles, and therefore has to be made accessible to those involved in the struggles at all levels. The lessons also include Sen's point that the framework of that knowledge must be open and subject both to elaboration in new contexts and to fundamental revision. Finally, they include the practical lessons that can be derived from the experience of Mahbub ul Haq's project: the elaboration and application of knowledge will have to be done in the hundreds of contexts, and as many vernaculars, as there are in the real-world struggles over the future of the global political economy.

Is it reasonable to imagine that critical IR could learn these lessons? Maybe not. Our visions, or at least the way we articulate them, have rarely been inspiring to audiences beyond our students. (None of us have had Barbara Ward's capacity with words, or even that of her students!). But perhaps we still can learn to speak to more audiences, and to learn from them, to commit ourselves as deeply to empathetic

[52] Amartya Sen, 'A Decade of Human Development', *Journal of Human Development*, 1:1 (2000), p. 22.
[53] Gasper, 'Values, Vision, Proposals and Networks', p. 6.
[54] Anantha Kumar Duraiappah, Flavio Comim, Davinder Lamba and Terry Hirst, *There is a Better Way! An Introduction to the 'Development as Freedom Approach'* (Nairobi: International Institute for Sustainable Development and the Mazingira Institute, 2003).
[55] *El Dessarrollo Humano en la Argentina del Siglo XXI* (Buenos Aires: UNDP, 2003).
[56] Murphy, *The United Nations Development Programme*, p. 255.
[57] Ibid., p. 259.

understanding of the larger world as we have proven ourselves to be to the archeology of our field and to the rejection of any social science that searches only for universally valid laws.

The difficulty in doing more

Students who are enamoured of critical IR (and who are probably our most valuable critics) often tell me that my 'practical' conclusions always seem to amount to a 'very reformist neo-Gramscianism', one that Antonio Gramsci would have distained. 'Can't committed, internationally-focused scholars do more than rededicate themselves to an empathetic understanding of the larger world?'

To explain my answer, that this is a necessary first step, I sometimes ask students to play a version of the game Victorian children called 'the Emperor of China', but that my students are more likely to know as 'Six Degrees of Kevin Bacon'. I ask, 'How many people would you have to go through to pass a personal message to China's President Hu Jintao? How about President Bush? Bill Gates?'

There is good argument and some empirical evidence that, if our social networks were random, the average number would be six.[58] In fact, in my introductory international relations class, there is usually at least one student who knows someone who knows President Hu and others who are one degree away from Bush and Gates, putting everyone in the class just two degrees away. The numbers may be larger in the classes of many who are reading this article, but the number is unlikely to be as large as six.

Then we play the game with people whose power and material conditions are typical of the world's majority. 'How many people would you have to go through to get to get a similar message to the last woman to be married in the village closest to a point 100 km north of the cathedral in Beira, Mozambique', or, 'the last man to leave the mosque after Friday noon prayer in the Chinese city with the tenth largest Muslim population'. These second chains are much harder to figure out, and they are always much longer: nine, ten, eleven individuals.

Then I ask students to play a second children's game, or just to imagine it: in the front row, three students playing 'Telephone', the student closely connected to President Hu, a student play-acting as her connection in-between, and then one acting as Hu. In the back row, twelve students play the connections between our class and any typical person. The same whispered message is passed down both lines, but the messages received at the other end are frighteningly different.

This is a model of the problem faced by critical IR: given the vastness of the inequalities that exist at a global level, the social worlds of critical IR scholars and those we wish to serve are so disconnected that it would be an incredible arrogance to claim that we could play a role in the transformation of the 'common sense' of the world's most disadvantaged into any sort of radical, Gramscian 'good sense'.[59] With

---

[58] A report of a recent experiment that includes a relevant bibliography is Peter Sheridan Dodds, Roby Muhamad and Duncan J. Watts, 'An Experimental Study of Search in Global Social Networks', *Science*, no. 301 (8 August. 2003), pp. 827–9.

[59] Focusing on these terms, and drawing from a number of places in the *Prison Notebooks*, Enrico Augelli and I outlined what we believed were Gramsci's main insights about intellectual leadership in *America's Quest for Supremacy and the Third World* (London: Pinter, 1988), pp. 16–25.

very few exceptions, we are all like Cox; there is no social group of the world's least advantaged with which we have any particularly close connection; it is very unlikely that we understand much at all about their life-worlds, self-understanding, or struggles.

It may be useful to think about the contrast between our situation and that of those early, globalist 'organic intellectuals' Karl Marx and Frederick Engels. They probably did stand fewer than six degrees away from most of the workingmen [sic] organising in the factories and mines in the smaller world in which they were a part. August Nimtz begins his discussion of these 'Prototypical Transnational Actors' with Engels's account of his daily reading in 1895:

I have to follow the movement in five large and a lot of small countries and the U.S. America. For that purpose I receive 3 German, 2 English, 1 Italian *dailies* and from Jan. 1, the Vienna daily, 7 in all. Of *weeklies* I receive 2 from Germany, 7 from Austria, 1 France, 3 America (2 English, 1 German), 2 Italian, and 1 each in Polish, Bulgarian, Spanish and Bohemian, three of which in languages I am still gradually acquiring.[60]

Engels was probably more linguistically skilled and was, perhaps, a more voracious reader than most critical IR scholars are, but there are other differences, as well. There is the matter of modesty: Francis Wheen's careful reading of the minute books of the International Workingmen's Association gives us a picture of 'indisputably . . . bourgeois intellectual[s]' who believed that they 'still had much to offer the association as long as they didn't pull rank or hog the limelight'.[61] Most importantly, there is the existence of concrete movements responding to similar situations (the transformation of working life by industrial capitalism) using similar tools (withdrawing work, fighting for representative democracy) in many sites across much of western and central Europe and a part of North America. The multiple (local) movements created the political space in which the transnational intellectual leaders had something to offer; it was not Marx and Engels who created those movements.

There is no single, global movement of the dispossessed fighting for the whole range of issues of concern to critical IR, no movement promoting Ashley's unpoetic, 'equality, justice, reproductive social norms interiorizing the actualization of humanity's potential within concepts of individual fulfillment, the free flow of information, and shared consciousness of the intimate interconnections of humanity and nature'. There are multiple movements in specific places. That is why the closest approximations to Marx and Engels that can be found in the Western academy today are scholars whose ethnographic research puts them in continuous and direct contact with a few of the social movements of the least advantaged in parts of the developing world. This is exactly why we should cherish such scholars, and expand their numbers.

I deeply admire the modesty and realism that leads Robert Cox to see himself as 'an observer, not a representative' who, nonetheless, can contribute critical 'analysis to the service of historical change'. The 'UN strategy' of his studies of the future of global governance provided significant space for such to-be-cherished scholars simply because they were the only ones in a position to inform Cox's own analysis of the

---

[60] Frederick Engels quoted in August Nimtz, 'Marx and Engels: The Prototypical Transnational Actors', in Sanjeev Khagram, James V. Riker and Kathryn Sikkink (eds.), *Restructuring World Politics: Transnational Social Movements, Networks, and Norms* (Minneapolis, MN: University of Minnesota Press, 2002), p. 245.

[61] Francis Wheen, *Karl Marx* (London: Fourth Estate, 1999), pp. 278–81.

possible 'social basis for an alternative social order';[62] they reduced the number of distorting 'Telephone' connections between Cox and those from whom he needed to learn.

The spaces for such scholars exist not only within our research projects, but also within our departments, our syllabi, our journals, and our professional associations. Making sure that they come to occupy such positions is a fundamental task for critical IR, one essential to our political as well as our analytical ends.

---

[62] Cox, 'Reflections and Transitions', p. 37.

Towards a sociology of global morals with an 'emancipatory intent'

ANDREW LINKLATER*

Abstract. First generation Frankfurt School critical theorists argued that global solidarity was possible because human beings have similar vulnerabilities to mental and physical suffering. This approach to solidarity remains significant for any discussion of the ethical aspirations of critical theory. It also has ramifications for efforts to develop a sociological approach to global moral codes which is influenced by the idea of an emancipatory social theory. Informed by certain themes which were developed by Simone Weil, this article draws on the writings of Fromm, Horkheimer, Adorno and Elias to consider how a sociology of international moral codes can be developed. One of the aims of this project is to consider how far global moralities have developed forms of solidarity around the recognition of shared vulnerabilities to mental and physical suffering which are part of the species' biological legacy.

Numerous thinkers have denied that the idea of shared humanity can provide the philosophical foundations for a cosmopolitan ethic, and many have rejected the belief that appeals to humanity will ever compete with the emotional attachments and the established norms of specific communities in determining human conduct.[1] But the idea that common humanity has profound ethical significance is not entirely friendless in recent moral and political theory. Gaita has drawn on Simone Weil's writings to defend an ethic of human concerns which is, in some respects, more fundamental than the social moralities which usually shape individual and group behaviour.[2] The central aim of this article is to link this idea with the notion of a sociology of global morals with an emancipatory intent. The principal objective is to build on previous endeavours to construct a mode of comparative sociological analysis that examines the extent to which basic considerations of humanity have influenced the conduct of international relations in different historical eras and may yet acquire a central role in bringing unprecedented levels of global connectedness under collective moral and political control.

The article begins by summarising Weil's thesis, noting that it raises significant problems for 'communitarian' arguments which deny that representative moral

---

* I am grateful to Toni Erskine, Stephen Mennell and Richard Shapcott for their comments on an earlier draft of this article.
[1] See David Hume's that 'there is no such passion in human minds, as the love of mankind, merely as such', in *A Treatise of Human Nature* (Harmondsworth: Penguin, 1969), p. 533, and the reservations about cosmopolitan motivation in Michael Walzer, 'Spheres of Affection', in Martha Nussbaum, *For Love of Country?* (Boston, MA: Beacon Press, 2002).
[2] Raimond Gaita, *A Common Humanity: Thinking about Love and Truth and Justice* (London: Routledge, 2002).

agents are motivated to act from considerations of humanity. The key contention is that Weil identifies certain humanist dispositions, which have probably existed to some degree in all or most times and places, and which have long contained the possibility of radically enlarging the moral and political boundaries of community. The second section identifies affinities between Weil's doctrine of humanity and critical-theoretical claims that common vulnerabilities to mental and physical suffering provide the most secure foundation for solidarity between strangers. This position has special significance for the task of reconstructing historical materialism and redirecting the course of the critical theory of society. Developing this theme, sections three and four consider the implications of these remarks for a sociology of global morals which analyses the extent to which the most basic forms of human solidarity have influenced international relations in different eras and may yet prove to be decisive in shaping the evolution of the species as a whole.

Universalisable sympathies

Weil maintained that a person stranded in the desert, but possessing ample water, would normally be expected to assist a stranger who was facing death because of thirst. Most moral agents, Weil observed, would assume that considerations of humanity would make rescue 'automatic'; in the circumstances, there would be no request for an explanation of the decision to assist. By contrast, most observers would think an explanation was called for, 'if having enough water in his canteen (the potential rescuer) simply walked past, ignoring the other person's pleas'.[3]

Weil maintained that the obligation to assist reflected a belief that the dignity of other persons can only be respected through efforts to deal with 'earthly needs'; and on this matter, she proceeded to argue, 'the human conscience has never varied'.[4] The extent to which her theologically-grounded empirical claims about human responsiveness to threats to survival can be generalised across human history is an interesting question. It seems reasonable to suppose that the anthropological record reveals great cultural variations with respect to ethical commitments to 'Good Samaritanism'; it may also show that displays of solidarity towards the members of other communities have often been actively discouraged or regarded as morally reprehensible or judged to warrant severe punishment. In many societies, persons in the circumstances which Weil described may have ignored the plight of strangers on the grounds that their ethnicity, colour, enemy status, sacrilegious beliefs or whatever condemned them to perish. But it will have been noted that Weil did not insist that humanitarian assistance will always be automatic in the desperate conditions she described, or believe that other social actors must always be so astonished by the

---

[3] See Raimond Gaita, 'Critical Notice', *Philosophical Investigations*, 17 (1994), pp. 616ff, and the discussion in Gaita, *Common Humanity*. Similar sentiments are present in the claim that: 'To no matter whom the question may be put in general terms, nobody is of the opinion that any man is innocent if, possessing food himself in abundance and finding someone on his doorstep three parts dead from hunger, he brushes past without giving him anything'. See Simone Weil, *The Need for Roots: Prelude to a Declaration of Duties Towards Mankind* (London: Routledge and Kegan Paul, 1952), p. 6.

[4] Weil, *Need for Roots*, p. 6 where she describes this obligation as 'eternal'.

failure to assist as to feel compelled to request an explanation. But if help has been virtually automatic or widespread in various encounters with 'outsiders' over the millennia, and if failures to assist have often led to bemusement, astonishment, indignation or disgust, then rather more might be said for the ethical importance of considerations of humanity than the critics have recognised.

Weil's argument can be modified in ways that consolidate her claims about the most basic forms of solidarity between strangers. One might ask if it would not seem odd if a person who is facing death because of a lack of water failed to ask or implore a passing stranger to help on the grounds of the invisible ties of common humanity. Here one must also allow for important exceptions. In some societies, such pleas may be regarded as violating cherished social norms, as bringing dishonour to the group, as risking cultural pollution or some such thing. Unbroken traditions of hostility and warfare may often have led to decisions not to place the self at the mercy of an alien other. In such circumstances, the decision to withhold the request for assistance may not prompt requests for an explanation.

Scepticism about the motivational power of common humanity is weakened significantly if at least some human beings in different historical eras have thought it was right to help a stranger in the circumstances described, if others have endorsed their course of action, and if they have sanctioned the failure to rescue. Distrust of the ties of humanity is dented if certain basic forms of solidarity with the suffering led at least some moral agents to assist others more or less automatically in different historical eras. Empirical evidence of levels of attachment to Good Samaritanism over time is unavailable, but it does not seem preposterous to speculate that complete strangers have been compelled to act by the ties of humanity in very different times and places. If this is right, and as already noted, then there is more to be said for the ethical significance of shared humanity than 'communitarian' objections to cosmopolitanism have allowed.

Weil's thesis raises several interesting claims about moral agency if it is the case that certain sympathies have been extended to strangers in the circumstances described in many historical epochs. First, the potential rescuer and the endangered do not have to belong to the same moral and political community to participate in the imagined ethical encounter. Second, the ethical exchange does not presuppose the capacity to communicate in the same spoken language. These points will be extended in a moment but, before doing so, it is important to stress what the encounter does presume, namely the existence of universally intelligible expressions and gestures, and a shared emotional vocabulary, which make it possible for the members of radically different groups to communicate distress to each other and to respond sympathetically. Given the significance of emotions such as empathy and sympathy for solidarity between strangers, it is worth pausing to note that, from Darwin to Ekman, analysts of the role of emotions in human behaviour have argued that all human beings possess a similar repertoire of facial expressions denoting fear, anger, joy, distress *et cetera* which ensure intelligibility between groups which are otherwise separated by differences of language and culture.[5] Various debates surround the question of whether, or how far, basic emotions such as fear are 'hard-wired', but Weil's argument which assumes that certain emotional responses to suffering will be

---

[5] Paul Ekman, *Emotions Revealed: Understanding Face and Feelings* (London: Weidenfeld and Nicholson, 2003), ch. 1.

automatic invites consideration of the claim that certain ethical potentialities have long been immanent within a universal vocabulary of moral emotions.[6]

The ability to communicate distress to another, and capacity to recognise suffering, are clearly essential if the Weilian 'primordial' ethical encounter is to occur, but they are not sufficient conditions. A complete explanation must include references to the rudimentary emotions of empathy and sympathy, emotions which can be usefully linked with Bentham's thesis about the centrality of sentience for the moral life. In a famous passage on the grounds for being moved by animal suffering, Bentham maintained that the central question is not whether the animal can speak or reason but whether it can feel pain and has the capacity for suffering. Sympathy for sentient creatures which are all condemned to feel pain and to suffer to some degree was at the heart of morality in Bentham's judgment.[7]

Just as the decision to assist a non-human animal does not assume the equality of human and non-human species, so the decision to help a stranger from another social group need not rest on a doctrine of the equality of all persons – or rather it need only recognise their equality to a very limited extent. Pragmatic considerations which have little or no place for a doctrine of equal rights can be the spur behind assistance; but if the 'Weil thesis' is right, there is often more to help than simple prudential calculations.[8] The main point to make is that the bonds and attachments between strangers may rest entirely on the almost universal experience of being similar to, but not necessarily equal with (or identical to) others, and in being exposed as part of one's biological heritage to similar vulnerabilities to mental and physical suffering. It is striking that some of the earliest formulations of the defence of cosmopolitanism in Western moral and political theory grounded the perspective in such universal vulnerabilities of the body.[9] This is hardly extraordinary given that mutual recognition of shared mental and physical vulnerability provides the most readily available means of projecting forms of solidarity across the boundaries of established communities – and across the boundaries that are deemed to exist between human and non-human forms of life.

It was noted earlier that the strangers in the 'Weilian condition' need not belong to the same community or speak the same language before they can engage in crucial moral encounters. One might extend the point by adding that no sophisticated 'labour of translation' is required to steer agents towards a Gadamerian fusion of ethical horizons.[10] Nor is any great process of societal rationalisation needed in which cultures transcend egocentric or parochial world-views and embrace highly abstract, post-conventional ethical dispositions – even though it is the case that transcendent religious perspectives have often been the social force that has led human beings to

---

[6] In *Upheavals of Thought: The Intelligence of Emotions* (Cambridge: Cambridge University Press, 2001), p. 169, Martha Nussbaum maintains that 'biology and common circumstances ... make it extremely unlikely that the emotional repertoires of two societies will be entirely opaque to one another'.

[7] Jeremy Bentham, *The Principles of Morals and Legislation* (Darien, CT: Hafner), pp. 311ff.

[8] Gaita, *Common Humanity*, p. 276 notes that a slave-owner might assist a slave in desperate circumstances, but in this case assistance does not rest on a doctrine of equal rights. The desire to protect another slave-owners' property, rather than human solidarity, may prompt an act of rescue.

[9] See H. C. Baldry, *The Unity of Mankind in Greek Thought* (Cambridge: Cambridge University Press, 1965), pp. 45ff.

[10] The idea of a form of universality that requires a complex labour of translation can be found in Judith Butler, 'Universality in Culture', in Nussbaum, *Love of Country*.

project relations of sympathy beyond in-groups.[11] As already noted, the precondi-
tions of the ethical encounter described above include certain emotional and
expressive capacities which revolve around mutually intelligible concerns about the
vulnerabilities of the body. Some such reference to inherent capacities which can bind
strangers together has a distinguished presence in the history of Western moral and
political thought. It is evident in Aristotle's claim that 'there is ... a general idea of
just and unjust in accordance with nature, as all in a manner divine, even if there are
neither communications nor agreement between them'.[12] The capacity for feeling pity
for others, he argued, stems from the agent's fears for his or her personal well-being,
a position which was defended by Adam Smith with the correct proviso that the root
of the capacity to sympathise with others is, at one and the same time, often the
reason for decisions to place the satisfaction of one's relatively minor interests before
the welfare of others.[13]

Aristotle's observations about certain intuitive understandings about justice that
can bind persons who have neither communicated with each other nor entered into
a previous pact, resonate with the claims made earlier about the most elementary
forms of human solidarity. The emphasis here is on how the vulnerabilities of the
person and the emotions such as sympathy which can be woven around them –
sensitivities which have existed to some degree in all ways of life – create the
possibility of 'embodied cosmopolitanism', that is the potentiality for extending
rights of moral consideration to all other human beings, and indeed to all creatures
that are sentient.[14] The emphasis is on the *potentialities* which arise from corporeality
or embodiment since, of course, rather more than recognition of this biological legacy
must be in place to convert mere possibilities into binding social practices.

We shall come back to the question of the factors which can intercede between
certain basic universal experiences and the structure of moral codes, but some prior
remarks about empathy and sympathy may be useful to capture the essential point.
As Smith emphasised, certain empathetic dispositions which are based on anxieties
about one's own welfare do not guarantee the development of sympathy for others.[15]
Empathy can make it easier for the torturer to estimate the victim's likely
breaking-point, and it may lead to the voyeuristic enjoyment of media spectacles of
distant suffering. Sympathy, which all societies must endeavour to inculcate in their
members to some degree, has almost always been largely confined to members of the
same 'survival group'.[16] Almost all social moralities have revolved around insider–
outsider distinctions that devalued the suffering of distant strangers and even
attached positive value to it. In such conditions, help for 'distant strangers' has not

---

[11] For Occidental rationalism and societial rationalisation, see Jurgen Habermas, *The Theory of Communicative Action*, vol. 1: *Reason and the Rationalisation of Society* (Boston, MA: Beacon Press, 1984).

[12] Aristotle, *The 'Art' of Rhetoric* (London: William Heinemann, 1959), Book 1.13.

[13] Adam Smith, *Theory of Moral Sentiments* (Indianapolis, IN: Liberty Fund, 1982), p. 9.

[14] See my 'Distant Suffering and Cosmopolitan Obligations', *International Politics*, 44:1 (2007), pp. 19–36.

[15] Adam Smith, *Moral Sentiments*, pp. 136–7 maintains that a person may be unable to sleep at night knowing that his or her small finger will be removed the following day, but the same person will sleep peacefully even though s/he knows that countless distant strangers face the most awful calamities – presuming, Smith added, that the person 'never sees them'. For further reflections on these matters, see my *Distant Suffering*.

[16] Or sympathy has been confined to some members of the survival group where forms of stigmatisation blocked its universal expression within the same society.

been 'automatic'. Aristotle observed that a person is more likely to pity another when the victim 'does not deserve it', when the 'evil' involved is of the kind that might afflict oneself or a friend and, crucially, when it 'seems near'.[17] As noted earlier, Smith made a similar point about the unequal moral significance of proximate and distant suffering. Such realities complicate but they do not undermine the claim that certain potentialities for supporting embodied cosmopolitanism have existed in all societies, and may have been realised from time to time, albeit fleetingly and exceptionally, in the relations between very different social groups. The interesting question for a sociology of morals is what has determined whether or not these potentialities have been realised, and what has decided how far cosmopolitan sympathies have influenced international relations.

Solidarity and suffering

Largely neglected sociological questions are raised by these observations about the sources and channels of human sympathy, questions which are directly linked with puzzles about the processes affecting 'the expansion and contraction of the boundaries of community', levels of 'emotional identification' between different societies and the 'scope of moral concern' in international states-systems. These matters have special significance for a mode of sociological investigation which is infused with the normative purposes associated with the Frankfurt School. In particular, they suggest new directions for a critical sociology of world politics with an emancipatory intent. To explain this point more fully, it is necessary to consider how notions of sympathy and compassion have been central to forms of ethical reasoning that challenge Kantian understandings of the relationship between reason and morality of the kind that inform Habermas's conception of critical social theory. It is especially important to consider the rather different approach to ethical reasoning which was advanced by early Frankfurt School reflections on suffering and solidarity; and it is also essential to show how these themes provide a new agenda for critical international theory, one that regards the prevalent attitudes to harm, suffering and vulnerability, and the dominant dispositions to cruelty and compassion, in different international states-systems as the principal object of sociological inquiry.

The starting point for this stage in the discussion is that the capacity to acquire sympathies which can be extended to distant persons is universal; this potentiality to extend 'the scope of moral concern' can be regarded as a 'species-power' which is immanent in most if not all social systems. A link can be forged between this contention and the philosophical claim that sympathy belongs among the more 'primitive' moral emotions, a proposition that does not regard sympathy as a natural endowment or as a biological trait but which contends that it is irreducible to more fundamental ethical dispositions. In deliberations of this kind, attention frequently turns to Wittgenstein's remarks on an 'attitude to a soul' which stressed forms of human recognition which have to be instilled in the course of early, routine socialisation processes before more complex ethical dispositions and relationships

---

[17] Aristotle, *Rhetoric*, Book II. Section 8. and Aristotle, *Poetics* (Harmondsworth: Penguin, 1995), Sections 7.2 and 7.4.

can develop.[18] Primitiveness in this context refers to the first stages in human moral development in which children are taught that other persons are independent centres of feeling and experience who can be made to suffer and be harmed in other ways by their actions.[19] Inculcating this awareness of sentience and recognition of the causal and possibly harmful effects of actions on other sentient creatures is essential to develop respect for the principles of moral responsibility which are intrinsic to every social group. The capacities for empathising with others, and for developing the separate but related moral ability to sympathise with suffering others, are the foundations on which all moral codes rest.

Schopenhauer, whose influence on Horkheimer will be considered later, placed these attitudes towards the soul at the heart of his ethical system, as is evident from an intriguing passage in his writings which reflects on the report of a mother who murdered one child by pouring boiling oil down its throat, and another by burying it alive. In the course of analysing the reasons for regarding such behaviour as despicable, he maintained that feelings of revulsion are not a response to the mother's failure to be deterred by the thought of divine sanctions, or to the astonishing disregard for the categorical imperative, but to the fundamental cruelty of the deed and the complete absence of compassion. The steeper the gradient between self and other, Schopenhauer added, the more reprehensible such acts are generally regarded.[20] His reflections on such matters did not consider how the 'gradient between self and other' has changed over history or varies in relations between members of the same society as a result of the dominant forms of inclusion and exclusion.[21] Clearly, there are sharp differences in the level of emotional identification between persons, and in the gradient between self and other, in the same society and indeed in the whole history of human societies. Notwithstanding these realities, his emphasis on the ethical significance of revulsion towards certain acts of cruelty, and on the lack of compassion, drew attention to dimensions of the moral code and related emotions which are almost certainly present in all functioning social systems.

Schopenhauer was a forceful critic of what has been regarded as Kant's excessive rationalism which denied that ethical principles can be grounded in the moral emotions. Philosophical inquiries into the relationship between ethics and the emotions are not the subject of this article although it is useful to pause to recall Kant's advice that moral agents should not strive to avoid sites of evident suffering. Direct encounters with suffering were vital, Kant argued, if agents were to develop moral sensibilities and inclinations which would lead them to do what reason required but might not always accomplish on its own.[22] The core issue here is the

---

[18] Ludwig Wittgenstein, *Philosophical Investigations* (Oxford: Basil Blackwell, 1974), Part II, Section 4. See also the discussion in Gaita, *Common Humanity*, pp. 259ff.

[19] Paul L. Harris, *Children and Emotion: The Development of Psychological Understanding* (Oxford: Blackwell, 1989), and Craig Taylor, *Sympathy: A Philosophical Analysis* (London: Routledge, 2004), p. 3.

[20] Arthur Schopenhauer, *On The Basis of Morality* (Oxford: Berghahn, 1995), p. 169 and pp. 204–5.

[21] These were crucial themes in the writings of Norbert Elias. For a summary of their significance for International Relations, see my 'Norbert Elias, the "Civilizing Process" and International Relations', *International Politics*, 41 (2004), pp. 3–35.

[22] Kant denied that an ethic could be grounded in the emotions, and indeed he expressed a preference for 'cold-blooded goodness' over the 'warmth of affection' precisely because the former was 'more reliable'. See Anthony Cunningham, *The Heart of What Matters: The Role for Literature in Moral Philosophy* (Berkeley, CA: University of California Press, 2001), p. 222. Justin Oakley, *Morality and the Emotions* (London: Routledge 1992), pp. 109ff, stresses that recent Kantians have been less

nature of ethical motivation. As various analyses of moral codes and the emotional life have revealed, compliance with social norms depends crucially on how far key principles are embodied in the emotional lives of moral agents and have the force of 'second nature'. None of these accounts denies the importance of the fear of external sanctions for agent conformity with moral codes. What all highlight in addition is the role of psychological factors such as experienced or anticipatory shame or guilt, and feelings of indignation, shock, disgust and so forth, in creating harmony between agents' engrained dispositions and the 'external' demands of moral systems. The gap between agent and structure is bridged (but not always successfully) to the extent that ethical responses are embodied and almost instinctive – that is, to the extent that the configuration of emotions and constitution of impulses make agent compliance with social principles virtually automatic.[23]

Mainstream and critical investigations of world politics are largely guilty of neglecting the psychological and emotional dimensions of social conduct and moral interaction.[24] These elements of human behaviour were central preoccupations of Freudian-influenced Frankfurt School theory, and they were also critical to how analysts such as Erich Fromm (an associate of the Frankfurt School of Psychoanalysis which existed alongside the Institute of Social Research) envisaged combining psychological and materialist approaches to the study of society and history (see below, p. 147).[25] For the purpose of stressing how far Frankfurt School critical theory – and related perspectives in the interwar period – moved the psychological and emotional features of human existence to the forefront of sociological analysis, it is important to recall Schopenhauer's distinctive influence on Horkheimer's reflections on solidarity and suffering, and also the place of the idea of 'injurability' in Adorno's ethical reflections on how modern societies should choose between forms of life. All of these preoccupations, it should be added, preserved core elements in Marx's critique of Hegelian idealism, and most obviously his claim that social investigation should start with concrete human beings or embodied selves which are required to satisfy basic biological needs which remind them of their origins in, and continuing membership of, the natural world. These emphases in Frankfurt School theory are central for the purposes of this article not only because they anticipated the recent sociological interest in the body,[26] but also because they foreshadowed parallel efforts to make vulnerability and frailty central to the defence of human rights.[27]

---

cautious about emotions such as compassion because of their importance for developing a sense of 'connectedness' with other persons. Not that this theme was wholly alien to Kant, as we have seen. Exposure to the poor, the sick and imprisoned could produce 'the pain of compassion', an impulse which had been created by Nature 'for effecting what the representation of duty might not accomplish by itself' (quoted in Cunningham, *Heart of What Matters*, p. 77 and p. 213).

[23] See Jack Barbalet, 'Introduction: Why Emotions are Crucial' in Jack Barbalet (ed.), *Emotions and Sociology* (Oxford: Blackwell, 2002). Interesting issues are raised here about how the emotions mark the point where the 'cultural' and the 'somatic' intersect. See Rom Harre and W. Gerrod Parrott, (eds.), *The Emotions: Social, Cultural and Biological Dimensions* (London: Sage, 1996), Introduction.

[24] Neta Crawford, 'The Passions of World Politics: Propositions on Emotions and Emotional Relationships', *International Security*, 24 (2001), pp. 116–56.

[25] Rolf Wiggershaus, *The Frankfurt School: Its History, Theories and Political Significance* (Oxford: Polity, 1993), p. 54.

[26] Embodiment was central to Elias's analysis of the civilising process which was first set out in the 1930s. Its significance for the Frankfurt School and for the critical sociology of world politics is considered on pp. 147ff.

[27] Bryan S. Turner, 'Outline of a Theory of Human Rights', *Sociology*, 27 (1993), pp 489–512.

First generation Frankfurt School theorists anticipated this last theme by insisting that the critical study of society has a responsibility 'to lend a voice to suffering' (this being a 'condition of all truth') and to 'abolish existing misery'.[28] In a parallel with Weil's thesis, Horkheimer argued that 'human solidarity' is best grounded in the 'shared experience of suffering and creaturely finitude'. Schopenhauer's worldly moral theory was a major influence on his attempt to unite 'materialism and morality'.[29] Similar commitments are evident in Horkheimer's claim that the foundation of 'correct solidarity' lies in the fact that human beings are 'finite beings whose community consists of fear of death and suffering' and who can sympathise with each others' 'struggle to improve and lengthen the life of all'.[30] Adorno's contention that the Holocaust demanded the ethical affirmation of the rights of the 'injurable animal' to receive protection and support defended broadly similar themes.[31] A 'new categorical imperative' was required in his view to ensure that the brutalities of the extermination camps did not occur again.[32] The new imperative would focus on absolute prohibitions rather than on the quest to realise some conception of the good life. Human beings, Adorno argued, 'may not know' what counts as the 'absolute good', but they have reached some shared understandings about 'inhuman' behaviour and about conceptions of the 'bad life' which should be resisted and opposed.[33]

[28] See respectively Theodor Adorno, *Negative Dialectics* (London: Routledge, 1990), pp. 17–18, and Max Horkheimer, 'Materialism and Morality', in Max Horkheimer, *Between Philosophy and Social Science: Selected Early Writings* (Cambridge: MIT Press, 1993), p. 32.

[29] See Seyla Benhabib et al. (eds.), *On Max Horkheimer: New Perspectives* (Cambridge: MIT Press, 1993), p. 5, and Stephen. E. Bronner, *Of Critical Theory and its Theorists* (Oxford: Blackwell, 1994), pp. 332–5 on the importance of such themes in Frankfurt School theory more generally.

[30] Horkheimer, quoted in Peter M. Stirk, *Max Horkheimer: A New Interpretation* (Hemel Hempstead: Harvester Wheatsheaf, 1992), p. 178. Vulnerability did not merely underpin solidarity with 'the community of men lost in the universe' – see Max Horkheimer, 'Schopenhauer Today' in Max Horkheimer, *Critique of Instrumental Reason* (New York: Seabury 1974), p. 75. Schopenhauer's defence of a post-anthropocentric ethic was reflected in Horkheimer's additional claim that the idea of vulnerability should underpin compassion for all sentient creatures and 'solidarity with life in general' (Horkheimer, *Materialism*, p. 36; see also Schopenhauer, *Basis of Morality*, pp. 175ff). For broadly similar views, see Adorno, *Problems*, p. 145 on the insights that can be learnt from Schopenhauer's 'crankiness'.

[31] The expression is used by J. M. Bernstein in 'After Auschwitz: Trauma and the Grammar of Ethics', in Robert Fine and Charles Turner (eds.), *Social Theory after the Holocaust* (Liverpool: Liverpool University Press, 2000), p. 122.

[32] See J. M. Bernstein, *Adorno: Disenchantment and Ethics* (Cambridge: Cambridge University Press, 2002), ch. 8.

[33] Theodor Adorno, *Problems of Moral Philosophy* (Cambridge: Polity, 2000), pp. 167ff. Whether Adorno overwrote this ethical argument is a question that goes beyond this discussion. Suffice it to add that his comments about an ethic which starts with the conditions of frailty and vulnerability find sympathy in many different areas of philosophical analysis. For comments on parallel themes in recent moral and political theory, see my 'The Harm Principle and Global Ethics', *Global Society*, 20 (2006), pp. 329–43. The rejection of what Onora O'Neill, *Towards Justice and Virtue: A Constructive Account of Practical Reason* (Cambridge: Cambridge University Press, 1996), pp. 165–6 calls the practice of placing 'the principle of injury' at the centre of social life can be traced back to the European Enlightenment. Charles Taylor, *Sources of the Self: The Making of Modernity* (Cambridge: Cambridge University Press, 1989) situates this within the broad cultural shift which supported 'the affirmation of ordinary life' and the parallel rejection of sacred suffering. Horkheimer's later reflections on theology and suffering (see Jurgen Habermas, 'Reflections on the Development of Horkheimer's Work', in Benhabib, *On Max Horkheimer*, ch. 3) invite the comment that several major faith traditions have regarded the capacity for suffering, and the potential for sympathy with the distressed, as the most natural point of solidarity between strangers. See John Bowker, *Problems of Suffering in the Religions of the World* (Cambridge: Cambridge University Press, 1970).

Such themes have not been at the forefront of attempts to construct a critical theory of international politics – at least, they have not been central to Habermasian-inspired developments. They have been more central to approaches which draw on Honneth's analysis of the 'struggle for recognition' which preserves certain early Frankfurt School preoccupations by stressing the part that 'moral injury' plays in generating social conflicts, whether by inflicting physical pain or injury, humiliating or demeaning others through 'the withdrawal or refusal of recognition' or by denying others a fair share of social resources.[34] The Habermasian discourse theory of morality has not ignored these themes entirely, but it cannot be said to have stressed them to anything like the same extent.[35]

The next two sections will comment on the Habermasian project of reconstructing historical materialism (and on its possible further reconstruction) but it is useful to pre-empt what is at stake in the discussion by recalling Habermas's specific claim about the cosmopolitan possibilities which were inherent in the first 'speech act' – in the first instances of communicative action which explored the prospects for reaching a shared understanding. The intriguing contention was that the very first speech act contained the promise of the moral and political unity of humankind – alternatively, that the presuppositions of everyday speech, wherever language has been used, have raised the possibility of a worldwide communication community in which all persons enjoy an equal right to advance claims about any decisions that may affect them and possess the same entitlement to influence deliberative outcomes. Collective learning processes over many centuries have brought these possibilities to light, and they have made them central to the advanced, 'post-conventional' moral codes and the associated democratic principles of legitimacy which must be included among the achievements of Occidental rationalism. But since these ethical and possibilities were immanent in the structure of communicative action in all previous phases of history, they were available at least in principle to every form of life.

Many critics have argued that the Habermasian approach to critical social theory rests on an 'excessive rationalism' and a 'limited conception of communication'.[36] Reflecting this concern, one might ask if Weil's claims about the most elementary forms of human solidarity do not suggest a rival conception of the cosmopolitan possibilities which have been immanent in all ways of life. The central issue is whether the very first humanitarian response to the pleas of an 'outsider' did not already contain a vision of universal ethical responsibilities which many ethical codes have developed further, most significantly in the claim that all members of the human race should enjoy the same rights of respect and protection irrespective of citizenship, nationality, race, gender and so forth. The question then is whether the first displays of sympathy for the stranger did not already embody the immanent possibility of

---

[34] See Axel Honneth, *The Struggle for Recognition: The Moral Grammar of Social Conflicts* (Cambridge: Polity, 1995) and Jurgen Hacke, 'The Frankfurt School and International Relations: On the Centrality of Recognition', *Review of International Studies*, 31 (2005), pp. 181–94. See also Axel Honneth, 'Mutual Recognition as a Key for a Universal Ethics', at: ⟨www.unesco.or.kr/kor/science_s/project/universal_ethics/asianvalues/honneth.htm⟩.

[35] With respect to exploitation, Jurgen Habermas, *Communication and the Evolution of Society* (Boston, MA: Beacon Press, 1979), p. 164, distinguishes between 'bodily harm (hunger, exhaustion, illness), personal injury (degradation, servitude, fear), and finally spiritual desperation (loneliness, emptiness) – to which in turn there correspond various hopes – for well-being and security, freedom and dignity, happiness and fulfillment'.

[36] Joel Whitebook, *Perversion and Utopia: A Study in Psychoanalysis and Critical Theory* (London: MIT Press, 1995), p. 9 and p. 183.

global relations of solidarity formed for the purpose of alleviating or ending unnecessary suffering.

It is not possible to do more than pose these questions here; clearly, further reflections are needed to develop and assess this conjecture and to ascertain whether the 'linguistic turn' in critical social theory failed to capitalise on early Frankfurt School reflections on suffering and solidarity for both normative and sociological purposes. Questions about the normative content of critical theory must be set aside because the priority is to extend the conception of a sociological project which has been outlined elsewhere, a project with the purpose of investigating how far the potentialities for global solidarity which can be derived from basic human concerns about vulnerability and injurability have been realised in different states-systems.[37] It is essential to consider Habermas's notion of the reconstruction of historical materialism, and his associated reflections on learning processes in the ethical sphere, before discussing how stronger links between International Relations and historical sociology might be developed.

Collective learning processes and social evolution

It is widely known that Habermas rejected the historical materialist claim that the labour process explains the evolution of humanity along with its exhausted conviction that the resolution of the main capitalist contradictions requires the transition to universal socialism. The reconstruction of historical materialism elevated the domain of communicative action to a position of equality with the labour-process; neither should be privileged, it was argued, in any account of the reproduction of any society or in the broader analysis of the evolution of humanity. An additional contention was that societies have undergone learning processes in the communicative realm which have been as important for the history of the species as the forms of social learning which had given rise to the unrivalled mastery of natural forces.

Habermas has claimed that the rise of reflective, universalistic ethical perspectives is one of the great accomplishments of Occidental rationalism and one of the most significant steps in the development of the species.[38] Collective learning processes replaced mythical narratives with 'rationalized world views' which valued 'argumentative foundations' and which broke through morally parochial ways of life.[39] Abstract ethical systems involved the 'decentration' of world-views, that is the movement from egotistical moral systems to commitments to the Kantian ideal of thinking from the standpoint of all others. They have been an essential part of long-term learning processes which have enabled the species to realise that consensual efforts to decide universalisable ethical principles represent its best hope of freeing global social and political relations from domination and force.[40]

The claim that there are 'homologies' between ego-formation in modern societies and the evolution of humanity as a whole which inform this account of social

---

[37] See my 'The Problem of Harm in World Politics: Implications for the Sociology of States-Systems', *International Affairs*, 78 (2002), pp. 319–38 and Linklater, *Norbert Elias*.
[38] Habermas, *Communication*, ch. 4.
[39] Ibid., p. 105.
[40] Ibid., chs. 3–4.

evolution preserves the early Frankfurt School's specific interest in psychological and psychoanalytical processes.[41] However, the focus on homologies contains few references to the role of collective and individual emotions in social systems – specifically in uniting 'agents' and 'structures' in the manner described earlier.[42] Generally lacking is any recognition of the significance of emotional responses to vulnerability, pain and suffering in understanding long-term patterns of change.[43] The relative silence about these matters underpins the criticism that Habermas's linguistic turn involves the 'decorporealization of Critical Theory'.[44] Honneth has advanced a similar claim by arguing that Habermas's approach 'is directed exclusively to an analysis of rules ... so that the bodily and physical dimension of social action no longer comes into view. As a result, the human body, whose historical fate both Adorno and Foucault had drawn into the center of the investigation ... loses all value within a critical social theory.'[45]

The lack of interest in corporeality may reflect the influence of Kant's ethical rationalism with its renowned distrust of the instinctual or impulsive.[46] Habermas is explicit that the human compulsion to satisfy the needs which form an important part of its biological legacy has no logical consequences for ethical reasoning; moreover, he insists that any leap from empirical observations about aversions to pain and injury to specific normative claims about how human beings should organise social and political life commits a 'naturalistic fallacy'.[47] No such problems arise, it is argued, for modes of ethical analysis which begin with the nature of communicative action rather than with the vulnerabilities of the body.[48]

There may be a link between Habermas's essentially Kantian ethical position and the neglect of the body and the emotions in his more sociological writings on

---

[41] See the discussion of psychoanalytical theory in Habermas, *Knowledge*, chs. 10–12 and the references to 'cognitive developmental psychology' in Habermas, *Communication*, p. 100; see also ch. 2 entitled 'Moral Development and Ego Identity'.

[42] Some critics regard this oversight as a weakness in Habermas's position, but not one that his approach is incapable of correcting. See Nick Crossley, 'Emotion and Communicative Action: Habermas, Linguistic Philosophy and Existentialism', in Gillian Bendelow and Simon. J. Williams (eds.), *Emotions in Social Life: Critical Themes and Contemporary Issues* (London: Routledge, 1998).

[43] Habermas, *Communication*, ch. 3. See also the references to the significance of 'affective expressions' in the evolutionary movement from primates to hominids on p. 134, and the more central concern with the development of 'structures of thought' which is expressed on p. 149.

[44] Joel Whitebook, 'Fantasy and Critique: Some Thoughts on Freud and the Frankfurt School', in David. M. Rasmussen (ed.), *The Handbook of Critical Theory* (Oxford: Blackwell, 1996), p. 300.

[45] Axel Honneth, *Critique of Power: Reflective Stages in a Critical Social Theory* (London: MIT Press, 1991), p. 281. What has been lost, it might be argued, is the 'underground history' which concerns the body and 'the fate of the human instincts and passions which are displaced and distorted by civilization': see Theodor Adorno and Max Horkheimer, *Dialectic of Enlightenment* (London: Verso 1972), p. 231.

[46] Contrasts can be drawn between broadly Kantian moral perspectives which privileged reason over the emotions and various conceptions of a sentimental ethic that support the emancipation of positive moral emotions.

[47] See, for example, the following claim in Habermas, *Communication*, p. 176: 'In living, the organisms themselves make an evaluation to the effect that self-maintenance is preferable to the destruction of the system, reproduction of life to death, health to the risks of sickness'. But from the 'descriptive statement that living systems prefer certain states to others' nothing follows ethically from the standpoint of observers.

[48] See the following claim in Habermas, *Communication*, p. 177): 'For a living being that maintains itself in the structures of ordinary language communication, the validity basis of speech has the binding force of universal and unavoidable – in this sense transcendental – presuppositions. The *theoretician* does not have the same possibility of choice in relation to the validity claims immanent in speech as he does in relation to the basic biological value of health' (italics in original).

long-term patterns of change in the modern West.[49] Not that Habermas has been entirely deaf to the influence of emotional or instinctual drives since he has argued for including in 'the natural basis of history, the heritage of natural history . . . consisting in an impulse potential that is both libidinal and aggressive', although he adds that emotional impulses are never encountered without the mediating effect of language and culture. There is explicit recognition here that an inquiry into moral learning which considers 'structures of thought' would be deficient if it neglected the natural 'heritage'. Nevertheless, his writings have not explained how a sociology of collective learning processes should proceed in the light of the fact that natural history 'determines the initial conditions of the reproduction of the human species'.[50]

Towards a sociology of global morals

In a lecture at the launch of the Institute of Psychoanalysis on 16 February 1929, Erich Fromm is reported to have stated that 'the most important psychological and sociological questions' of the era should endeavour to explain the 'connections' between 'the social development of humanity, particularly its economic and techno-logical development, and the development of its mental faculty, particularly the ego-organisation of the human being'.[51] Fromm argued for a materialist approach to 'psychological categories' which recognised that every society 'has not only its own economic and political but also its specific libidinous structure'.[52] Five years later, Horkheimer stressed the importance of integrating psychological approaches into the materialist interpretation of history.[53] Commenting on the Frankfurt School in the 1940s, Wiggershaus maintains that Horkheimer and Adorno seem to have leaned towards a form of 'biological materialism' in the belief that 'there was a utopian potential in instinctual structures'.[54] Reflecting similar themes, Marcuse later dis-tinguished between 'basic repression' and the 'surplus repression' of the instincts which modern civilisation requires. The transition to socialism, he added, would involve not only the reconfiguration of the relations of production but also fundamental changes in the constitution of the human psyche which would include 'a different sensitivity' involving 'different gestures' and 'impulses' and 'an instinctual barrier against cruelty, brutality (and) ugliness'.[55] A striking feature of those comments is their commitment to a critical approach to society which analyses the interplay between material structures or forces and the organisation of the libidinal and emotional dimensions of individual and collective selves.

Frankfurt School theorists have not been the sole advocates of the need for 'historical psychology'. By the late 1930s, the aspiration to develop more sophisti-cated understandings of the connections between the material dimensions of any society and the dominant personality types had already been promoted by Elias's

[49] Jurgen Habermas, 'History and Evolution', *Telos*, 39 (1979), pp. 5–44.
[50] See Habermas, *Knowledge*, pp. 256 and 285.
[51] Wiggershaus, *Frankfurt School*, p. 55.
[52] See Wiggershaus, *Frankfurt School*, p. 55, and Erich Fromm, 'Politics and Psychoanalysis', in S. E. Bronner and D. M. Kellner (eds.), *Critical Theory and Society* (London: Routledge, 1989), p. 216.
[53] Thomas A. McCarthy, *The Critical Theory of Jurgen Habermas* (London: MIT Press, 1981), p. 193.
[54] Wiggershaus, *Frankfurt School*, p. 271.
[55] Herbert Marcuse, *An Essay on Liberation* (Harmondsworth: Pelican, 1972), pp. 29–30.

analysis of the 'sociogenetic' and 'psychogenetic' elements of the European 'civilizing process' which gathered pace in the 1500s. Elias's legacy in the shape of figurational sociology, as well as Annales histories and the more recent subfield of emotionology all have particular importance for the mode of sociological investigation of international politics to which we now turn in conclusion.[56] At the heart of this approach is the suggestion that the most basic forms of solidarity between strangers are grounded in the shared sense of vulnerability to mental and physical suffering and in the related capacity to enlarge the scope of ethical concern to include the members of all other social groups. The main sociological question is how far commitments to embodied cosmopolitanism, which have been possible in all forms of life, emerged from under the shadows of pernicious systems of exclusion to influence the historical development of relations between societies. It is how far these ethical orientations have been central to collective learning processes in different societies of states; it is how far a world-historical approach to the human species, one that focuses on how social groups spread to all parts of the world and became more closely interconnected over thousands of years, can profit from analysing the development of moral capacities including the potentiality for the development of cosmopolitan forms of solidarity and sympathy.[57] In this perspective, international societies are the key level of analysis because they have been the main steering mechanisms which independent communities have devised for organising increasing levels of global interconnectedness. As organisers of humanity, they have been the vehicles through which certain universal ethical potentialities could be released and embedded in collective efforts to ensure that the relations between social groups do not cause unnecessary suffering to peoples everywhere.

It has been suggested that Horkheimer, Adorno, Fromm and others developed a conception of the critical theory of society which aimed to understand the connections between social-structural forces and psychological dynamics, and it has been maintained that Elias's figurational sociology is the main realisation of that aspiration. It is fitting that this article should end with some brief comments on the significance of Eliasian sociology for Frankfurt School critical theory, beginning with the fact that Elias was a member of the Department of Sociology in Frankfurt in the early 1930s, in the period when Horkheimer, Adorno and Fromm were engaged in developing a critical approach to society which incorporated Freudian insights into sociological analysis. Elias was not a member of the Frankfurt School, nor did he subscribe to partisan social inquiry, although his contention that the ultimate purpose of Sociology is to enable human beings to exercise control over uncontrolled social processes, including the complex forms of interdependence which now exist globally, might be said to share the humanist objectives of the Frankfurt School.[58] It

---

[56] Norbert Elias, *The Civilizing Process: Sociogenetic and Psychogenetic Investigations* (Oxford: Blackwell, 2000). See also the writings of Lucien Febvre collected in Peter Burke (ed.), *A New Kind of History from the Writing of Lucien Febvre* (London: Routledge and Kegan Paul, 1973), p. 24, and Peter N. Stearns and Carol Z. Stearns, 'Emotionology: Clarifying the History of Emotions and Emotion Standards', *American Historical Review*, 90 (1985), pp. 813–36. See Linklater, *Elias* for a list of key works in figurational sociology which are also relevant to the argument of this article.

[57] For an overview of the relevant literature, see Patrick Manning, *Navigating World History: Historians Create a Global Past* (Basingstoke: Palgrave, 2003).

[58] Elias moved to Frankfurt University when Karl Mannheim was appointed to the Chair of Sociology in 1929. For further details, see Artur Bogner, 'Elias and the Frankfurt School', *Theory, Culture and Society*, 4 (1987), pp. 249–85, and Wiggershaus, *Frankfurt School*. See also Chris Rojek, 'An

is especially important to stress the affinities between Elias's analysis of the modern West and the sociological directions which members of the Institute of Psychoanalysis and the Institute of Social Research started to explore in the late 1920s and early 1930s (and to lament the continuing fracturing of that discourse into separate branches of Sociology which was initially caused by the rise of Fascism).[59] A sociology of states-systems which draws on Elias's analysis of changing emotional responses to public and private acts of violence and cruelty in Western Europe over five centuries, and on his related examination of how the scope of emotional identification widened in the era in question, at least between members of the same bounded communities, can reinvigorate Frankfurt School social inquiry and develop the account of collective learning processes which was at the core of Habermas's account of social evolution. That sociological project must also address Elias's question of whether unprecedented global interconnectedness might yet extend the scope of emotional identification at the level of humanity and increase the sense of moral responsibility for the imperilled in other societies.[60] Finally, it must embrace his question, which was central to the more overtly normative project of Frankfurt School theory, of whether humanity can organise its social and political affairs with the minimum of force, domination and humiliation during its remaining time on earth.

Conclusion

Many thinkers such as Schopenhauer, Weil, Horkheimer and Adorno have placed solidarity with the suffering at the centre of their conceptions of ethical life. Their approach has the merit of highlighting moral sentiments which have been essential for the reproduction of all forms of life, and which may have had some salience in relations with other groups in very different historical eras. The most accessible forms of cosmopolitanism draw on universal capacities for sympathising with the suffering, but how far embodied cosmopolitanism has shaped different states-systems, and has an unusual influence in the modern world, are matters for a sociological project which can usefully combine Frankfurt School theory with Elias's analysis of civilising processes. Investigating these questions is critical to understanding how the human race may yet come to organise its political affairs so that all individuals and communities are released from constraints which are not absolutely necessary for the reproduction of society, which are grounded in gross asymmetries of power, in the

---

Anatomy of the Leicester School of Sociology: An Interview with Eric Dunning', *Journal of Classical Sociology*, 4 (2004), pp. 337–59.

[59] It is idle to speculate – but irresistible nonetheless – about how critical social theory might have developed if Adorno's discussions with Elias had continued beyond the 1930s so that Horkheimer and Adorno's *The Dialectic of Enlightenment* had engaged directly with *The Civilising Process* (the former was first published in 1944, the latter in 1939). It is equally tempting to speculate about how an explicit engagement with Frankfurt School critical theory might have shaped Elias's own project and the fate of European Sociology more generally.

[60] See Norbert Elias, *The Germans: Power Struggles and the Development of Habitus in the Nineteenth and Twentieth Centuries* (Cambridge: Polity Press, 1996); Stephen Mennell, 'The Formation of We-Images: A Process Theory', in Craig Calhoun (ed.), *Social Theory and the Politics of Identity* (Oxford: Blackwell, 1994); and Abram De Swaan, 'Widening Circles of Identification: Emotional Concerns in Sociogenetic Perspective', *Theory, Culture and Society*, 12 (1995), pp. 25–39.

dominion of sectional interests, in disrespect for other persons or groups, and in forms of fear, distrust and insecurity that are intrinsic to intractable social conflicts. The purpose of a global sociology of morals with an emancipatory intent is to understand how human beings might yet learn to live together without such crippling infestations and afflictions.

Between Kant and Pufendorf: humanitarian intervention, statist anti-cosmopolitanism and critical international theory

RICHARD DEVETAK*

Abstract. Immanuel Kant and Samuel Pufendorf were both exercised by the relationship between politics, morality and lawful authority; a relationship that goes to the heart of the sovereign state's existence and legitimacy. However, while Kant defended the authority of the moral law, believing morality provides higher authoritative norms than the sovereign state, Pufendorf defends the political morality of authority, believing the sovereign state should submit to no higher moral norms. The rivalry between these two positions is reprised in current debate between cosmopolitanism and statism over humanitarian intervention. Arguing against statism, this article defends a Habermasian-style critical international theory which affords a 'cosmopolitanism without imperialism'.

Introduction

Born in 1632 in the Saxon town of Dorfchemnitz, Samuel Pufendorf grew up having experienced the horrible brutality and senseless violence of the Thirty Years War. He held university appointments at Heidelberg and Lund before eventually working as historian and counsellor to the Swedish and then Brandenburg courts. Immanuel Kant was born in 1724 in the Prussian port city of Königsberg and lectured at its local university. He apparently never left his home town, but on his daily walks the urbane philosopher of enlightenment must have travelled the world in his mind, conjuring ideas of a cosmopolitan system of rights for all peoples across the globe. No such cosmopolitan thoughts occurred to the well-travelled Pufendorf. His political thought remained scaled at the level of the sovereign territorial state that was taking shape across Europe. But for all the differences of personal biography and political outlook, both Kant and Pufendorf were exercised by the relationship between politics, morality and lawful authority: a relationship that goes to the heart of the sovereign state's existence and legitimacy.

The Prussian and the Saxon offer two distinct approaches to the question of how politics, morality and law ought to be understood and related. Kant defends the authority of the moral law: that is, morality provides higher authoritative norms than

* I am grateful to Alex Bellamy, Roland Bleiker, Andrew Linklater and Richard Shapcott for useful feedback on earlier drafts. I am especially thankful to Ian Hunter for his generous engagement with and learned comments on an argument about which he would hold strong reservations. I wish I could have responded to all their comments more fully.

the authority of the sovereign state to his mind. This is what persuades Kant that the establishment of perpetual peace requires the sovereign state's subordination to international and cosmopolitan law. It will ensure that moral duties are not limited to fellow citizens but extended to all humans. By contrast, Pufendorf defends the political morality of authority: that is, the civil authority of the sovereign state submits to no higher moral power or norms. For Pufendorf, duties to humanity, inasmuch as they are valid at all, are best served through a states-system because rights and duties can only be established and maintained by a functioning sovereign state.

Writing long before Kant's birth, and drawing the ire of the towering figure of Gottfried Leibniz, Pufendorf's critique was aimed at proposals for universal principles of justice that transcend territoriality.[1] Pufendorf not only considered the states-system as the most rational way of politically organising the planet,[2] he also held that civil society's laws ought not be grounded in abstract metaphysical natural laws as championed by Leibniz.[3] Appeals to divine authority would do nothing but initiate, exacerbate and prolong religious wars because rulers who held to different confessional beliefs could be charged with heresy and thus delegitimised and attacked. Moral and political norms were to be grounded instead in the positive law of the state. Justifications of political norms could not refer to a higher moral law or authority, but only to worldly authorities.

The rivalry between the Kantian and Pufendorfian positions is being replayed today in international relations theory. On the one hand we have Kantian-universalist arguments mobilised to support, or at least consider, humanitarian intervention, universal human rights and cosmopolitan democracy; and on the other we have statists who reject calls for humanitarian and cosmopolitan transformation on the grounds that sovereign states and international law ought to be preserved in their present form as the most effective and practical modes of political organisation. Though the statists do not usually invoke the name of Pufendorf directly, I think it can be shown that they reflect the kind of argument Pufendorf advanced in the mid- to late-seventeenth century against pre-Kantian universalists like Leibniz: one that is deeply suspicious of appeals to humanity.

The trouble for critical international theorists is that Kant's writings have been influential in strains of liberal internationalism that give expression to belligerence and neo-imperialism. This 'Wilsonianism with boots', as some have named it, which has been associated with the administrations of Bill Clinton and George W. Bush in the USA, and with Prime Minister Blair in the UK, uses liberal notions of freedom and human rights to defend the extensive use of military force. While so many controversial wars are waged under the banner of liberal ideals associated with Kant, the Enlightenment and cosmopolitanism, critical international theory will need to ensure that its arguments are not co-opted by or aligned with such war-mongering. It will need to distinguish its position all the more clearly from liberal imperialism.

---

[1] For examples of Leibniz's position see his 'Meditation on the Common Concept of Justice' and 'Opinion on the Principles of Pufendorf', both collected in Leibniz, *Political Writings*, trans. and ed. Patrick Riley (Cambridge: Cambridge University Press, 1988).

[2] Andrew Linklater, 'Men and Citizens in International Relations', *Review of International Studies*, 7:1 (1981), pp. 23–37, at 28.

[3] Ian Hunter, 'Conflicting Obligations: Pufendorf, Leibniz and Barbeyrac on Civil Authority', *History of Political Thought*, 25:4 (2004), pp. 670–99.

This article argues that a certain amount of misunderstanding has generated unwarranted concerns about Kantian cosmopolitanism, but that if critical international theory is to avoid being tainted by association with liberal imperialism, as it is by some International Relations scholars,[4] it must distance itself from uncritical promotion of humanitarian intervention just as it must distance itself from uncritical acceptance of the sovereign state.

Critical theory and IR

Written during the Second World War, Max Horkheimer and Theodor Adorno's *The Dialectic of Enlightenment* offered a startling critique of Enlightenment thought and industrial society.[5] Despite the promise to liberate humanity from all manner of domination, Horkheimer and Adorno accused the Enlightenment of lending greater force to logics of domination through its privileging of instrumental rationality. In civilisation's drive to extend its domination over nature it could not immunise human social relations against the same drive. Domination over humans followed domination over nature. They believed that modern forms of domination in totalitarian societies were not an outcome of anti-Enlightenment logics, but the realisation of the Enlightenment itself. In fact, they asserted that 'Enlightenment is totalitarian'.[6] Both totalitarianism and liberal capitalism developed out of the same logic – instrumental rationality, and tend towards a utilitarian politics of uniformity. For years to come their devastating critique would haunt optimistic assessments about human progress, especially in the liberal-capitalist societies of the West.

Horkheimer and Adorno were far from being the only or even the first critics of the Enlightenment. From Edmund Burke and G. W. F. Hegel, through Alexis de Tocqueville to J. L. Talmon and Zygmunt Bauman, concerns, both radical and conservative, have been raised about the Enlightenment's complicity with Terror and totalitarianism. But even in their most pessimistic mood the Frankfurt School theorists continued to advocate a critical social philosophy that refused to hypostasise extant social and political reality.[7] In recent years though, Jürgen Habermas, a student of Adorno and major figure in the second generation of Frankfurt School critical theory, has led attempts to defend and renew aspects of the Enlightenment.[8]

In IR, Andrew Linklater's writings have perhaps been most directly influenced by Habermas's revisioning of the Enlightenment project. But R. B. J. Walker, though

---

[4] Helen Thompson notes this unfortunate association in a most thoughtful and non-dogmatic defence of statism, 'The Case for External Sovereignty', *European Journal of International Relations*, 12:2 (2006), pp. 251–74, at 262.

[5] Max Horkheimer and Theodor Adorno, *The Dialectic of Enlightenment* (London: Allen Lane, 1973).

[6] Ibid., p. 6.

[7] On the Frankfurt School's contribution to an emancipatory social theory of international relations see Martin Weber, 'The Critical Social Theory of the Frankfurt School, and the "Social Turn" in IR', *Review of International Studies*, 31:1 (2005), pp. 195–209. Also see my 'Critical Theory', in Scott Burchill, Andrew Linklater, Richard Devetak, Jack Donnelly, Matthew Paterson, Chris Reus-Smit and Jacqui True, *Theories of International Relations*, 3rd edn. (London: Palgrave, 2005).

[8] See Jürgen Habermas, *The Philosophical Discourse of Modernity: Twelve Lectures*, trans. Frederick G. Lawrence (Cambridge: Polity Press, 1987).

not indebted directly to Habermas, has clearly positioned himself in relation to debates about the Enlightenment's legacy for thinking about global politics.[9] From different angles both Linklater and Walker have developed robust critiques of the modern system of sovereign states and reflected upon the possibilities of replacing them with less exclusionary practices and structures. For all their differences, and they are substantial, the critical international theories of Linklater and Walker are sustained philosophico-historical critiques of the assumptions surrounding the sovereign state as the dominant form of political community.[10] Both reject the supposition of 'recurrence and repetition' without any historical differentiation, both remain deeply sceptical of claims about the moral necessity or historical inevitability of the sovereign state as a political community.

In recent years, however, there has been a resurgence in IR theory of statism and anti-cosmopolitanism. Global events have refocused attention on the sovereign state once again, with defenders arguing that the growing preference for cosmopolitanism, which undermines the sovereign state, is hastening capitalist expansionism and social anomie, especially in member states of the European Union; moreover, and more pertinently for my purposes here, cosmopolitanism is thought to be enlarging the scope for political violence and threatening long-term international instability and conflict through humanitarian interventions.

This article will first provide a brief survey of critiques of humanitarian intervention, focusing especially on claims about the autonomy of the political realm and the steadfast defence of the non-intervention rule. The purpose is not to resolve debates over the rights and wrongs of humanitarian intervention, but to highlight how humanitarian intervention has revitalised statism and generated greater scepticism towards moral claims in international relations. In the process, dogmatic positions either for or against humanitarian intervention make a just response more difficult.

Humanitarian intervention and the critique of cosmopolitanism

During the last decade of the twentieth century the discourse of humanitarian intervention became a frequent refrain in international relations. Rwanda and Bosnia are just two place-names associated with calls for humanitarian intervention to prevent or stop war crimes, crimes against humanity and genocide. But a third name, Kosovo, has attracted most discussion. It brought to the surface all the ethical, legal and political dilemmas associated with resorting to force to save strangers. David Rieff observes that the Kosovo war, 'the first war ever waged by the NATO alliance,

---

[9] I have argued elsewhere that the Frankfurt School Critical Theory-inspired writings of Linklater and the more post-structuralist inclined writings of Walker may be interpreted as different moments of a broader project of modernity insofar as both are concerned to elaborate the conditions of possibility for emancipation. See Devetak, 'The Project of Modernity and Theories of International Relations', *Millennium*, 24:1 (1995), pp. 27–51.

[10] See Andrew Linklater, *The Transformation of Political Community: Ethical Foundations of the Post-Westphalian Era* (Cambridge: Polity Press, 1998), and R. B. J. Walker, *Inside/Outside: International Relations as Political Theory* (Cambridge: Cambridge University Press, 1993). For the differences, see Walker, 'The Hierarchicalization of Political Community', *Review of International Relations*, 25:1 (1999), pp. 151–6.

was undertaken more in the name of human rights and moral obligation than out of any traditional conception of national interest'.[11] The fifty years old human rights discourse was now beginning to have telling effects on the 'Old Westphalian system, in which state sovereignty was held to be well-nigh absolute', he noted.[12] This remains a typical assessment; it is more or less accepted by both defenders and critics of humanitarian intervention that the post-Cold War era has witnessed a greater willingness to use moral arguments in international relations. Much is at stake, including whether or not, and the degree to which, this 'post-Cold War moralization of international politics', as Rieff calls it, represents a progressive step.[13] Critical international theorists need to ask whether, as Ken Booth argues, humanitarian intervention not only honours, legitimises and encourages war, but, by perpetuating 'human wrongs', erodes moral and political resources capable of extending human freedom.[14] They should also ask whether humanitarian intervention actually gives succour to the West's imperialist tendencies rather than enhances prospects of cosmopolitan justice.

Humanitarian intervention: cosmopolitan or imperial?

This section outlines arguments of some of the leading proponents of humanitarian intervention. It does not seek to provide an exhaustive analysis of the arguments so much as highlight key assumptions that have attracted strong criticism.

Firstly, there is the very idea that war may be legitimately fought for humanitarian reasons. This places humanitarian intervention squarely in the Just War tradition, recognising that because of war's horrors, it may also occasionally be necessary to resort to force in order to prevent worse catastrophes, but that restraints should be observed.[15] Proponents of humanitarian intervention are willing to consider armed intervention in another sovereign state when human rights abuses take place on a massive scale. Moreover, some believe that it is not just a *right* of capable states to intervene, but a *duty*.[16] In this respect, humanitarian intervention is simply viewed by proponents as the latest, post-metaphysical instantiation of the Just War tradition in arguing that under some circumstances – to promote human rights or to end human wrongs – it is both right and reasonable to wage war. In Christopher Coker's words:

Metaphysics has been abandoned along with the invocation of God as a justification for war or legitimisation of its practise. Instead, we have regrounded war on humanism, we have put humanity back at the centre of our philosophical and ethical systems of

---

[11] David Rieff, 'A New Age of Liberal Imperialism?', *World Policy Journal*, 16: 2 (1999), pp. 1–10, at 1.

[12] Ibid.

[13] Ibid.

[14] Ken Booth, 'Ten Flaws of Just Wars', in Booth (ed.), *The Kosovo Tragedy: The Human Rights Dimension* (London: Frank Cass, 2001).

[15] The most important book published on humanitarian intervention is Nick Wheeler's *Saving Strangers: Humanitarian Intervention in International Society* (Oxford: Oxford University Press, 2000). Also see Alex Bellamy's chapter on humanitarian intervention in his *Just Wars: From Cicero to Iraq* (Cambridge: Polity Press, 2006), ch. 10.

[16] Philippe Garigne, 'Intervention-Sanction and "*Droit d'Ingérence*" in International Humanitarian Law', *International Journal*, XLVIII (1993), pp. 669–86.

thought – hence the interest in humanitarian warfare, and the importance attached to 'humanity' in the wars we now fight.[17]

Coker is not a critical international theorist, but his claims find echoes in their writings, especially the appeal to humanity.

A second assumption that has attracted much criticism is the belief that humanitarian intervention contributes to a more cosmopolitan system of world politics. While holding serious reservations about the employment of humanitarian intervention, Habermas, Linklater and Lynch are all willing to countenance the possibility that humanitarian intervention may enhance the movement towards more just world orders, or at least halt the slide to greater injustice. Habermas, for example, contemplates whether or not humanitarian intervention may be part of the same Kantian agenda that seeks to transform the 'classical international law of states' into a 'cosmopolitan law of a global civil society'.[18] Similar considerations are contemplated by Lynch: that if all reasonable, diplomatic attempts fail, then humanitarian intervention by democratic countries acting with international public support may be a 'progressive force' for change.[19]

The combination of these two assumptions has found more bullish expression in some strands of liberal internationalism, particularly as part of a wider global strategy to restore international peace and security in the so-called 'war on terror'. Writers such as Robert Cooper, Anne-Marie Slaughter and Fernando Tesón best represent this strand of liberal thought that has become virtually inseparable from the neo-conservative project driving US foreign policy at present.[20]

The statist anti-cosmopolitan critique of humanitarian intervention

In this section I present the statist critique of cosmopolitanism. Railing against what it perceives as abstract rationalism, statist anti-cosmopolitanism sees critical international theory as simply extending the Enlightenment's complicity with violence, revolution and terror. There are two main strands to this critique: firstly, a critique of moral criticism of politics, and secondly, a defence of the sovereign state and its claimed rights. Both are deemed essential to achieving a peaceful, law-governed world order.

Patricia Owens, in a chapter primarily concerned with Hannah Arendt's contribution to thinking about organised violence in international politics, estimates that future Western military campaigns are as likely to be legitimated by reference to humanitarianism as the war on terror. She expresses concern that 'cosmopolitanism

---

[17] Christopher Coker, *Humane Warfare* (London: Routledge, 2001), p. 5.

[18] Habermas, 'Bestiality and Humanity: A War on the Border between Legality and Morality', *Constellations*, 6:3 (1999), pp. 263–72, at 263–4.

[19] Marc Lynch, 'Critical Theory: Dialogue, Legitimacy, and Justifications for War', in Jennifer Sterling-Folker (ed.), *Making Sense of International Relations Theory* (Boulder, CO: Lynne Rienner, 2005), p. 182.

[20] Robert Cooper, *The Breaking of Nations: Order and Chaos in the Twenty-First Century* (London: Atlantic Books, 2004), Lee Feinstein and Anne-Marie Slaughter, 'A Duty to Prevent', *Foreign Affairs*, 28:3 (2004), pp. 136–55, Fernando Tesón, 'Ending Tyranny in Iraq', *Ethics and International Affairs*, 19:2 (2005), pp. 1–20. For a detailed critique of liberal internationalism's succumbing to imperialist tendencies, see Anthony Burke, 'Against the New Internationalism', *Ethics and International Affairs*, 19:2 (2005), pp. 73–89.

commitments to defend human rights', encompassing the thought of Christopher Coker as well as Jürgen Habermas, Mary Kaldor, and Marc Lynch among others, have revealed too sanguine a view of military force.[21] Her inference is that cosmopolitanism has become closely associated with the ideology and practice of what Noam Chomsky calls the 'new military humanism'.[22] If Owens is right, despite its normative appeal, cosmopolitanism collapses into a new form of colonial violence insofar as it supports humanitarian intervention.[23]

Owens believes that humanitarian discourses, unwittingly perhaps, open a space for violence.[24] A collateral effect of their approach, she says, 'is the violent externalization of the project of liberal democracy under the label "humanitarian intervention" '.[25] In opposition to advocates of humanitarian intervention, Owens asserts that '[w]e ought to be suspicious of efforts to legitimate wars in the name of "humanity" '.[26] Though she will employ Arendt to try to expose the folly of such humanitarian wars, she resorts in the first instance to the argument of Carl Schmitt. She quotes at length from his *Concept of the Political*.[27] The passage in question is the one where Schmitt criticises the concept of humanity. Wars waged in its name, he says, are never actually waged 'for the sake of humanity'. Instead, such wars merely 'usurp a universal concept' so as to depict the enemy not just as the state's enemy, but as humanity's enemy. In other words, appeals to humanity are dubious attempts to claim the high moral ground, to dress up a grubby war of competing interests in the praiseworthy language of universal values. Humanity operates as little more than a 'useful ideological instrument' to rationalise wars of aggression and expansion. Owens, unfortunately, ends the quote just before Schmitt's pithy conclusion: 'whoever invokes humanity wants to cheat'.[28] But her point is clear: although states will always try to justify violence by appeal to universal values, it can never be legitimate.[29] Owens adds that, although she is 'sympathetic' to Schmitt's critique, her intention lies more in mobilising Arendt's insights into the question of organised violence in international politics.[30] But it is noteworthy nonetheless that Schmitt's

---

[21] Patricia Owens, 'Hannah Arendt, Violence, and the Inescapable Fact of Humanity', in Anthony Lang Jr and John Williams (eds.), *Hannah Arendt and International Relations: Readings Across the Lines* (London: Palgrave, 2005), pp. 42–3.

[22] Noam Chomsky, *The New Military Humanism: Lessons from Kosovo* (Monroe, ME: Common Courage Press, 1999).

[23] Owens, 'Hannah Arendt'.

[24] Ibid., p. 46. In fact, it is not altogether clear that Owens believes the violence is unintentional. Despite saying that 'Habermas and his followers ... do not consciously seek to replicate in the global arena the ills of contemporary liberal society, ..., she also says, 'not only is there an implicit structural violence in the deliberative rationality assumed by discourse ethics, there is an explicit effort to rationalize violence in the form of "humanitarian" war'. Ibid., pp. 57, 50.

[25] Ibid., p. 57.

[26] Ibid., p. 43.

[27] Trans. by George Schwab (Chicago, IL: University of Chicago Press, 1996), p. 54.

[28] Schmitt's 'anti-humanism' inspires the title and argument of Danilo Zolo's *Invoking Humanity: War, Law and Global Order*, trans. Federico and Gordon Poole (London: Continuum, 2002), see especially pp. 38–42.

[29] Owens, 'Hannah Arendt', p. 53.

[30] Ibid., p. 43. Schmitt, it hardly needs saying, is enjoying an extraordinary revival at present. See Chantal Mouffe, *On the Political* (London: Routledge, 2005) for a sympathetic account of his work. For useful accounts of his relevance to IR theory, see Michael C. Williams, 'Words, Images, Enemies: Securitization and International Politics', *International Studies Quarterly*, 47:4 (2005), pp. 511–31, and Jef Huysmans, 'Know your Schmitt: A Godfather of Truth and the Spectre of Nazism', *Review of International Studies*, 25:2 (1999), pp. 323–8.

argument against humanity is highlighted; the implication being that moral rationalisations of violence should carry no political weight.

Jeremy Moses similarly offers a critique of humanitarian intervention, but his objections are based more on a rigid defence of state sovereignty and the rule of non-intervention, and a critique of neo-Kantian interpretations of Kant. In essence, Moses believes, and thinks Kant agrees, that non-intervention is an absolute, non-derogable principle. From a reading centred around Kant's fifth preliminary article to *Perpetual Peace*, Moses concludes that 'it is clear that Kant supported a very strong notion of non-intervention'.[31] Moses does not elaborate on the difference between very strong and absolute support for non-intervention, but given the dogmatism of his objection to intervention we can safely assume that 'very strong' is tantamount to 'absolute' in Moses' mind.[32]

Moses is particularly exercised by the notion that has become fashionable among some liberals, that state sovereignty is 'conditional'. This is an argument that Feinstein and Slaughter, and Fernando Tesón, a target of Moses, among others, have advocated. Moses quotes Tesón asserting that non-intervention is contingent on the internal political arrangements of a state, and that '[s]overeignty is to be respected only when it is justly exercised'.[33] There is, to be sure, much to be concerned about in such arguments.[34] But the main issue here is Moses' argument about sovereignty and non-intervention in relation to human rights. After quoting former Czech President Vaclav Havel's argument in favour of NATO's Kosovo intervention on the grounds of human rights law, 'a law that ranks higher than the law which protects the sovereignty of states' in Havel's mind, Moses delivers his most important criticism. This type of argument, says Moses, 'puts forward the supremacy of individual rights as an unquestionable fact, and bases this upon "conscience", the definition of which has long been the self-appointed domain of "civilised" international lawyers'.[35] The

---

[31]   Jeremy Moses, 'Challenging Just War and Democratic Peace: A Critical Perspective on Kant and Humanitarian Intervention', in Christian Enemark (ed.), *Ethics of War in a Time of Terror*, Canberra Papers on Strategy and Defence, no. 163 (Canberra, 2006), p. 72.

[32]   Here is not the place to dispute Moses' reading of Kant, but a more critical reading of Kant would acknowledge that some ambivalence exists in his historico-political writings regarding state sovereignty and the rule of non-intervention. At the very least it should be noted that Kant steers clear of any absolute commitment to non-intervention; as even in the fifth preliminary article Kant allows for 'interference' in another state when its sovereign can no longer claim exclusive authority. For an argument supporting Moses' interpretation of the fifth preliminary article, see Thomas Mertens, 'Cosmopolitanism and Citizenship: Kant against Habermas', *European Journal of Philosophy*, 4:3 (1996) pp. 328–47, for one that notes Kant's ambivalence, see Howard Williams, 'Back from the USSR: Kant, Kaliningrad and World Peace', *International Relations*, 20:1 (2006), pp. 27–48.

[33]   Moses, 'Challenging Just War', p. 73.

[34]   In fact, I express similar concerns in a chapter of the same volume that carries Moses' chapter. My argument there is that distinctions between liberal and non-liberal states are part of a broader attempt by the North (or West) to spatialise the sources of terrorist violence; that is, to identify terrorism with the South. This spatialisation not only exculpates the North, but opens opportunities for the North either to wage war against enemies in the South or to impose their preferred forms of political and economic governance. Devetak, 'Failed States, Rogue States and the Sources of Terrorism: How the North Views the South', in Enemark (ed.), *Ethics of War*. For a powerful and persuasive critique of Tesón see Terry Nardin, 'Humanitarian Imperialism', *Ethics and International Affairs*, 19:2 (2005) pp. 21–6.

[35]   Moses, 'Challenging Just Wars', p. 74. It is interesting that Moses pinpoints 'conscience' as a problem. Although he mentions only contemporary Finnish lawyer Martti Koskenniemi in his footnote, he might also have mentioned Thomas Hobbes who dismantled 'conscience' which such devastating effect over three hundred and fifty years ago in *Leviathan*. As we shall see, this

problem, as Moses sees it, is that liberal cosmopolitan arguments in favour of humanitarian intervention not only suppose universal agreement about human rights' primacy at the expense of state sovereignty, but that 'self-appointed' representatives of civilisation arrogate to themselves the right to decide when intervention is warranted. Here Moses brings his defence of state sovereignty into alignment with a critique of 'moralism' in international politics.

These two strands of statist anti-cosmopolitanism are brought together in David Chandler's *From Kosovo to Kabul*,[36] a withering critique of cosmopolitan attempts to defend and promote human rights in international relations. He seeks to unmask the human rights movement's progressive agenda as little more than a myth. It may promise empowerment of marginalised peoples, but the human rights movement actually works in the opposite direction by enabling Western elites and governments to impose their agenda, by force if necessary. Worst of all, Chandler believes, the human rights agenda is undermining international order by eroding classical international law and expanding the reasons for waging war.

A central theme running through Chandler's argument is that as 'old' humanitarianism has given way to the 'new' human-rights based humanitarianism, neutrality and universality have been replaced by partiality and selectivity. Instead of 'operating separately from political mechanisms', the new humanitarianism, says Chandler, sees itself 'as an alternative guide to policy-making'.[37] Once safely segregated from politics, humanitarianism has increasingly, and problematically, encroached on politics, aspiring to substitute itself for elected government, as Chandler sees it. In short, his complaint is that the 'new' humanitarianism is effecting a moralisation of international politics.

Underlying Chandler's entire analysis is a binary opposition between human rights and state sovereignty. Chandler believes that human rights discourse always contradicts and undermines state sovereignty. But this binary opposition only proves to be a reflection of a deeper dichotomy between politics and morality, or as he alternatively puts it, law and ethics. Chandler repeatedly frames the 'problem' with human rights as a privileging of morality and ethics over politics and law. As he puts it in his Introduction, for example, 'The idea of human-centred rights putting people first, . . . derives more from the spheres of morality and ethics than that of politics'.[38] And again:

The human rights critique is in many ways a stunningly confident attack on the political sphere under the cover of ethics and morality. Transcendental moral values are portrayed as the progressive solution to the problems of the narrow political sphere.[39]

The dichotomies do not end there though; a parallel distinction is also drawn between facts and values, practices and principles.[40] For Chandler, only the *politiques* and lawyers deal in facts whereas the ethicists and moralists focus on values, and, in their complicity with human rights activists, 'sidestep factual criticism'.[41] With this series

---

dismissal of conscience connects Moses' argument much more directly to the arguments of Schmitt, Koselleck, Saunders and Hunter that we explore below.
[36] David Chandler, *From Kosovo to Kabul* (London: Pluto Press, 2002).
[37] Ibid., p. 38.
[38] Ibid., p. 5.
[39] Ibid., p. 107.
[40] Ibid., p. 16.
[41] Ibid., p. 16. It may or may not be true that on occasion proponents of the so-called 'new' humanitarianism have handled facts in less than satisfactory ways; but the same criticism can easily

of binary oppositions firmly in place – politics/morality, facts/values – Chandler proceeds to rebuke human rights-based humanitarianism for its normative or moral critique of politics. His objection to the new humanitarianism is neatly summed up in his accusation that it is an 'anti-political critique'.[42] By implication, normative and critical theorists are dismissed for ignoring 'the real and the profane' in favour of 'moral critique'. Moreover, in their 'thoroughly critical' and 'thoroughly radical' critique of actually existing states, Chandler thinks they attribute the twentieth century's horrors to democracy and state sovereignty, two things Chandler wants to place beyond criticism.[43]

Chandler says that his critique seeks to 'expose the elitist assumption behind the human rights "movement" and reassert the contemporary relevance of the universal values of political equality and democracy'.[44] He defends state sovereignty as an absolute principle, no matter whether or not states respect the values of political equality or democracy in their own domestic spheres. The accusation against elites is a typical gesture of the statist anti-cosmopolitan position; that, '[F]ar from giving a voice to the excluded, the elite advocates are empowered on the basis of their vicarious association with moral causes'.[45] Universal human rights are a cloak behind which colonial patterns can be restored and maintained, thereby overturning the 'assumptions and processes of representative democratic government'.[46] All that has changed in the twenty-first century, he says, is that colonial patterns of domination are no longer legitimised by a conservative elite peddling claims of racial superiority, but 'by a liberal elite' peddling claims of 'ethical superiority'.[47] Chandler is sceptical of the motive behind the human rights movement because he thinks it has less to do with altruism than with elites and intellectuals trying to plug themselves back into the circuits of power, which is why he believes international lawyers and NGOs are battling it out with elected politicians for 'the job of running the world'.[48]

If statist anti-cosmopolitans are right, critical international theory is anti-political (for its moral critique of politics) and violent (for its alleged unstinting support of humanitarian intervention). As we shall see in the next section, this type of argument is not new and is not confined to International Relations theory.

Kant versus Pufendorf: the state and early modern political thought

In this section I sketch the contours of a statist anti-cosmopolitanism that has been presented in the history of political thought. I shall focus particularly on the writings

---

be applied to absolutist defenders of state sovereignty like Chandler. Facts relating to large-scale and systematic forms of state violence are never mentioned. Either they do not matter or Chandler believes we live in a world free of violence thanks to the sovereign state. In any case, Chandler stands exposed for sidestepping facts in his Panglossian apologia for 'the best of all possible worlds'.

[42] Ibid., p. 111.
[43] Ibid., p. 107. Whilst it is true that critical international theorists charge the sovereign state with various forms of domination, exclusion and perhaps horrors, it is false to say that they attribute these problems to democracy. Quite the opposite is true.
[44] Ibid., p. 19.
[45] Ibid., p. 119.
[46] Ibid.
[47] Ibid., p. 156.
[48] Ibid., p. 210.

of Ian Hunter and David Saunders, but will also mention two other twentieth-century German scholars upon whom they draw, Carl Schmitt and one of his students, Reinhart Koselleck. The essence of this argument parallels the one presented above: that Enlightenment-influenced cosmopolitanism's moral critique of the state runs aground on the shores of the political. By contrast with critical international theories, the position defended by these historians of political thought is profoundly statist and equally profoundly sceptical of appeals to humanity. Instead of being a cause of peace, the Enlightenment project behind Kantian cosmopolitanism, with its appeals to reason and humanity, is actually perceived as a cause of warfare. These statist anti-cosmopolitans contend that the 'post-scholastic' natural law doctrines of Thomas Hobbes, Samuel Pufendorf and Christian Thomasius, rather than the 'neoscholastic' ethical universalism of Gottfried Leibniz, Christian Wolff or Immanuel Kant, afford the only politically prudent principles for achieving peace in a conflictual world. Revisiting this intellectual rivalry should help refine the differences between cosmopolitanism and statist anti-cosmopolitanism.[49]

Absolutism, sovereignty and the political: civil philosophy's critique of metaphysical philosophy

Saunders and Hunter follow Schmitt and Koselleck in adopting a Hobbesian statist position against Kantian cosmopolitanism. In essence, their argument is that Kantian cosmopolitanism replicates the political problem identified by Hobbes in the middle of the seventeenth century: in appealing to alternative sources of authority, cosmopolitanism inevitably leads to war and the undermining of the sovereign state, the *sine qua non* of domestic and international peace. The sovereign state is thus placed more or less beyond criticism within both historical and contemporary discourses of statist anti-cosmopolitanism. To understand why appeals to alternative authorities outside or beyond the sovereign state, including moral laws, are thought to be dangerous, it will help if we briefly return to Hobbes's denunciation of conscience.

Hobbes, it will be recalled, is scathing of conscience in *Leviathan* because on his diagnosis it is the leading source of state dissolution. In chapter XXIX, 'Of those things that Weaken, or tend to the DISSOLUTION of a Common-wealth', Hobbes argues that conscience, which grants to each private individual the right to judge good and evil, is a seditious poison.[50] He wants to deny the presumption of individuals to make themselves judges of good and evil because he believes it to be repugnant to civil society, threatening to unleash a 'war of all against all' once again. Private consciences are only private opinions, he says dismissively; 'the Law is the

---

[49] There are, of course, different interpretations of the seventeenth and eighteenth century 'histories of morality', the best known being Richard Tuck's *The Rights of War and Peace: Political Thought and the International Order from Grotius to Kant* (Oxford: Oxford University Press, 1999). He sees things rather differently to Hunter and Saunders, admitting a greater continuity between Hobbes and Kant than between Hobbes and Pufendorf. For another historical narrative that affirms statism against cosmopolitanism, see Blandine Kriegel, *The State and the Rule of Law*, trans. Marc LePain and Jeffrey Cohen (Princeton, NJ: Princeton University Press, 1995).

[50] Thomas Hobbes, *Leviathan*, ed. C. B. Macpherson (Harmondsworth: Penguin Books, 1968), p. 366.

publique Conscience', and it alone should be obeyed.[51] Hobbes brings the issue into stark relief by drawing out the consequences of allowing the exercise of religious beliefs or private consciences in public affairs. Ultimately, he says, it leads to challenges to sovereign authority, the setting up of '*Supremacy* against the *Soveraignty*; *Canons* against *Lawes*; and a *Ghostly Authority* against the *Civill*'.[52] When conscience enters politics through religion, individuals erect alternative sources of authority; rival kingdoms grounded on different laws compete for the same citizens and territory, invariably leading to bloody conflict. In this context of confessional conflict, Hobbes says, 'ghostly' authorities are set up to counter the 'temporal' authority of the sovereign state, meaning that individuals will be torn between the two.

For seeing the *Ghostly* Power challengeth the Right to declare what is Sinne it challengeth by consequence to declare what is Law, (Sinne being nothing but the transgression of the Law;) and again, the Civill Power challenging to declare what is Law, every Subject must obey two Masters, who both will have their Commands be observed as Law; which is impossible. Or, if it be but one Kingdome, either the *Civill*, which is the Power of the Common-wealth, must be subordinate to the *Ghostly*, and then there is no Soveraignty but the *Ghostly*; or the *Ghostly* must be subordinate to the *Temporall* and then there is no *Supremacy* but the *Temporall*. When therefore these two Powers oppose one another, the Common-wealth cannot but be in great danger of Civill warre, and Dissolution.[53]

Either two rival authorities (religious-ghostly and civil-temporal) battle it out with the victor assuming sole supreme authority, or one subsumes the other within it. In any case, says Hobbes, civil war and the dissolution of the state are the likely outcomes of appeals to religious conviction under the guise of 'conscience'.

As Koselleck glosses Hobbes, when conscience pretends to 'mount the throne', it does not become the judge of good and evil, so much as 'the source of evil itself'. 'Instead of being a *causa pacis*, the authority of conscience in its subjective plurality is a downright *causa belli civilis*'.[54] It is this confessional conflict that the absolutist state was meant to remedy. Fiercely intolerant religious factions had, since the latter stages of the sixteenth century, made the temporal authority of civil sovereignty very fragile. In the midst of this 'legitimation crisis', rivals fought bloody battles to impose their confessional beliefs on others, only to encounter determined resistance. As long as the condition of religious diversity fuelled mutual intolerance and violent conflict, public peace could never be guaranteed. A means therefore needed to be devised to smother or neutralise this confessional strife. As Koselleck puts it, drawing on Schmitt, 'Not until the State had suppressed and neutralised religious conflict could progressive reason unfold in the newly vacated space'.[55]

The absolutist response to what Saunders calls 'the high-minded butchery that went with inter-communal strife', was twofold: the decoupling of politics and religion and the establishment of a supreme civil authority as sovereign.[56] The end result, if

---

[51] Ibid., p. 366.

[52] Ibid., p. 370.

[53] Ibid., pp. 370–1.

[54] Reinhart Koselleck, *Critique and Crisis: Enlightenment and the Pathogenesis of Modern Society* (Oxford: Berg, 1988), pp. 28–9.

[55] Ibid., p. 34. Carl Schmitt, 'The Age of Neutralizations and Depoliticizations', *Telos*, 96 (1993), pp. 130–42.

[56] David Saunders, *Anti-Lawyers: Religion and the Critics of Law and State* (London: Routledge, 1997), p. 4.

Saunders' account is correct, is that a 'state emerged that set itself above the theological doctrines and moral absolutes that had bonded the warring confessions into communities of mutual hatred'.[57] To outline this absolutist response we can usefully employ Pufendorf, one of the heroes of Hunter's narrative, for he provides a clear example of each of these responses.

Pufendorf's whole argument in *On the Duty of Man and Citizen* begins from a demarcation of natural law from moral theology.[58] Whilst natural law is concerned with external human behaviour, moral theology is concerned with the mind's inner workings and conformity to God's will.[59] Pufendorf sees natural law and moral theology as producing two distinct types of moral personae, the moral (read Christian) 'man' and the political 'citizen'. His emphasis is on natural law because it is 'confined within the orbit of this life', concerned with shaping sociable and socially useful individuals.[60] This contrasts with moral theology where the end is salvation in 'the life to come'.[61] Once again we find the split between the ghostly and the temporal.

On this account, absolutist natural law marked a vital step forward in decoupling politics and religion. The desacralised absolutist state Hobbes and Pufendorf envisage will need to eradicate 'ghostly authority' from the political realm. The purpose, as Saunders notes, was to 'disengage the demands of spiritual life from civil government, the dictates of moral conscience from law'.[62] Only by delegitimising alternative sources of moral authority could the state take its rightful place above the fray of sectarian bickering as a neutral civil authority – it would take no position on the truth or otherwise of asserted religious doctrines. The de-theologisation or de-sacralisation of politics was intended to neutralise the bloody conflict generated by proselytising religions. It had one very important consequence for how modern thought defines the political. In relegating religion to the private realm, politics was simultaneously carved out as an autonomous realm. Morgenthau's famous second principle of political realism, which notes the autonomy of the political, comes to him from early modern thought via Weber and Schmitt.[63]

Following Bodin, Hobbes and Pufendorf also seek to establish civil authority as the sole sovereign. In the same way that Hobbes argued that individuals could not be subject to two masters and two laws in social life, favouring the supremacy of temporal over ghostly authority, so too did Pufendorf. Sovereignty denotes a singular

---

[57] Ibid.

[58] Originally published in 1673, *On the Duty of Man and Citizen According to the Law of Nature* is a condensed version of the massive *On the Laws of Nature and Nations* which had been published in the previous year. Since the argument is essentially the same, nothing shall be lost by focusing on the shorter and more widely available text. See James Tully, 'Editor's Introduction', to Samuel Pufendorf, *On the Duty of Man and Citizen*, trans. Michael Silverthorne, ed. James Tully (Cambridge: Cambridge University Press, 1991), p. xxi.

[59] Pufendorf, *On the Duty*, p. 9.

[60] Ibid., pp. 8 and 35.

[61] Ibid., p. 9.

[62] Saunders, *Anti-Lawyers*, p. 88.

[63] Hans Morgenthau, *Politics Among Nations: The Struggle for Power and Peace*, brief edn. (New York: McGraw-Hill, 1985), ch. 1. Also see Martti Koskenniemi, 'Carl Schmitt, Hans Morgenthau, and the Image of Law in International Relations', in Michael Byers (ed.), *The Role of Law in International Politics: Essays in International Relations and International Law* (Oxford: Oxford University Press, 2000), and Michael C. Williams, 'Why Ideas Matter in International Relations: Hans Morgenthau, Classical Realism, and the Moral Construction of Power Politics', *International Organization*, 58 (2004), pp. 633–65.

and exclusive authority and power. 'Every authority [*imperium*] by which a state [*civitas*] is ruled . . . has the characteristic of supremacy [*summum*]', says Pufendorf.[64] He continues, 'its exercise is not dependent on a superior; it acts by its own will and judgment; its actions may not be nullified by anyone on the ground of superiority'. In short, sovereignty, for the early modern statist, is the supreme authority which neither recognises nor answers to any other power, ghostly or temporal. It is also, importantly, 'an authority whose powers include the right of life and death', in Pufendorf's words.[65]

Absolutism's positing of an autonomous political realm seemed to flow naturally into the idea of *raison d'état* (reason of state) – a form of reason that, as Friedrich Meinecke puts it in his classic history of the concept, transcends 'the bounds of law and morality' in maintaining 'the health and strength of the State'.[66] Although *raison d'état* thinking emerges in the late sixteenth and early seventeenth centuries through the rise of Tacitism, scepticism and neo-Stoicism, according to Richard Tuck, it gradually joins up with the 'new' natural law thinking of Hobbes and Pufendorf.[67] It is not just, as Edward Keene notes, that natural law thinking increasingly adopts the empirico-historicist methods of *raison d'état* thinking,[68] but that in disengaging politics from 'higher' moral norms it opens the way for sovereigns to pursue more instrumental forms of politics. As Tuck observes, the religious wars of the late 1500s had 'sharpened the perception of contemporaries about what kind of politics was necessary in the modern world'.[69] The reason or interest of state thenceforth became paramount, freeing the Prince's hand from the constraints of law when necessity demanded. In Koselleck's opinion, *raison d'état* enabled the absolutist state to establish 'an area where politics could unfold regardless of moral considerations'.[70]

This narrative of early modern European politics finds agreement in the arguments of both Hunter and Saunders. In Hunter's view, this story has been largely obscured by 'histories of morality' that accord too much importance to Immanuel Kant, treating his work as the crowning philosophical moment in achieving a reconciliation between rationalism and voluntarism, idealism and empiricism, universal and particular.[71] Hunter's is a brilliant work of revisionist historiography that sees Kant's critical philosophy as unable to dialectically assimilate the civil philosophies of Pufendorf and Thomasius which cultivate quite different understandings of the relationship between politics and morality. By staking out the debate in this way as a clash between rival intellectual cultures, Hunter wishes to 'measure the distance to be travelled from post-Kantian conceptions of a unified "humanity" or "reason"'.[72]

[64] Pufendorf, *On the Duty*, p. 146.
[65] Ibid., pp. 132–3.
[66] Friedrich Meinecke, *Machiavellism: The Doctrine of* 'Raison d'État' *and Its Place in Modern History*, trans. Douglas Scott (New York: Frederick A. Praeger, 1965), pp. 15, 1.
[67] Tuck, *Rights of War*, ch. 2.
[68] Edward Keene, *International Political Thought: A Historical Introduction* (Cambridge: Polity Press, 2005), p. 100.
[69] Richard Tuck, *Philosophy and Government, 1572–1651* (Cambridge: Cambridge University Press, 1993), p. 33.
[70] Koselleck, *Critique and Crisis*, p. 16.
[71] Ian Hunter, *Rival Enlightenments: Civil and Metaphysical Philosophy in Early Modern Germany* (Cambridge: Cambridge University Press, 2001). Linklater's narrative in *Men and Citizens in the Theory of International Relations* (London: Macmillan, 1982) would appear to tell just such a story.
[72] Ibid., p. x.

He also wants to give due regard to a philosophy that, in its prizing of state sovereignty, is 'neither capable nor in need of a higher moral grounding'.[73]

Hunter's historical focus is on the seventeenth century, especially the political and legal history of German lands from the religious wars through the Peace of Westphalia (1648) to the Treaty of Basel (1795). He argues that the clash between metaphysics and civil philosophy that distinguishes the post-Westphalian intellectual terrain marks out opposing responses to the decoupling of civil and religious authority. On the one side are Hobbes, Pufendorf and Thomasius who want to defend and consolidate this separation, says Hunter, developing 'a doctrine of natural law in which the exercise of political power (the "civil kingdom") was segregated from the sphere of life in which the pursuit of moral perfection took place (the "kingdom of truth")'.[74] On the other side are Leibniz, Wolff and Kant, who, by contrast, envisaged a rational reconciliation of politics and religion at a higher level, the metaphysical. According to Hunter, the latter offered theories aimed at rising 'to the domain of transcendent perfections'.[75] This type of argument, which mixed theology and philosophy, took shape in a university metaphysics (*Schulmetaphysik*) that asserted its claim to moral oversight of the spheres of politics and jurisprudence. It had the terrible consequence, according to the civil philosophers, of heightening the 'legitimation crisis' by blurring ghostly and temporal authority and giving rise to war-mongering confessional states. The confessional conflict was, according to Hunter, partly fuelled 'by a reason whose passion for transcendence made its claims non-negotiable'.[76] At this point the similarity with Koselleck's argument is manifest; Hunter's quarry too is 'an anti-political and anti-juridical metaphysical philosophy' he identifies with Kant's cosmopolitan philosophy.[77]

Given that the interference of abstract moral claims was thought by 'post-scholastic' civil philosophers to be inimical to political order and security, it comes as no surprise that Kant is seen by Koselleck, Hunter and Saunders as a threat to the sovereign state. In their view, Kant merely repeats the problems of the religious enthusiasts. In espousing a politics aimed at the regeneration of citizens' moral virtue in *Religion within the Limits of Reason Alone* and *Metaphysics of Morals*,[78] for example, Kant overreaches the proper limits of civil philosophy; his critical philosophy endangers the quarantining of conscience from the public realm. In rejecting *raison d'état* and conceiving politics and law as branches of moral philosophy, Kant constituted 'a direct attack on the desacralisation of politics' by conceiving of a higher law than that of the state.[79] This leads Hunter to argue that 'Kant's theory of the state represents an anti-political reduction of civil to moral governance'.[80] Kant's thought merely continues the *Schulmetaphysik* that Pufendorf and Thomasius had sought to discredit, an abstract rationalism that mixed moral philosophy and

---

[73] Ian Hunter and David Saunders, 'Introduction', in Hunter and Saunders (eds.), *Natural Law and Civil Society: Moral Right and State Authority in Early Modern Thought* (London: Palgrave, 2002), p. 4.

[74] Hunter, *Rival Enlightenments*, p. xi.

[75] Ibid., p. xii.

[76] Ibid., p. 8.

[77] Ibid., p. 9.

[78] I. Kant, *Religion within the Limits of Reason Alone*, trans. Theodore M. Greene and Hoyt H. Hudson (New York: Harper, 1960), and 'The Metaphysics of Morals', in *Kant's Political Writings*, ed. Hans Riess (Cambridge: Cambridge University Press, 1970).

[79] Ibid., p. 316.

[80] Ibid., p. 336.

theology with dangerous social consequences.[81] The main task of the civil philosophers therefore was to limit the civil power of the 'clergy' for fear of them inflaming
religious civil war, and establish an 'extra-religious, supra-partisan' state – a secular
civil authority positioned above politics.[82]

To summarise, the writings of Koselleck, Hunter and Saunders are interesting and
important because they directly impact on contemporary debates in politics and
international relations. Firstly, they present a critique of Enlightenment cosmopolitanism's persistent moral argumentation. The inference is that contemporary
exponents of critical theory, notwithstanding claims to secular rationalism, merely
continue 'religion by other means'.[83] Secondly, they offer a powerful defence of the
sovereign state as the *sine qua non* of civil peace and security. Critical theorists are
thought to undo all the good work done by the seventeenth century's introduction of
the non-sectarian, absolutist state. Indeed, Hunter wonders whether modern critical
theory is 'indicative of a "moral forgetting" of the work of the state in pacifying
fratricidal religious and ethnic communities'.[84]

Defending critical international theory against statist anti-cosmopolitanism

In this final section I want to examine the statist anti-cosmopolitan arguments and
sketch a defence of cosmopolitanism from a critical international theory perspective.
There are three parts to what follows. Firstly, I argue that statist anti-cosmopolitans
take too much metaphysical comfort in the sovereign state. Secondly, I argue that
their dogmatic prioritisation of politics over morality is simply an inversion of the
problem they mistakenly identify in Kantian cosmopolitanism. Finally, I argue that
there are no good reasons for critical international theory to take an *a priori* stance
on humanitarian intervention one way or the other, for that would be more seriously
anti-political.

The metaphysical comfort of the state

In a critical essay on Schmitt, Habermas accuses the controversial German jurist of
retaining 'the bearing of a metaphysician' in his quest to arrest the 'disenchantment

---

[81] Koselleck continues this critique in depicting Enlightenment critics of the absolutist state as
dangerous, hypocritical utopians blind to their own will to power. In a manner similar to J. L.
Talmon's argument in *The Origins of Totalitarian Democracy* (London: Sphere Books, 1970),
Koselleck says that the Enlightenment 'succumbed to a Utopian image which, while deceptively
propelling it, helped to produce contradictions which could not be resolved in practice and
prepared the way for the Terror and for dictatorship', in Koselleck, *Critique and Crisis*, p. 2. See
also Carl L. Becker's argument in *The Heavenly City of the Eighteenth Century Philosophers* (New
Haven, CT: Yale University Press, 1932) that the French Revolution 'took on the character of a
religious crusade', not only in the sense that it had its own forms of worship and its own saints,
but in the sense that it 'was sustained by an emotional impulse, a mystical faith in humanity, in the
ultimate regeneration of the human race', p. 155.
[82] Koselleck, *Crisis and Critique*, p. 27.
[83] Saunders, *Anti-Lawyers*, ch. 2.
[84] Hunter, *Rival Enlightenments*, p. 317.

of a state power that had once been sacred'.[85] The same could be said of the statist anti-cosmopolitans discussed here. The intensity with which Chandler, for example, defends the state's honour against normative critiques takes on a quasi-religious enthusiasm. It becomes an article of faith not only that the state must be protected, but that its critics must be denounced.[86]

The Schmittean conception of politics that pervades statist anti-cosmopolitanism conceals a zeal for state security – a notion of security left entirely in the hands of governmental machinery that need not offer justifications for the harms done to its own or foreign citizens, and that need not adhere to international (or even domestic) laws when 'necessity' demands. The sovereign state is thus apparently positioned outside and above the law, with its own laws and its own reason (*raison d'état*). From this position, the sovereign power is immunised against criticism so long as it trades in the terms of security and the national interest. But, parodying Schmitt we might say, 'Whoever invokes the national interest wants to cheat'.[87] Given how notoriously slippery and indeterminate the concepts of 'security', 'national interest', 'reason of state' and 'state of exception' are, it is surprising that they should be used so uncritically by statists in efforts to deride the concept of 'humanity'.

Another indication of the metaphysics associated with the sovereign state is in the uncritical assumption that states relate to human rights as the concrete relates to the abstract. Chandler and Moses both discuss the state and human rights as if they were two terms of a binary opposition reflecting the deeper contrast between the concrete and the abstract. Moses, for example, is quick to dispute the claim that human rights are 'an unquestionable fact',[88] while remaining silent about the state. The state's existence may or may not be in question, but the rights (and duties) ascribed to sovereign states are precisely what are being questioned in discussions about humanitarian intervention and more generally in international relations theory. To imply otherwise, is to suppose that sovereign states' rights are, like natural rights, somehow beyond history and politics. It is to dehistoricise the state, to reify it as an abstraction, as if it fell from the heavens fully formed. But any rights, including state rights, are socially and historically constructed; that is, they are constituted in time through socially produced rules and norms inseparable from changing structures and processes of interaction, recognition and legitimacy.[89]

Perhaps most disturbing is the statist anti-cosmopolitan blindness to state violence. Though Chandler claims that in pursuit of the ideal it is the 'new' humanitarians who ignore 'the real and the profane', statists might be similarly accused of ignoring the real and profane violence committed by sovereign power in the name of security and *raison d'état*. This is why Chandler's suggestion that human rights discourses disdain the notion of democratic self-government is as absurd as it

---

[85] Jürgen Habermas, *The New Conservatism: Cultural Criticism and the Historians' Debate*, trans. Shierry Weber Nicholsen (Cambridge: Polity Press, 1989), p. 133.

[86] Chandler, *From Kosovo*.

[87] Schmitt, *Concept of the Political*, p. 54.

[88] Moses, 'Challenging Just War', p. 74.

[89] On the social construction of sovereign states and their rights, see Thomas Biersteker and Cynthia Weber (eds.), *State Sovereignty as Social Construct* (Cambridge: Cambridge University Press, 1996) and Chris Reus-Smit, 'Human Rights and the Social Construction of Sovereignty', *Review of International Studies*, 27:4 (2001), pp. 1–20. Also see John Dunn's deft 'deconstruction' of the idea that human rights and the modern state are 'diametrically opposed', in *The Cunning of Unreason: Making Sense of Politics* (London: HarperCollins, 2000), pp. 89–90.

is false.[90] The state's well-established capacities to prevent the exercise of autonomy and to obstruct full participation in government are precisely what the human rights movements combat. Ultimately, Chandler and Moses have nothing to say for citizens who might perish at the hands of sovereign power. States' victims become the silent remainders of a politics that cannot countenance rights other than those attaching to sovereign states.

The dogmatic prioritisation of the political over the moral

Statist anti-cosmopolitans consistently emphasise the autonomy of the political and its priority over and against other realms as the above discussion of Chandler showed. They find moral criticism of politics futile, lamentable and potentially dangerous. As Saunders remarks, drawing in equal measure from twentieth century German scholars Schmitt and Koselleck as from early modern post-scholastic thinkers, contemporary cosmopolitans use the figure of humanity in their attempts to restore moral community, but all they really do is unleash the kind of sectarian conflict that ravaged early modern Europe.[91] The problem, as statists see it, is that moral claims muddy the clear waters of politics even while they aspire to transcend grubby politics by appealing to higher, purer moral laws. Hunter and Saunders make clear that the questioning of state sovereignty 'in the name of a higher moral principle, whether this be invested in humanity or society, self-governing individuals or self-determining peoples', ought to be questioned.[92] In short, morals are best kept out of politics.

An inescapable presence here is Schmitt and his definition of the political as a realm necessarily distinguishable from the moral, the legal, the economic and the aesthetic. Each realm, according to Schmitt, is characterised by its own expressive distinction. The moral realm is defined by the distinction between good and evil, the legal by the distinction between right and wrong, the economic by the distinction between profitable and unprofitable, and the aesthetic by the distinction between the beautiful and the ugly.[93] The political, however, is characterised by the distinction between friend and enemy, a distinction, says Schmitt, that denotes 'the most intense and extreme antagonism'.[94] The final point to note for our discussion is that for Schmitt, the state is the decisive or authoritative entity.[95] The political realm is tied ineluctably, in Schmitt's view, to the sovereign state, for it is the sovereign alone who designates the enemy and who 'decides on the exception'.[96] It is on the basis of the state's right of self-preservation that the exceptional measure of

---

[90] Chandler, *From Kosovo*, p. 101.

[91] Saunders, *Anti-Lawyers*, p. 88.

[92] Hunter and Saunders, 'Introduction', pp. 1–2. The implication of their position is that arguments like Chandler's which appeal to self-determination are equally guilty of the metaphysical resort to higher laws.

[93] Schmitt, *Concept of the Political*, p. 26.

[94] Ibid., p. 29.

[95] Ibid., pp. 43–4.

[96] Carl Schmitt, *Political Theology: Four Chapters on the Concept of Sovereignty*, trans. George Schwab (Cambridge, MA: MIT Press, 1985), p. 5. For the most important recent analysis of the 'state of exception', see Giorgio Agamben, *State of Exception*, trans. Kevin Attell (Chicago, IL: University of Chicago Press, 2005), ch. 1.

suspending the rule of law is invoked. In the exception, Schmitt says, 'The decision frees itself from all normative ties and becomes in the true sense absolute'.[97] But the right to self-preservation, as Samuel Weber remarks, is still a normative appeal.[98] So it happens that even in extreme and intense political moments, like 'states of exception' when the state feels under existential threat, the political cannot break entirely free of the normative, it is still in contact with moral claims and legal norms.

This suggests that politics can never be successfully quarantined from morality. Indeed, politics is often the clash between different value rationalities or moral criteria for judging practices and policies. We might say that politics is defined by the fact that it is never autonomous, never entirely closed in on itself, never finally separated from the moral, legal, economic and even aesthetic spheres.[99] This conclusion is supported by Michael C. Williams, who, in an insightful reading of Morgenthau, has shown that the exiled-German classical realist, though influenced by Schmitt, learned from Max Weber that political actions always combine strategic *and* value rationalities.[100] Williams reveals that Morgenthau recognised that 'the political sphere (like all others) is in reality never pure, and that all spheres interpenetrate in ways that reflect the structures of power and interest operating in different ways at different times and places'.[101] Morgenthau's conception of politics thus begins with recognition of the disenchanted context in which rival values are espoused and contested and in which power struggles occur. In fact, the value claims and counter-claims are power struggles themselves. This contrasts with the metaphysical aspiration of statist anti-cosmopolitanism to restore the purity of the political by quarantining it from other spheres and reducing politics to the security interests of the state.

A further dimension of this precept about the autonomy of the political takes shape in the dogmatic anti-intervention position. Building on Schmitt's conception of the political, Koselleck explained the historical advance embodied in the absolutist state as a shift away from moral judgments of good and evil to political ones regarding peace and war.[102] Westphalia and the United Nations Charter are viewed by statists as codifying 'positive' laws aimed at ensuring peaceful co-existence. As 'positive' laws they contrast with the alleged inscrutability of human rights. Because they are predicated on the political goal of international order, they are thought to transcend the moral alternative between good and evil. But this is surely questionable: statists are just as likely to transpose good and evil onto peace and war. Indeed, the denunciation of humanitarian intervention in Chandler, Moses and Owens inevitably becomes moral in positing non-intervention as good and intervention as evil. Statist anti-cosmopolitans therefore rarely escape the normative ties they try to shrug off, despite their best efforts.

---

[97] Ibid., p. 12.

[98] Samuel Weber, 'Taking Exception to Decision: Walter Benjamin and Carl Schmitt', *Diacritics*, 22:3–4 (1992), pp. 5–18, at 10.

[99] There has been growing research interest in the aesthetic dimensions of international relations in recent years. See the special issues of *Millennium* on aesthetics and the sublime, 30:3 (2001) and 34:3 (2006).

[100] Williams, 'Why Ideas Matter'.

[101] Ibid., p. 653.

[102] Koselleck, *Critique and Crisis*, p. 25.

Critical international theory and the question of humanitarian intervention: constitutionalism and cosmopolitanism from Kant to Habermas

In this final section I outline a brief defence of Kantian cosmopolitanism by linking it to the work of Habermas and Linklater, before turning lastly to the question of how critical international theory might think about humanitarian intervention. I shall argue that cosmopolitanism has the resources to overcome the objections posed by statist anti-cosmopolitans and to articulate a more nuanced view of humanitarian intervention that avoids the dogmatic extremes of statist anti-cosmopolitanism and liberal imperialism.

Midway through the discussion of his second 'definitive article' of *Perpetual Peace*, Kant fires a famous broadside at Hugo Grotius, Samuel Pufendorf and Emmerich Vattel, branding them 'sorry comforters'.[103] His accusation is that they are little more than apologists for war. Their treatises on the law of nations 'do not and cannot have the slightest *legal* force', he says, 'since states as such are not subject to a common external constraint'. The chief task then is to develop concrete legal and political institutions which will restrain the international interactions of states. It is in this context that Kant prescribes the six preliminary articles and three definitive articles of perpetual peace. These articles have, understandably, been the focus of most critical attention, and need no elaboration here; the main point is that Kant, unlike Pufendorf, was willing to consider the prospects of transforming state power through the development of republican, international and cosmopolitan constitutional principles.[104] These would have a constitutive as well as regulative impact on states.

The two appendices that accompany Kant's missive, however, are often overlooked despite their importance for understanding Kant's view of the relationship among politics, morality and law. Politics and morality are, in Kant's mind, both branches of the theory of right (*Rechtslehre*), belonging as they do to the practical sphere. However, while Kant believes there should be no conflict between the two, this is because he does indeed appear to subordinate politics to morality. Nonetheless, in the first appendix Kant distinguishes between the 'moral politician' and 'political moralist'.[105] The former is someone who manages to make political expediency conform to moral principles, while the latter bends morality to serve political interests. The political moralist, acting according to hypothetical imperatives, begins with an objective and then fashions a moral justification to achieve that goal. Kant would say that the 'sorry comforters' provide political moralists with extensive resources to justify morally dubious wars. The moral politician will, by contrast, adopt the categorical imperative and act in accordance with principles that can be universalised.[106]

To borrow Habermas's terms, Kant's law must establish an internal relation between coercion and freedom if it is to be legitimate.[107] This contrasts with

---

[103] Kant, 'Perpetual Peace', in *Kant's Political Writings*, p. 103.
[104] For useful accounts of Kant's views on international relations, see James Bohman and Matthias Lutz-Bachmann (eds.), *Perpetual Peace: Essays on Kant's Cosmopolitan Ideal* (Cambridge, MA.: MIT Press, 1997); Linklater, *Men and Citizens*, ch. 6, Mertens, 'Cosmopolitanism and Citizenship'; and Howard Williams, 'Back from the USSR'.
[105] Kant, 'Perpetual Peace', p. 118.
[106] Ibid., p. 122.
[107] Habermas, *Between Facts and Norms: Contributions to a Discourse Theory of Law and Democracy*, trans. William Rehg (Cambridge: Polity Press, 1997), p. 28. For a useful discussion in International

Pufendorf for whom legitimate law establishes an internal relation between coercion and security. For Kant, as Habermas explains, law must always be in the service of freedom; legal coercion is necessary, but can only be justified on the grounds of preventing or removing harmful limits on freedom.[108] Kant's point, which is picked up by critical theorists, is that law bereft of moral standards appertaining to freedom, like Pufendorf's, is morally and politically dangerous.[109]

Contemporary critical theorists adopt Kant's constitutionalism but, unlike the philosopher of Königsberg, tie it closely to democracy. This allows the exercise of political power to be filtered through the rule of law and democracy. It thus marks some distance from the statism found in Schmitt which not only grants sovereign states wide scope to suspend the rule of law, but also ridicules democratic deliberation as 'everlasting conversation'.[110] Schmittean statists are intolerant of deliberation and negotiation, practices that are integral to Habermasian discourse ethics, where political principles or decisions must be capable of meeting with the approval of all who stand to be affected by them if they are to be valid.[111]

In a sense, as Linklater suggests, it is an attempt to put into practice Kant's ideal of a community of co-legislators embracing the whole of humanity.[112] But there are three important differences between critical theory's discourse ethics and Kant's categorical imperative. Firstly, whereas Kant puts the generalisability of principles to the test in an *imaginary* dialogue, discourse ethics recommends an *actual* dialogue of speaking and listening human beings arguing and deliberating over criticisable validity claims. Secondly, Habermas reconstructs practical reason via a theory of communicative action. This shift from practical to communicative reason is oriented to redeeming validity claims in dialogue with others, not to providing 'substantive orientation for managing practical tasks'.[113] A third important difference to note is that critical theory does not subordinate politics to morality, or positive law to natural or moral law as Kant ultimately did. Instead, it sees legal, moral and political rules as complementary. As Habermas expresses it:

a legal order can be legitimate only if it does not contradict basic moral principles. . . . But this moral reference must not mislead us into ranking morality above law, as though there were a hierarchy of norms. *The notion of a higher law (i.e., a hierarchy of legal orders) belongs to the premodern world.* Rather, autonomous morality and the enacted law that depend on justification stand in a complementary relationship [emphasis added].[114]

Habermas, in fact, understands and is sympathetic to Schmitt's complaint that an 'unmediated moralization of politics' may be politically harmful by corroding the

---

Relations see Jürgen Haacke, 'The Frankfurt School and International Relations: On the Certainty of Recognition', *Review of International Studies*, 31:1 (2005), pp. 181–94, especially at 182–6.

[108] Habermas, ibid., and Kant, 'Metaphysics of Morals', p. 134.

[109] Having said that, Kant does align himself with Pufendorf in denying citizens the right of resistance. See Kant, 'Metaphysics of Right', pp. 143–7 and Pufendorf, *On the Duty*, pp. 146–7.

[110] Schmitt, *Political Theology*, p. 53.

[111] Habermas, *Justification and Application: Remarks on Discourse Ethics*, trans. Ciaran Cronin (Cambridge: Polity Press, 1993), p. 151.

[112] Linklater, *The Transformation*, pp. 84–9.

[113] Habermas, *Between Facts and Norms*, pp. 4–5. See also Habermas, *The Theory of Communicative Action*, vol 1: *Reason and the Rationalization of Society*, trans. Thomas McCarthy (London: Heinemann, 1984).

[114] Habermas, *Between Facts and Norms*, p. 106.

barriers societies build to protect legal persons.[115] But Habermas believes the Schmittean response to the moralisation of politics – quarantining politics from law and law from morality – would be a mistake if we are committed to the principles of constitutional democracy. Maintaining the close proximity of politics to law and law to morality is crucial to constitutional democracy according to Habermas. The legitimation of coercive force on which constitutionalism depends rests on political and legal predicates, and the democratic sanctioning of law is intended to preserve its moral legitimacy – without which the state would be an arbitrary power. In short, Kantian-inspired critical theory recognises the important mediating function morality and law serve in keeping a check on the state and maintaining its legitimacy, both domestically and internationally.

The cosmopolitan approach of critical international theory simply extends the constitutional and democratic principles incompletely enunciated by Kant and then revised and expanded by Habermas. It does not place morality above politics, rather it identifies an internal relation between them and law that is broken by Pufendorf and his statist disciples to allow sovereign authority almost unimpeded rights by appealing to *raison d'état*.

These remarks should also make plain the fact that the moral critique of politics practiced by critical international theory does not descend from the heavens, does not derive from 'ghostly' authority. Rather, it develops out of socially produced 'temporal' authority (constitutionalism) in conjunction with historically unfolding (democracy) norms. That is to say, critical international theory does not transform politics into abstract moral theorising, rather it develops a politics out of 'positive' civil laws and concrete agreements arrived at discursively, including human rights instruments. Statists are therefore wrong to suppose that appeals to human rights are appeals to abstract moral claims. As Habermas insists, *contra* Havel, in a context where there is 'no higher law', '[h]uman rights should not be confused with moral rights'.[116] They exist in state-sanctioned legal orders, not in 'transcendental purity'.[117]

In summary, critical international theory accepts the Kantian argument that morality can and should evaluate politics and law, refuting the claimed autonomy of the political, and countering the attempt to purify politics of moral and legal norms. This together with a rejection of the metaphysical comfort invested in the state make critical international theory's cosmopolitanism more defensible than statist anti-cosmopolitanism. The recognition by critical international theorists that the state has lost its sacred aura should not however be mistaken for a dogmatic anti-statism. There has been no 'moral forgetting' of the state's political importance. From Kant to Habermas and Linklater, the state's social, political and moral function has been acknowledged. Indeed, constitutional and cosmopolitan democracy arguments of the type articulated by Habermas and Linklater are predicated on the democratic advances made by the modern state being deepened further and raised higher. If critical international theory objects to anything, it is sovereignty; calling instead for

---

[115] Habermas, 'Kant's Idea of Perpetual Peace: At Two Hundred Years' Historical Remove', in Habermas, *The Inclusion of the Other: Studies in Political Theory* (Cambridge: Polity Press, 1998), p. 199.

[116] Ibid., p. 201.

[117] Habermas, *Between Facts and Norms*, p. 129.

a more 'differentiated' conception of state that might enhance the prospects of 'good international citizenship'.[118] It is precisely this prospect that is raised by humanitarian intervention: the possibility that states might act on behalf of wider moral and legal obligations. But this should not be mistaken for an uncritical acceptance of humanitarian intervention.

While Habermas, Linklater and Lynch have been painted by statist anti-cosmopolitans as unhesitating advocates of humanitarian intervention, nothing could be further from the truth. All three heavily qualify their support for a principle of humanitarian intervention. Habermas, for example, holds grave concerns about the Kosovo war. He expresses disquiet over NATO's self-authorisation, a negotiation strategy that left no room for non-military solutions, and the expediency of air strikes. Indeed, Habermas goes so far as to admit some doubts over his position of 'legal pacifism'.[119] But in the end he returns to the thought that, 'When nothing else is possible, neighbouring democracies should be allowed to rush to provide emergency help as legitimated by international law'.[120] But precisely because global civil society remains underdeveloped, 'a special sort of sensitivity' is required when considering humanitarian intervention. At the very least, according to Habermas, 'Existing institutions and procedures are the only available controls over the fallible judgments of a party aspiring to act on behalf of the common interest'.[121] Constitutional procedures in the UN, for example, must be respected as the best source of international legal rules and norms.

Linklater reveals similar doubts to Habermas. The main question, according to Linklater, is 'whether humanitarian intervention should be avoided in all cases – or in all but the most extreme cases – because of the danger of eroding barriers to the use of force'.[122] Linklater makes plain his view that humanitarian intervention remains a question; decisions must be taken on a case by case basis, after assessing the facts and making normative evaluations and prudential calculations. There can be no pre-determined decision about whether or when humanitarian intervention is legitimate. Lynch too is sceptical about NATO's intervention in Kosovo, but sees no reason to discard humanitarian intervention completely. His concern is that NATO failed to engage in genuine dialogue prior to military action. He also recognises the 'mismatch between NATO's moral rhetoric and the human costs of a campaign fought from the air'.[123] In the end, Lynch concludes that NATO's Kosovo war lacked both 'procedural and substantive legitimation'.[124]

---

[118] The notion of a 'differentiated' conception of state sovereignty is discussed in Kenneth Baynes, 'Communitarian and Cosmopolitan Challenges to Kant's Conception of World Peace', in Bohman and Lutz-Bachmann (eds.), *Perpetual Peace*, and 'good international citizenship' is discussed in Linklater, 'What is a Good International Citizen?', in Paul Keal (ed.), *Ethics and Foreign Policy* (Sydney: Allen and Unwin, 1992). There is a very large literature criticising sovereignty, but see Walker's *Inside/Outside* for one of the most devastating critiques.

[119] Habermas, 'Bestiality and Humanity', p. 267.

[120] Ibid., p. 271.

[121] Ibid.

[122] Linklater, 'The Good International Citizen and the Crisis in Kosovo', in Albrecht Schnabel and Ramesh Thakur (eds.), *Kosovo and the Challenge of Humanitarian Intervention* (Tokyo: UN University Press, 2000), p. 488.

[123] Lynch, 'Critical Theory', p. 192.

[124] Ibid., p. 185. For a qualified defence of NATO's Kosovo war, see Bellamy, *Kosovo and International Society* (London: Palgrave, 2002).

Conclusion

This article has sought to show that the statist critique of cosmopolitanism is unconvincing. Critical international theory does not run aground on the shores of the political after all. In fact, quite the opposite is true. By maintaining a critical openness on the question of humanitarian intervention, critical international theory avoids the anti-political gesture of applying preordained support or objection to specific cases. It acknowledges that violence is an ineradicable aspect of politics and that decisions themselves can entail violence, even if they are arrived at discursively. Attuned to the changing patterns of inclusion and exclusion, critical international theorists are better placed than statist anti-cosmopolitans to notice the different 'economies of violence' that arise in politics.[125]

Turning specifically to the question of humanitarian intervention, critical international theory must recognise that both the rule of non-intervention and the rule of humanitarian intervention entail violence. The sovereign closure effected by the rule of non-intervention promises to secure international order by maintaining peaceful coexistence. But it is always possible that the domestic and international peace secured by non-intervention permits sovereign states to inflict internal political violence and human rights abuses. By the same token, although armed intervention justified under international humanitarian law promises to save strangers from unnecessary harm, it is always possible that levels of violence will simply escalate, exacerbating and spreading violence further. To adopt an *a priori* assumption that humanitarian intervention is always wrong or evil, as statist anti-cosmopolitans tend to do, is simply an inversion of the liberal imperialist assumption that humanitarian intervention is always right and good when led by the West. Neither position can be acceptable if politics is not to be reduced to the dogmatic or technical application of predetermined rules. The problem with these extreme positions is that, denials notwithstanding, they foreclose politics by invoking fixed, preordained rules without sufficient attention to context or human suffering.

Ultimately, there is a violence associated with non-intervention just as there is with intervention. But deciding whether or not armed intervention may be legitimate for humanitarian purposes must surely be a matter for judgment depending on particular circumstances, not something one can judge in advance. It requires assessment of facts, complex calculations based on normative and prudential evaluations and, at a minimum, dialogue with all parties to the conflict, but especially those on all sides bearing the burden of violence. There is no escaping the tension between facticity and validity that Habermas identifies.[126] In the end, there may not be a choice for critical international theory to make between Kant and Pufendorf, just endless attempts to resolve the tensions between morality, politics and law in response to political violence.

---

[125] I borrow the phrase 'the economy of violence', from Sheldon Wolin's classic *Politics and Vision: Continuity and Innovation in Western Political Thought* (Boston, MA: Little Brown, 1960), pp. 220–35.

[126] Habermas, *Between Facts and Norms*.

Index

www.ingramcontent.com/pod-product-compliance
Ingram Content Group UK Ltd.
Pitfield, Milton Keynes, MK11 3LW, UK
UKHW012021280225
455719UK00011B/431